War and the City

War (Hi) Stories

Edited by

Frank Jacob, Sarah K. Danielsson,
Hiram Kümper, Sabine Müller, Jeffrey M. Shaw

Vol. 6

Tim Keogh (Ed.)

War and the City

The Urban Context of Conflict and Mass Destruction

Ferdinand Schöningh

Cover illustration:
Aerial view of the ruins of Rotterdam. From World War II Photos call no. 208-PR-10L-3, Digital Photography Collections, National Archives. https://www.archives.gov/files/research/military/ww2/photos/images/ww2-184.jpg.

Bibliographic information published by the Deutsche Nationalbibliothek

The Deutsche Nationalbibliothek lists this publication in the Deutsche Nationalbibliografie; detailed bibliographic data available online: http://dnb.d-nb.de

www.schoeningh.de

Cover design: Nora Krull, Bielefeld
Production: Brill Deutschland GmbH, Paderborn

ISSN 2511-5154
ISBN 978-3-506-70278-4 (paperback)
ISBN 978-3-657-70278-7 (e-book)

Contents

1. Introduction 1
   Tim Keogh

2. Learning the "Grammar" of Urban Operations: The United States Army and Urban Combat in World War II 17
   Jonathan A. Beall

3. Saxon Cities in the Great Northern War (1700–1717) 45
   Alexander Querengässer

4. Panic in London? Attitudes of Civilians to Air Attacks in 1917/18 and 1944/45 67
   Linda Parker

5. The Death of a City: The Yugoslav Peoples Army Siege of Vukovar, 1991, Refugee Crisis, and Its Aftermath 85
   James Horncastle

6. "Government Forces Dare Not Penetrate": Urban Arab Palestine, No-Go Areas, and the Conflicted Course of British Counter-Insurgency during the Great Rebellion, 1936–1939 105
   Simon Davis

7. Occupied Naples and the Politics of Food in World War II 139
   Stefan Laffin

8. Rebuilding after the Reich: Sacred Sites in Frankfurt, Leipzig, and Wrocław, 1945–1949 167
   Andrew Demshuk

Contributors 195

Index 197

CHAPTER 1

Introduction

Tim Keogh

> There is a direct reciprocity between war and cities ... the latter are more thoroughgoing constructs of collective life, containing the definitive human places. War is the most thoroughgoing or consciously prosecuted occasion of collective violence that destroys places.[1]

Scholars believe history's first recorded battle occurred around 3,500 BCE at Hamoukar, a city bordering modern-day Syria and Iraq, then situated along the major trade route between Mesopotamia and Anatolia. Residents had clearly prepared for battle, ringing the city with sophisticated defensive walls, and during the siege from an unknown enemy, the inhabitants had turned clay pits into defense factories, "quite literally throwing everything they could find at the aggressors" as archaeologist Clemens Reichel puts it. Unfortunately, their efforts did not prevent the city's destruction: the enemy lodged nearly 2.300 sling bullets into the walls and eventually burned Hamoukar to the ground. The casualties were then buried into the ruined walls.[2] The archaeological site is merely the earliest example of a pervasive feature in Ancient Mesopotamia: fortified cities, sieges, structural and human casualties. This is hardly surprising since the origins of organized warfare and of the city-state are inseparable. As James C. Scott argues, the 'grain-population complex' was the nucleus of political power upon the advent of agriculture and therefore the target of raids, which the victor either sought to destroy, transfer whatever assets that could be moved, or absorb the city into their own collection of grain-population complexes. It is not that city inhabitants witnessed the first wars; raids and organized violence long predated city-state formation. But cities, as sites of immense concentrations of wealth, engines of technological innovation, centers of political and ideological legitimacy, and strategic locations near resources made them the source and targets of sophisticated organized

1 Ken Hewitt, "Place Annlihilation: Area Bombing and the Fate of Urban Places," *Annals of the Association of American Geographers* 73:2 (1983), 258.

2 William Harms, "Evidence of Battle at Hamoukar Points to Early Urban Development," *The University of Chicago Chronicle* 26:8, January 18, 2007. Accessed March 28, 2018. http://chronicle.uchicago.edu/070118/hamoukar.shtml.

 | DOI:10.30965/9783657702787_002

violence that we have come to define as 'warfare,' with its attendant monument destruction, crop burnings, mass enslavement, and at its most extreme, total state obliteration.[3]

The tight relationship between cities and organized armed conflict remained long after "cities" and "states" were synonymous: Alexander and Tyre, the Romans and Carthage, the Ottomans and Constantinople, Acre, Tenochtitlan, Vicksburg, Nanjing, Nagasaki, or most recently, Mosul. While popular conceptions of battles pit lines of soldiers facing off in open fields, or tanks and cannons firing at one another across trench lines and undulating hills (think of how most toy soldiers are constructed for example), in reality sieges, and more broadly urban warfare, dominated military conflict throughout history. It was only a small period, from roughly the mid-eighteenth century through the early twentieth century, that decisive battles took place in open fields rather than cities, a consequence of new military technologies, the changing layout of cities, and the preferred military strategies of leading tacticians, Napoleon above all.[4] Indeed, while warfare has been understood most often as clashes between states, state power has often been fragmented and transitory; the effective reach of states are among its controlled cities, which have historically served as the source of their survival and therefore target of violence.[5] And throughout history, warfare and urbanization have intensified in tandem. Max Weber famously referred to the city as the "fusion of fortress and market," protecting property owners who designed the fundamental building blocks of capitalism.[6] Military innovations have similarly had their greatest expression in cities, the instant vaporization of cities and their inhabitants the penultimate example; alternatively, a more optimistic view posits how cities have tempered war, acting as civilizing crucibles of the "humanitarian revolution" that have made the present an allegedly less violent age.[7]

---

3 James C. Scott, *Against the Grain: A Deep History of the Earliest States* (New Haven: Yale University Press, 2017), ch. 6, "Politicide: Wars and Exploitation of the Core" (ebook format).

4 Louis DiMarco, *Concrete Hell: Urban Warfare from Stalingrad to Iraq* (Oxford: Osprey, 2012), 15-26.

5 Martin Shaw, "New Wars of the City: Relationships of 'Urbicide' and 'Genocide'," in *Cities, War, and Terrorism: Towards an Urban Geopolitics*, ed. Stephen Graham (London: Wiley-Blackwell, 2004): 141-153.

6 Max Weber, *Economy and Society* (Berkeley: University of California Press, 1978), 1223; For quantitative evidence, see Mark Dincecco and Massimiliano Gaetano Onorato, "Military Conflict and the Economic Rise of Urban Europe," *Journal of Economic Growth* 21:3 (2016), 259-282.

7 Steven Pinker, *The Better Angles of our Nature: Why Violence has Declined* (New York: Penguin Press, 2012), 177-186.

Despite the intimate connection between cities and war, scholarship studying urban warfare in its broadest terms throughout history has until recently been meager. The classic strategists set the stage for this blindspot. Sun Tzu infamously warned that sieging cities was only a strategy of last resort that would likely lead to troop exhaustion and protracted warfare:

> As for fortified cities that are not assaulted: We estimate that our strength is sufficient to seize it. If we seize [a city], it will not be of any advantage to the fore; if we gain it we will not be able to protect it at the rear. If our strength equals theirs, the city certainly will not be taken. If, when we gain the advantages of a forward (position) the city will then surrender by itself, while if we do not gain such advantages (the city) will not cause harm to the rear – in such cases, even though the city can be assaulted, do not assault it.[8]

For Carl von Clausewitz, cities presented an uncertain environment, a more prominent 'fog of war' complicating strategic planning and goals. While neither contended urban warfare should be avoided at all costs, they, and military tacticians generally, preferred the relatively empty stage of open fields or seas for the clash of war technology and troops without the physical and moral messiness of buildings, homes, and civilians.[9] Historians for their part not only work from the records and ideas of military strategists, generals, and campaign materials, all of which derive from manuals and strategies that have rarely addressed war's urban dimensions, but also operate within sub-disciplinary boundaries with distinct questions, terms, literatures, and methodologies. Only recently have both military and urban history branched out beyond their borders, incorporating the sources, approaches, and influences of social, cultural, transnational and global history, combining the insights of these diverse fields to investigate urban warfare in its broadest terms, from literal fighting to the very memory of war inscribed into the physical and psychic landscape of cities themselves. This edited volume seeks to push this recent historiographical shift further, bridging the most cutting-edge research and methodologies within military and urban history to better understand all the dimensions of what has and what will surely continue to be the dominant site of warfare.

---

8 Quoted in Louis DiMarco, "Attacking the Heart and Guts: Urban Operations Through the Ages," in *Block by Block: The Challenges of Urban Operations*, eds. William G. Robertson and Lawrence A. Yates (Fort Leavenworth KS: US. Army Command and General Staff College Press, 2003): 3.

9 Christian Aditya Niksch, "The Strategic Challenges of Urban Warfare," (M.A. Thesis: University of Denver, 2017), 6, 43.

Urban and Military History, Old and New

Though military history has a long tradition and remains a popular subject among the public, urban history is a relatively recent subfield, with its own distinct methodology and questions emerging in the tilt toward social history in the 1960s and 1970s. Prior to the 1960s, 'urban' history was a field with a 'meta-narrative,' as historians investigated the role of cities in human development generally or wrote urban biographies to explain a particular city's rise to prominence.[10] Scholars like Arthur M. Schlesinger exemplified the trend, making the case for cities as the driver of American history for example, overturning Frederick Jackson Turner's once-dominant idea that the American frontier drove change.[11] Lewis Mumford took the idea further in his magistral *The City in History*, contending that cities emancipated humanity itself from primitivism and irrationality, which as products of science and technology, civilized the world. Early urban histories didn't avoid the relationship between war and urbanization; on the contrary, Mumford admits that

> War and domination, rather than peace and co-operation, were ingrained in the original structure of the ancient city ... Thus both the physical form and the institutional life of the city, from the very beginning of the urban implosion, were shaped in no small measure by the irrational and magical purposes of war.[12]

But while the book ends as it starts, with a stern warning about the potential for total urban destruction, war is nonetheless but one subject among many in his generalized study of urbanization, a trait shared with the myriad of early city biographies.

The 'new' urban history, a sub-field of the social history revolution in the 1960s and 1970s, turned inward, no longer concerned with justifying the importance of cities in history, but instead investigating the historical origins to contemporary urban problems, the process of urbanization itself, and unearthing the lived experience of urban residents who otherwise left no record of their

---

10 Timothy Gilfoyle, "Michael Katz on Place and Space in Urban History," *Journal of Urban History* 41:4 (2015): 572-584.

11 Arthur M. Schlesinger, *The Rise of the City, 1878–1898* (Columbus, OH: Ohio State University Press, 1999); Richard C. Wade carries this argument further. See Richard C. Wade, *The Urban Frontier: The Rise of Western Cities 1790–1830* (Cambridge UK: Cambridge University Press, 1959).

12 Lewis Mumford, *The City in History: Its Origins, Its Transformations, and its Prospects* (New York: Harcourt, Brace & World, 1961), 44-45.

existence.[13] Through this research lens, war and its close relationship to cities became a modest subject of study. Urban warfare remained at the sidelines; Bowyer Bell's comparative study of mid-twentieth century urban sieges and Christopher Duffy's *Siege Warfare* remain standouts.[14] The one key exception was aerial bombardment and nuclear war, itself so grounded in the urban that scholars had to engage key urban questions.[15] But in broader terms, scholars employed social scientific tools to understand broader links between war and cities. Roger W. Lotchin's edited collection, *The Martial Metropolis*, makes the case that urbanization not only depends on the conventional variables of demography, regional economic strength and local politics, but state defense spending and militarization, influencing city planning, politics, education, infrastructure, and the local economy, a 'metropolitan-military' complex in the U.S.[16] Conversely, Philip Benedict's celebrated *Rouen During the Wars of Religion* employs quantitative analysis to reveal how the sixteenth-century religious wars were a "profound social and cultural crisis affecting the entire society," shaping municipal government, class politics, even the use of urban space among Protestants and Catholics.[17] *Capital Cities at War* epitomizes the very best in this line of research, a collaborative comparative history of Paris, London and Berlin during the first World War from respected social historians. Departing from the usual focus on nation-state mobilization, the authors contend that war is experienced at the local, community level, not at the 'imagined' national level, and the city is where these lived experience and the 'imagined' national community coalesce. Seventeen chapters illustrate how war shaped housing, public health, labor, prices, and how administrators managed food, public order, and energy amidst the upheaval of war to varying degrees of success across the three cities, and more broadly, how the psychological and physical impact of war rested unevenly across class-stratified neighborhoods.[18]

---

13 Margaret Marsh, "Old Forms, New Visions: New Directions in United States Urban History," *Pennsylvania History: A Journal of Mid-Atlantic Studies* 59:1 (1992), 21-28.

14 Bower J. Bell, *Besieged: Seven Cities under Siege* (Philadelphia: Chilton, 1966); Christopher Duffy, *Siege Warfare: The Fortress in the Early Modern World* (London: Routledge, 1979).

15 For examples, see Hans Rumpf, *The Bombing of Germany* (New York: Rinehart and Winston, 1962); Tom Harrisson, *Living Through the Blitz* (London: Collins, 1965); Hewitt, "Place Annihilation," 257-284.

16 Roger W. Lotchin, ed. *The Martial Metropolis: U.S. Cities in War and Peace* (New York: Praeger, 1984).

17 Philip Benedict, *Rouen during the Wars of Religion* (Cambridge: Cambridge University Press, 1981), ix.

18 Jay M. Winter and Jean-Louis Robert, eds. *Capital Cities at War: Paris, London, Berlin, 1914–1919* (New York: Cambridge University Press, 1999).

Though the 'new' urban history opened up avenues for inquiry and "validated the importance of the city as an essential locus of cultural, class, and gender accomodation as well as conflict," the quantitative focus, sometimes narrow questions, and dominance of case studies to prove or disprove broad theories nonetheless limit the scope of study. Perhaps Phillippa Levine's review of *Capital Cities at War* illustrates the boundaries of the 'new' urban history best when she calls the book a 'descriptive' analysis "so intimidatingly reliant on statistical inquiry and on economic and demographic data ... which rarely goes beyond the presentation of carefully gathered and precise data to examine the meaning – and the problems – of the authors' notion of "community." With a focus on wage changes, coal supplies, or material sacrifice among urban residents, the authors fail to address bigger problematics beyond the assertion that war affected cities.[19] Levine's criticism exemplifies the shift away from the 'new' urban history's narrow methodologies starting in the 1980s, as scholars drew on a much broader array of interpretive paradigms. The cultural turn has been particularly influential, permitting a veritable explosion in the field, examining such wide-ranging topics as the construction of social identities linked to physical locales, the role of gender in shaping street discourse or public space, meanings inscribed into the built environment, the relationship between urban infrastructure and values or culture, and examinations of language's influence on urban political behavior, among others.[20] The 'spatial' turn has been equally important. Both place and space are now understood as having influence over how and why events happen, not as fixed entities, 'stages' where human drama occurs, but as places imbued with meaning that shapes human activity or as a social construction by people; the influence of space and place, the *where*, is elevated alongside change over time in historical thinking. Events or historical concepts are understood to have uneven spatial and historical consequences.[21]

This most recent methodological shift has greatly benefitted the study of war and cities. After all, military history underwent its own revolution alongside the latest cultural and spatial turns in urban history. The 'old' military history,

---

19 Phillippa Levine, Review of *Capital Cities at War: Paris, London, Berlin, 1914–1919*, *The Journal of Modern History* 71:2 (1999), 445-447.

20 Timothy J. Gilfoyle, "White Cities, Linguistic Turns, and Disneylands: New Paradigms of Urban History," *Reviews in American History* 26:1 (1998), 175-204.

21 Charles J. Withers, "Place and the Spatial Turn in Geography and History," *Journal of the History of Ideas* 70:4 (2009), 637-658; David Livingstone, "The Spaces of Knowledge: Contributions Towards a Historical Geography of Science," *Environment and Planning D: Society and Space* 13 (1995), 5-34; John Agnew and James Duncan, eds. *The Power of Place* (Boston: Unwin Hyman, 1990).

with its focus on weapons, tactics, war operations, and campaigns, its narratives resting on the 'great' leaders and battles has given way to a "new military history," histories of war connected to society, economics, politics, and culture, aspects of war no less important but nonetheless distinct from the narrow and sometimes pedantic concerns of traditional studies.[22] Robert M. Citino contends that the new military history "has developed over the past few decades into the very epitome of the big tent," with all sorts of new branches growing from the military history tree: 'war and society' scholarship, operational historians who more deeply analyze the hows and whys of warfare, those studying memory and culture, scholars integrating questions of race, gender, and class into histories of warfare or military composition, among other subjects.[23] If anything, new military histories are "accused of being interested in everything about armies except the way they fought, interested in everything about war except campaigns and battles."[24] While histories of war have remained a perennially popular subject among the public, the new directions in military history have reinvigorated the sub-field within the academy, and American scholars Tami Davis Biddle and Robert M. Citino correctly believe that "scholars in our field are well-positioned to draw linkages and build bridges among subfields in history, and to engage in interdisciplinary work."[25]

Those bridges include linking military and urban history, which since the turn of the century has blossomed across both sub-disciplines, with some scholars building upon earlier work, while others taking war and urban history in radically new directions. Operational historians for their part make the forceful case for urban warfare as a central element of warfare itself. Antony Beevor re-popularized the urban warfare biography with award-winning books, including *Paris after the Liberation, 1944–1949*, *Stalingrad*, *Berlin – The Downfall 1945*, and most recently *Arnhem: The Battle for the Bridges, 1944*, mixing urban operational narrative with compelling portraits of those who experienced the

---

22 Peter Paret, "The New Military History," *Parameters* 21 (1991), 10-18; Joanna Bourke, "New Military History," in *Palgrave Advances in Modern Military History*, eds. Willliam J. Philpott and Matthew Hughes (London: Palgrave MacMillan, 2004), 258-280; Yuval Noah Harari, "The Concept of "Decisive Battles" in World History," *Journal of World History,* 18:3 (2007), 251-266.

23 Robert M. Citino, "Military Histories Old and New: A Reinterpretation," *American Historical Review* 112 (2007), 1070.

24 Ibid., 1071.

25 Tami Davis Biddle and Robert M. Citino, "The Role of Military History in the Contemporary Academy," *A Society for Military History White Paper* (2014), 5. Accessed, April 13, 2018. https://www.acls.org/uploadedFiles/News/SMHWhitePaper.pdf.

repercussions of urban warfare firsthand: combatants, civilians, children, etc.[26] Scholarly works investigating key questions about the nature of urban warfare include Gregory J. Ashworth's *War and the City*, which surveys the changing spatial layout of cities for the purpose of defense in early modern Europe, showing how defensive construction evolved over history from a concern with invasions from beyond city borders to insurgencies and rioting from within, reshaping how military planners built for violence.[27] Paul K. Davis meanwhile surveys siege warfare from ancient Jericho to Sarajevo in the 1990s.[28] *Block by Block: The Challenges of Urban Operations* is an edited collection with a general overview of urban operations throughout history along with ten case studies of urban warfare since World War II, all serving to re-conceptualize urban operations given its dominance throughout history and growing importance in the present. It rightly takes into account the broader context of urban warfare and the fact that while military theory has been slow to catch onto urban operations, history has many case studies of the often improvised and experimental ways militaries have fought, secured, and policed urban environments.[29] And scholarship on recent history, including urban operations in the Iraq War and War on Terror, have sparked a re-engagement with the nature, efficacy, and outcomes of urban warfare.[30]

Scholars have also taken urban warfare further, conceiving of cities as sites of war in the broader sense. The fraught concept of 'urbicide,' generally the annihilation of city structures or cities themselves as the strategic object of violence, well beyond the bounds of 'military necessity,' has been a fruitful lens to consider war's impact on cities.[31] The concept has been employed both explicitly and implicitly. Histories of aerial bombardment illustrate how

---

26 Antony Beevor and Artemis Cooper, *Paris After the Liberation, 1944–1949* (New York: Penguin Books, 2004); Antony Beevor, *Stalingrad* (London: Viking, 1998); Antony Beevor, *Berlin: The Downfall 1945* (London: Penguin Books, 2002); Antony Beevor, *Arnhem: The Battle for the Bridges, 1944* (London: Viking, 2018).

27 Gregory J. Ashworth, *War and the City* (New York: Routledge, 1991).

28 Paul K. Davis, *Besieged: 100 Great Sieges from Jericho to Sarajevo* (Santa Barbara, CA: ABC-CLIO, 2001).

29 William G. Robertson and Lawrence A. Yates, eds. *Block by Block: The Challenges of Urban Operations* (Fort Leavenworth KS: U.S. Army Command and General Staff College Press, 2003).

30 For some examples, see Stephen Graham, ed. *Cities, War, and Terrorism: Towards an Urban Geopolitics* (Malden, MA: Blackwell Publishing, 2004); Alice Hills, *Future War in Cities: Rethinking a Liberal Dilemma* (London: Frank Cass, 2004).

31 David Campbell, Stephen Graham, and Daniel Bertrand Monk, "Introduction of Urbicide: The Killing of Cities?" *Theory & Event*, 10:2 (2007); Martin Coward, *Urbicide: The Politics of Urban Destruction* (London: Routledge, 2009).

cities became "battlespaces" in the modern era, due to their sites as military-industrial centers, homes to the enemy population, and their cultural significance to morale. As Martin Shaw contends, urbanization and bombing went hand in hand, as bombardment "moved from the selective destruction of key sites within cities to extensive attacks on urban areas, and, finally, to instantaneous annihilation of entire urban spaces and populations."[32] Urbicide has likewise been useful to understanding colonial practices of domination in conquered cities, which some link to urban renewal's urbicidal destruction of the places in imperial capitals.[33] Beyond urbicide, historians have also flipped the relationship of cities and war, using an expansive notion of 'urban' to claim that battlefields themselves constitute urban forms, particularly as soldiers and civilians remake bomb shelters and trenches into familiar urban spaces, or as in the case of Russia's largely peasant population, experience urban rituals and spaces for the first time in these densely populated tight spaces they share with urbanized comrades.[34]

Urban historians though have went beyond urban warfare, building upon the older histories of war and urbanization to explore themes and concepts relevant to the most recent trends in both fields. These include urban reconstruction and renewal, relationships between city and countryside during wartime, organized violence, and segregation, among other topics.[35] Winter and Robert's second volume of *Capital Cities at War* for example covers topics scantily addressed in their initial collection: landscapes, identity, cultural meanings inscribed into place, nostalgia and memory, rituals of mourning, and contested struggles for public space in Paris, Berlin, and London during the

32 Martin Shaw, *War and Genocide: Organised Killing in Modern Society* (New York: John Wiley & Sons, 2015), 131.

33 Marshall Berman, "Falling Towers: City Life after Urbicide," in *Geography and Identity*, ed. Dennis Crow (Washington: Maisonneuve, 1996), 172-192; Neil Smith, *The Urban Frontier: Gentrification and the Revanchist City* (London: Routledge, 1996); Stephen Graham, "Cities as Strategic Sites: Place Annihilation and Urban Geopolitics," in *Cities, War, and Terrorism: Towards an Urban Geopolitics*, ed. Stephen Graham (London: Blackwell, 2004), 31-53.

34 Tan Gang, "Living Underground: Bomb Shelters and Daily Lives in Wartime Chongqing (1937–1945)," *Journal of Urban History*, 43:3 (2017), 383-399; Brandon Schechter, *Government Issue: The Material Culture of the Red Army 1941–1945* (Cornell University Press, forthcoming).

35 For some examples, see Jeffry M. Dießendorf, *In the Wake of War: The Reconstruction of German Cities after World War II* (New York and Oxford: Oxford University Press, 1993), 43; Marcus Funck and Roger Chickering, eds. *Endangered Cities: Military Power and Urban Societies in the Era of the World Wars* (Boston: Brill, 2004); Toby Lincoln, The Rural and Urban at War Invasion and Reconstruction in China during the Anti-Japanese War of Resistance, "The Rural and Urban at War Invasion and Reconstruction in China during the Anti-Japanese War of Resistance," *Journal of Urban History* 38:1 (2012), 114-132.

first World War.[36] Carl Nightingale's *Global Segregation* meanwhile situates the origins of urban racial segegregation in the crucible of war and conquest. As he argues, English colonization of Ireland entailed plowing seventy miles of earthworks around Dublin's hinterland to keep out the Irish, "the pale" that separated barbarity from civilization, and their spread of Protestant power included walling off city sections to separate Catholics from city centers, a practice corresponding to other colonial urban policies in Portuguese, Dutch, and Spanish colonies.[37] And urban scholars have found new angles in the seemingly saturated field of the American Civil War, making a compelling case for cities, even in the rural Confederate South, as the center of critical military-related themes, from gender, emancipation, and the causes and course of the war, to the destruction of the rebel nation itself.[38]

Contributions

This is hardly an exhaustive summary, particularly as the scholarship continues to evolve. The sub-field's exciting growth led to the 2017 Conference in New York City that brought together scholars to assess the state of research and consider future scholarship. The present volume is the fruit of this conference, and the chapters build off two decades of recent scholarship with cutting-edge research demonstrating where histories of war and cities are going. The volume is organized from the inside out, starting with urban warfare in the more conventional sense and then moving outward toward post-conquest urban occupation and refugee management, and finally to postwar urban reconstruction and memory. Jonathan Beall provides a case study of an all-too often reality of urban warfare: troops, untrained for urban environments, having to figure out the 'grammar' of urban operations in an ad-hoc basis, at the cost of lives and military losses. His example is the U.S. Army's 1st Infantry Division during World War II, who experienced urban fighting within hours of landing in North Africa in November 1942 despite having no training or field manuals to prepare them for such fighting, which forced them to improvise, augment their weapons and tactics, learn from mistakes, and develop an urban strategy on the ground as they repeatedly faced the Axis powers in urban settings

36 Jay M. Winter and Jean-Louis Robert, eds. *Capital Cities at War: Paris, London, Berlin 1914–1919*, vol. 2: *A Cultural History* (Cambridge: Cambridge University Press, 2007).

37 Carl Nightingale, *Segregation: A Global History of Divided Cities* (Chicago: University of Chicago Press, 2012).

38 Andrew L. Slap and Frank Towers, eds. *Confederate Cities: The Urban South During the Civil War Era* (Chicago: University of Chicago Press, 2015).

through to their march to Bonn in 1945. Alexander QUERENGÄSSER examines the intimate connections between the warfront and urban homefront in Early Modern Saxony during the Great Northern War (1700–1717), contending that early modern cities filled in for deficiencies of pre-modern militaries. They not only provided the conventional needs for war (as fortifications for civilians, sources of credit, material, etc.), but served as hospitals, housing, jails, even job markets for idle troops. These functions, usually provided by modern states or private contractors in the last two centuries, were filled in by city inhabitants and municipal governments, illustrating the deep and personal connections urban residents had with war in Early Modern Germany. Finally, Linda PARKER compares civilian and British government responses to German air attacks on London in World War I and World War II. She contends that the air raids did serve their purpose of eroding civilian morale in their destruction of the physical landscape, a result not only of the raids themselves, but flawed government information campaigns and preparation procedures, which she deftly illustrates through her careful analysis of state archives and newspaper reports.

The next section covers the complications of urban military occupation and the fallout from urban sieges. James HORNCASTLE investigates the role of urbicide in shaping international responses to war. In this case, the 1991 siege of Vukovar's global media coverage decisively swayed international opinion from ambiguity and toward Croatian sympathy. Serbian aggression, inscribed in the destroyed buildings, the denial of aid to residents, and the refugees fleeing the city, shaped public opinion in Croatia's favor, which played a critical role in the outcome of the globally-influenced Yugoslav War. Simon DAVIS explores the Great Rebellion in British Mandate Palestine from a novel urban angle overlooked in histories that favor Palestine's rural insurgencies. It was the British colonialist framing of urban Arab Palestine, a place of lawlessness, filth, and general dysfunction, which fed a general apathy and avoidance of places like Jaffa, which in turn produced the conditions to protest and organize an insurgency that far surpassed the small uprisings British police forces were accustomed to, leading to a violent counter-insurgency. Stefan LAFFIN uses the politics of food provision in Allied-controlled Naples during World War II as a lens to understand urban military occupation. As he puts it, adequate food supply or distribution networks was the 'real test' of occupation for the Allied military government, and the Allies failed in this regard, as soldiers cleaned out shops, the occupiers doled out rations in a hierarchy of privilege, and relief proved inadequate, forcing Neapolitans to turn to the exploitative dense urban black market. From the vantage of urban residents, the failure to provide food blurred the lines between the retreating fascist regime and Allied 'liberators,' and the popular narrative of the resistance and Allied liberation formed from small villages and Southern Italy, not from the endless breadlines, corrupt black market, and food uprisings in cities like Naples.

The final chapter address postwar urban reconstruction and public memory, particularly the role of urban architecture in constructing national identities following massive upheaval to established states. Andrew DEMSHUK compares reconstruction between one war and another: the rebuilding of 'sacred sites' in Frankfurt, Leipzig, and Wrocław, cities formerly under German control during World War II, as they came under the control of divided ideologies and nation-states during the Cold War: liberal democracy, socialist utopianism, and Polish nationalism, respectively. In each case, planners, the public, local officials, and architects exploited urban destruction to 'reinvent a usable past' from sites that would situate the city within a new national story, and though each pursued different forms of reconstruction to fit their various still-gestating ideological/national narratives, a 'usable' past and vision for the future emerged in all three, each with relatively broad public support and good-will.

Though collectively the chapters cover the breadth of the new urban and military history, from urban operations to urbicide, occupation, and reconstruction, there are limits. The volume remains decidedly Euro-centric; only one chapter moves beyond Europe, a particular weakness given the recent explosion of global urban history.[39] In addition, the chapters are set in the modern era, despite the fact that urban warfare is at least as old as cities and organized conflict itself, as noted earlier. And while questions of identity emerge throughout, particularly ethnicity and nationality, gender is little discussed, an exciting theme in both sub-fields. Despite these omissions, the need for this volume is more important than ever. Military scholars now recognize that the present and future of war will be primarily urban, but as Antonio Sampaio notes, urban operational literature still fails to "consider the broader social, poiltical, and economic dynamics that affect the urban environment as part of military strategy." Sampaio implores military strategists to think of cities as "socially constructed spaces, with their densely built areas being a material envelope for a deeper set of human and institutional connections that are the true drivers of the success or failure of a given security or stabilization

39 For an overview of the long global urban 'concept,' see Stuart Schrader, "Henri Lefebvre, Mao Zedong, and the Global Urban Concept," *Global Urban History Blog*, May 1, 2018. Accessed, May 2, 2018. https://globalurbanhistory.com/2018/05/01/henri-lefebvre-mao-zedong-and-the-global-urban-concept/.

mission."[40] A more holistic view of warfare's impact on cities, which the chapters in this volume and recent urban military histories more generally examine, is critical for grappling with what is sure to continue and proliferate. With more than half of the global population living in cities as of 2008, and with urban real estate replacing industry as the driver of global capitalism in the past few decades, urban destruction threatens the majority of humanity directly through violence or indirectly through its effect on the global market.[41] Therefore, questions of cities as sites of war production, warfronts themselves, food provision, reconstruction, insurgency, and memory, all covered in this volume, are only increasingly relevant. Lastly, the volume represents the thrust of recent scholarship, and more importantly, offers avenues which scholars need to explore further.

Works Cited

Agnew, John and James Duncan, eds. *The Power of Place*. Boston: Unwin Hyman, 1990.

Ashworth, Gregory J. *War and the City*. New York: Routledge, 1991.

Beevor, Antony and Artemis Cooper. *Paris After the Liberation, 1944–1949*. New York: Penguin Books, 2004.

Beevor, Antony. *Arnhem: The Battle for the Bridges, 1944*. London: Viking, 2018.

Beevor, Antony. *Berlin: The Downfall 1945*. London: Penguin Books, 2002.

Beevor, Antony. *Stalingrad*. London: Viking, 1998.

Bell, Bower J. *Besieged: Seven Cities under Siege*. Philadelphia: Chilton, 1966.

Benedict, Philip Benedict. *Rouen during the Wars of Religion*. Cambridge: Cambridge University Press, 1981.

Berman, Marshall. "Falling Towers: City Life after Urbicide." In *Geography and Identity*, edited by Dennis Crow, 172-192. Washington: Maisonneuve, 1996.

Biddle, Tami Davis and Robert M. Citino. "The Role of Military History in the Contemporary Academy." *A Society for Military History White Paper* (2014), https://www.acls.org/uploadedFiles/News/SMHWhitePaper.pdf (accessed April 13, 2018).

Bourke, Joanna. "New Military History." In *Palgrave Advances in Modern Military History*, edited by Willliam J. Philpott and Matthew Hughes, 258-280. London: Palgrave MacMillan, 2004.

40 Antonio Sampaio, "The Utility of Force in Cities: Future Challenges of US Army Urban Stabilization Efforts," in *The Future of US Warfare*, eds. Scott N. Romaniuk and Francis Grice (New York: Routledge, 2017): 173-183.

41 "Urban Population (% of total)," Wold Bank Open Data, *The World Bank*, https://data.worldbank.org/indicator/sp.urb.totl.in.zs (Accessed April 25, 2018); Peter Marcuse, *In Defense of Housing* (New York: Verso, 2016), 8-9.

Campbell, David, Stephen Graham, and Daniel Bertrand Monk. "Introduction of Urbicide: The Killing of Cities?" *Theory & Event*, 10:2 (2007), https://muse.jhu.edu/ (accessed April 23, 2018).

Citino, Robert M. "Military Histories Old and New: A Reinterpretation," *American Historical Review* 112 (October 2017): 1070-1090.

Coward, Martin. *Urbicide: The Politics of Urban Destruction*. London: Routledge, 2009.

Davis, Paul K. *Besieged: 100 Great Sieges from Jericho to Sarajevo*. Santa Barbara, CA: ABC-CLIO, 2001.

Dießendorf, Jeffry M. *In the Wake of War. The Reconstruction of German Cities after World War II*. New York and Oxford: Oxford University Press, 1993.

DiMarco, Louis. *Concrete Hell: Urban Warfare from Stalingrad to Iraq*. Oxford: Osprey, 2012.

Dincecco, Mark and Massimiliano Gaetano Onorato. "Military Conflict and the Economic Rise of Urban Europe," *Journal of Economic Growth* 21:3 (September 2016): 259-282.

Duffy, Christopher. *Siege Warfare: The Fortress in the Early Modern World*. London: Routledge, 1979.

Funck, Marcus and Roger Chickering. eds. *Endangered Cities: Military Power and Urban Societies in the Era of the World Wars*. Boston: Brill, 2004.

Gang, Tan. "Living Underground: Bomb Shelters and Daily Lives in Wartime Chongqing (1937–1945)." *Journal of Urban History*, 43:3 (May 2017): 383-399.

Gilfoyle, Timothy J. "White Cities, Linguistic Turns, and Disneylands: New Paradigms of Urban History," *Reviews in American History* 26:1 (March 1998): 175-204.

Gilfoyle, Timothy J. "Michael Katz on Place and Space in Urban History," *Journal of Urban History* 41:4 (July 2015): 572-584.

Graham, Stephen. ed. *Cities, War, and Terrorism: Towards an Urban Geopolitics*. Malden, MA: Blackwell Publishing, 2004.

Harari, Yuval Noah. "The Concept of "Decisive Battles" in World History," *Journal of World History*, 18:3 (September 2007): 251-266.

Harms, William. "Evidence of Battle at Hamoukar points to early Urban Development," *The University of Chicago Chronicle* 26:8 (January 18, 2007). http://chronicle.uchicago.edu/070118/hamoukar.shtml (Accessed March 14, 2017).

Harrisson Tom. *Living Through the Blitz*. London: Collins, 1965.

Hewitt, Ken. "Place Annlihilation: Area Bombing and the Fate of Urban Places," *Annals of the Association of American Geographers* 73:2 (June 1983): 257-284.

Hills, Alice. *Future War in Cities: Rethinking a Liberal Dilemma*. London: Frank Cass, 2004.

Levine, Phillippa. Review of *Capital Cities at War: Paris, London, Berlin, 1914–1919, The Journal of Modern History* 71:2 (June 1999): 445-447.

Lincoln, Toby. "The Rural and Urban at War Invasion and Reconstruction in China during the Anti-Japanese War of Resistance," *Journal of Urban History* 38:1 (January 2012): 114-132.
Livingstone, David. "The Spaces of Knowledge: Contributions Towards a Historical Geography of Science," *Environment and Planning D: Society and Space* 13 (1995): 5-34.
Lotchin, Roger W. ed. *The Martial Metropolis: U.S. Cities in War and Peace*. New York: Praeger, 1984.
Marcuse, Peter. *In Defense of Housing*. New York: Verso, 2016.
Marsh, Margaret. "Old Forms, New Visions: New Directions in United States Urban History." *Pennsylvania History: A Journal of Mid-Atlantic Studies* 59:1 (January 1992): 21-28.
Mumford, Lewis. *The City in History: Its Origins, Its Transformations, and its Prospects*. New York: Harcourt, Brace & World, 1961.
Nightingale, Carl. *Segregation: A Global History of Divided Cities*. Chicago: University of Chicago Press, 2012.
Niksch, Christian Aditya. "The Strategic Challenges of Urban Warfare." M.A. Thesis: University of Denver, 2017. https://digitalcommons.du.edu/cgi/viewcontent.cgi?article=2285&context=etd (Accessed April 20, 2018).
Paret, Peter. "The New Military History," *Parameters* 21 (Autumn 1991): 10-18.
Pinker, Steven. *The Better Angles of our Nature: Why Violence has Declined*. New York: Penguin Press, 2012.
Robertson, William G. and Lawrence A. Yates, eds. *Block by Block: The Challenges of Urban Operations*. Fort Leavenworth KS: U.S. Army Command and General Staff College Press, 2003.
Rumpf, Hans. *The Bombing of Germany*. New York: Rinehart and Winston, 1962.
Sampaio, Antonio. "The Utility of Force in Cities: Future Challenges of US Army Urban Stabilization Efforts." In *The Future of US Warfare*, edited by Scott N. Romaniuk and Francis Grice. 173-183. New York: Routledge, 2017.
Schelsinger, Arthur M. *The Rise of the City, 1878–1898*. Columbus, OH: Ohio State University Press, 1999.
Schrader, Stuart. "Henri Lefebvre, Mao Zedong, and the Global Urban Concept," *Global Urban History Blog*, May 1, 2018, https://globalurbanhistory.com/2018/05/01/henri-lefebvre-mao-zedong-and-the-global-urban-concept/ (Accessed May 2, 2018)
Scott, James C. *Against the Grain: A Deep History of the Earliest States*. New Haven: Yale University Press, 2017.
Shaw, Martin Shaw. *War and Genocide: Organised Killing in Modern Society*. New York: John Wiley & Sons, 2015.
Slap, Andrew L. and Frank Towers, eds. *Confederate Cities: The Urban South During the Civil War Era*. Chicago: University of Chicago Press, 2015.

Smith, Neil. *The Urban Frontier: Gentrification and the Revanchist City*. London: Routledge, 1996.

Wade, Richard C. *The Urban Frontier: The Rise of Western Cities 1790–1830*. Cambridge: Cambridge University Press, 1959.

Weber, Max. *Economy and Society*. Berkeley: University of California Press, 1978.

Winter, Jay M., and Jean-Louis Robert. eds. *Capital Cities at War: Paris, London, Berlin, 1914–1919*. New York: Cambridge University Press, 1999.

Winter, Jay M., and Jean-Louis Robert. eds. *Capital Cities at War: Paris, London, Berlin 1914–1919; Volume 2: A Cultural History*. Cambridge: Cambridge University Press, 2007.

Withers, Charles J. "Place and the Spatial Turn in Geography and History," *Journal of the History of Ideas* 70:4 (October 2009), 637-658.

CHAPTER 2

Learning the "Grammar" of Urban Operations: The United States Army and Urban Combat in World War II

Jonathan A. Beall

When American forces fought the Mexican Army inside the streets of Monterey, Mexico in September 1846, a Texan described the urban fight as "a most strange and *novel* scene of warfare."[1] As the 19th Massachusetts Volunteer Infantry floundered in the streets of Fredericksburg in December 1862, one officer recalled that it "was not only *novel* but a great strain upon the moral and physical courage."[2] In September 1944, Major General Walter Robertson's slugged through the streets of Brest. Although the popular term for urban combat in World War II was "street fighting," Robertson recorded that "the term 'street fighting' is a misnomer, for the street was one place we could not go ... Our procedure was to go from house to house blasting holes through the walls with satchel charges."[3] Early examinations of the nine-month long battle of Mosul in Iraq in 2016 and 2017 has invited comparisons to earlier urban clashes such as Stalingrad in from 1942 to 1943 and Hue in 1968. For all the advanced technology at the anti-ISIS coalition's fingertips, combatants had to deal with booby traps, snipers, and a brutal, house-by-house, dismounted fight in the Old City's narrow, winding streets.[4] While twenty-first century technology clearly affected the urban fight for Mosul, the battle was waged in ways very similar to the urban battles of past wars. These historical examples point to urban combat's distinctive nature that sets it apart from other environments.

1 Samuel C. Reid, Jr. *The Scouting Expeditions of McCulloch's Texas Rangers; of The Summer and Fall Campaign of the Army of the United States in Mexico – 1846; Including Skirmishes with the Mexicans, and an Accurate Detail of the Storming of Monterey; also the Daring Scouts at Buena Vista; Together with Anecdotes, Incidents, Descriptions of Country, and Sketches of the Lives of the Celebrated Partisan Chiefs, Hays, McCulloch, and Walker* (Philadelphia: G. B. Zieber and Co., 1848), 192. Italics added.

2 John G.B. Adams, *Reminiscences of the Nineteenth Massachusetts Regiment* (Boston: Wright & Potter Printing Company, 1899), 50. Italics added.

3 "Fighting in the City of Brest," *Twelfth Army Group Battle Experiences* 50 (28 September 1944), 1.

4 For an early analysis of the long battle for Mosul, see Ben Watson, "What the Largest Battle of the Decade Says About the Future of War," *Defense One*, 28 June 2017. http://www.defenseone.com/feature/mosul-largest-battle-decade-future-of-war/.

 | DOI:10.30965/9783657702787_003

This reality is true whether armies, like those in the 1800s, have no doctrine for urban combat or, like many armies in the twenty-first century, invest more heavily in urban combat training.

Policy analyst Alice Hills argues that urban operations are unique because they possess their own grammar, or guidelines and rules that influence methods and conduct.[5] Hills borrows from a singular line in Carl von Clausewitz's 1832 *On War* where he writes that "its [war's] grammar, indeed, may be its own but not its logic."[6] Or, more commonly: war has its own grammar but not its own logic. In explaining the grammar-logic metaphor, Clausewitz scholar Antulio Echevarria describes the "grammar" of war as the fundamental principles in the conduct of war that pertain to the operational and tactical levels of warfighting. The logic of war, Echevarria continues, includes the different political goals that nations hope to achieve by going to war and the strategic means to achieve those goals. In this understanding, why a nation chooses to fight a war – the logic – changes even as the conduct of war – the grammar – has long continuities that guide warfighting.[7]

Alice Hills applies Clausewitz's grammar-logic concept to argue that urban combat forcefully imposes its own grammar of war upon armies because "cities represent a man-made environment that interact with armies in a way jungles do not."[8] That radically different grammar is influenced by the nature of urban geography in that, first, cities are simultaneously three-dimensional and spatially confining. While fighting at street level, forces must deal with the enemy moving through subterranean routes below as well as firing from multiple stories above street level. At the same time, streets and buildings confine attacking forces and a defender may channel the attacker down prepared ambush routes. Tall buildings often interfere with radio communications, thus exacerbating friction and uncertainty. It is because of cities' restrictive spatial nature that urban combat is often more violent and chaotic than in other environments. Secondly, cities' interconnected infrastructures and

5 Alice Hills, "Continuity and Discontinuity: The Grammar of Urban Military Operations," in *Cities, War, and Terrorism: Towards an Urban Geopolitics*, ed. Stephen Graham (Malden, MA: Blackwell Publishing, 2004), 231-246. See also Alice Hills, *Future War in Cities: Rethinking a Liberal Dilemma* (London: Frank Cass, 2004). For a discussion on the nature of urban battle and the Battle of Mosul, see John Amble, host, "The Battle for Mosul, with Col. Pat Work," *The Modern War Institute Podcast* (MP3 podcast), 14 February 2018. https://mwi.usma.edu/mwi-podcast-battle-mosul-col-pat-work/.

6 Carl von Clausewitz, *On War*, trans. Michael Howard and Peter Paret (Princeton: Princeton University Press, 1984), 605.

7 Antulio J. Echevarria II, "Reconsidering War's Logic and Grammar," *Infinity Journal* 2 (Spring 2011), 4-7.

8 Hills, "Continuity and Discontinuity," 236.

complex social networks influence how combatants conduct an urban battle. In describing cities as living organisms, General Don Starry explains that cities' "interrelated systems in the organic infrastructure" can affect how belligerents conduct offensive and defensive operations.[9] For instance, as an attacking army cuts a city's power grid, so it must also find a way to run hospitals and supply clean water. Lastly, the presence of large numbers of civilian noncombatants is a characteristic exclusive to the urban environment. The deaths of large numbers of civilians can have a larger strategic and political impact but if an attacking army's rules of engagement are too tight, it may lead to more soldiers' deaths.[10] Hills also warns that the brutal nature of urban combat is often at odds with Western ways of humanitarian war. Furthermore, the grammar of urban operations involves more than tactics and fighting techniques; it often includes a host of complex issues that armies must confront, involving elements such as logistics, civil affairs, military government, and military law. Armies must master this unique "grammar" if they hope to be effective in the urban environment.[11] For soldiers, fighting within cities can mean fighting within a difficult and often confusing geography, amongst civilians, in intense close-quarters battles that can negate technology, with strained logistics, against strengthened defenders, in decentralized units, and often devolving into savagery.

This chapter examines how one infantry division, the U.S. Army's 1st Infantry Division, grappled with that distinct grammar in World War II before the development of any urban operations doctrine and training and within the logic of the American war effort against Germany. The 1st Infantry Division, or the "Big Red One," was part of the invasion of North Africa in November 1942 and experienced its first urban fight within hours of landing. It fought in Sicily and then trained in England for the invasion of northern France. The Big Red One landed on Omaha Beach and fought its way through Germany and, by 1945, had encountered significant urban combat. Although this division fought throughout America's war in Europe and was hailed as one of the Army's finest combat units, it was also composed primarily of drafted citizen-soldiers rather

9 Don A. Starry, foreword to *Block by Block: The Challenges of Urban Operations*, edited by William G. Robertson and Lawrence A. Yates (Fort Leavenworth: U.S. Army Command and General Staff College Press, 2003), ix-x. See also John Spencer and John Amble, "A Better Approach to Urban Operations: Treat Cities Like Human Bodies," 13 September 2017. https://mwi.usma.edu/better-approach-urban-operations-treat-cities-like-human-bodies/. To see the state of the dialogue between national security and military professionals on urban operations, see The Small Wars Journal's urban operations webpage at https://smallwarsjournal.com/urban_operations/main.

10 William G. Rosenau, "'Every Room Is a New Battle': The Lessons of Modern Urban Warfare," *Studies in Conflict and Terrorism* 20:4 (1997), 389-390.

11 Hills, "Continuity and Discontinuity," 231, 243-244.

than military professionals and had to learn the grammar of urban combat. It serves as a good example of how many American divisions learned over the course of World War II. The 1st Infantry Division is also significant in that it fought one of America's most significant urban battles when it seized Aachen, Germany in October 1944. Tracing the division's path through World War II affords an opportunity to understand the nature of conventional urban combat as well as see a combat unit's learning curve during wartime. The Big Red One shows elements consistent with the U.S. Army in World War II; namely, that as the Americans became more adept at combined-arms fighting and appreciated the urban environment's unique challenges, so it became fluent in the grammar of urban operations.[12] It also shows the constants that modern militaries must face and overcome in the urban environment regardless of time and place.

The Interwar Period was a busy time for the U.S. Army. The officer corps hotly disputed to what extent World War I had changed warfare while debating changes in military organization and infantry doctrine, the natures of air power and mechanized warfare, and developing amphibious warfare doctrine. By 1941, the Army's infantry divisions were "triangular." Each of the three infantry regiments partnered with a field artillery battalion to form "regimental combat teams." Each infantry regiment was composed of three battalions; each battalion had three rifle companies (and a heavy weapons company); each rifle company had three rifle platoons (and a weapons platoon); each rifle platoon had three squads.[13] The authorized size of an infantry division fluctuated around 14,000 men during the war.[14] The Big Red One was no different: the 16th, 18th, and 26th U.S. Infantry Regiments were each paired with a field artillery battalion, which helped create strong infantry-artillery teamwork. At the same time, uncertainty regarding the purpose and role of the tank minimized effective infantry-armor coordination and teamwork during this period. Combat inside towns and cities received virtually no attention. The closest that the United States Army came to an urban combat doctrine was

12 Simply put, combined-arms fighting means the coordination of all weapons systems on hand: in the World War II context, that meant combining and coordinating all infantry weapons with artillery, armor, engineers, and air power. See Jonathan M. House, *Combined Arms Warfare in the Twentieth Century* (Lawrence: University Press of Kansas, 2001).

13 Companies, battalions, and regiments can be denoted through a form of shorthand. For example, A Company, First Battalion, 18th U.S. Infantry Regiment is written as A/1/18; Second Battalion, 16th Infantry would be simply 2/16; and K Company, Third Battalion, 26th Infantry would be K/3/26. This form of shorthand will be used throughout this essay.

14 Virgil Ney, *Evolution of the U.S. Army Division, 1939–1968*, CORG-M-365 (Fort Belvoir: Combat Operations Research Group, 1969), 33.

a few paragraphs in its 1939 and 1941 field service regulations, in a section entitled "Combat in Woods and Cities."[15] An isolationist Congress and American public, along with already-low budgets slashed lower by the Great Depression, caused enough worries for military leaders that building mock villages was not a priority. There was no training for urban combat during the Interwar Period.

Due to a variety of internal and external factors, the U.S. Army was not prepared for war when it came in December 1941.[16] Large-scale exercises in Louisiana and the Carolinas in 1939 and 1941 indicated the Army's need for improved training and its need for tank-infantry cooperation. As such, urban operations were a distant problem and the army did not go to war with a well-defined, well-integrated, or well-understood doctrine on the urban environment.

To be clear, the United States was not alone in this regard: no other major army seriously considered the possibility of urban combat. The beginning of World War II in 1939 forced the consideration of urban combat, and ideas began to appear in professional military journals in the succeeding years. In September 1942, *Infantry Journal* published the ideas of Bert Levy, a Spanish Civil War veteran from Great Britain, regarding urban warfare. He warned that urban combat was proving unavoidable and that soldiers needed to know how to fight within these locations. His article included advice on how to plan, move within, defend, and attack a town or city. He also argued that supporting weapons such as artillery, airpower, and tanks had no effective place in an urban battle. Writing from experience, Levy concluded that urban combat was an infantry fight through and within buildings.[17] Despite Levy's article, the lack of prewar urban combat training meant that the army would have to learn when it went to war, including those in the 1st Infantry Division.

That learning process began early. In November 1942, the Big Red One was one of a handful of American divisions that invaded North Africa with Operation TORCH. When the 1st Infantry Division landed in Algeria on November 8, 1942 to seize the port city of Oran, its campaign plan had little coordination with any armored units. The movement to Oran from the landings in the Gulf of Arzew to the east meant passing through the small town of

15 See U.S. War Department, *Field Manuel 100-5: Tentative Field Service Regulations, Operations* (Washington, D.C.: Government Printing Office, 1939), 218-20; U.S. War Department, *Field Manuel 100-5: Field Service Regulations, Operations* (Washington, D.C.: Government Printing Office, 1941), 209-10.

16 David Johnson explores the internal and external factors that hindered American readiness for war in 1941 in great detail. See David E. Johnson, *Fast Tanks and Heavy Bombers: Innovation in the U.S. Army, 1917–1945* (Ithaca, NY: Cornell University Press, 1998).

17 Bert Levy, "Street Fighting," *Infantry Journal* 51 (1942), 23, 29.

St. Cloud. When the division's 18th U.S. Infantry Regiment attacked St. Cloud, the infantrymen advanced with little support.

St. Cloud housed four thousand residents and its garrison included French Foreign Legionnaires, paramilitary fascists, and colonial infantry and artillery supported by mortars, machine guns, and various types of artillery.[18] According to an intelligence report, the defenders were rated as "second- or third-class military troops."[19] The regiment's attack, supported only by its own organic weapons and lacking artillery and armor, did not go well. The town's stout buildings augmented the French defense, the 18th Infantry's attack was completely exposed and unsupported, and the inexperienced Americans were getting their first taste of battle. The 18th Infantry Regiment's 1st Battalion, or 1/18, made the opening attack, but even when the balance of the regiment joined the fight, the town did not fall.

Fighting continued the next day as small St. Cloud delayed the division's advance toward its objective at Oran. The division ordered and then cancelled an artillery bombardment because the commanding general did not want to kill French civilians at a time of tense Franco-American relations. Finally, the commanding general ordered the division to speed toward Oran while 1/18 remained to take St. Cloud. Progress inside the town was slow, poorly coordinated, hesitant, and exposed the absence of prewar training in cities. What intelligence had rated as second and third-class easily repulsed soldiers from one of America's top infantry divisions. St. Cloud demonstrated how urban terrain could multiply a defenders' combat power. Fighting in this small Algerian town resumed for a third day and steadier progress was made until the authorities in Oran – who had surrendered to the 1st Division – ordered St. Cloud to cease fighting. On the afternoon of 10 November, St. Cloud was in American hands.[20]

Reflections on this small urban fight credit the French with a strong defense and criticize the inexperienced Americans for a lack of coordination and for struggling to maintain command and control. Two battalion commanders

18 George F. Howe, *Northwest Africa: Seizing the Initiative in the West* (Washington, D.C.: Office of the Chief of Military History, Department of the Army, 1957), 208; Rick Atkinson, *An Army at Dawn: The War in North Africa, 1942–1943* (New York: Henry Holt & Co., 2002), 125; James Scott Wheeler, *The Big Red One: America's Legendary 1st Infantry Division from World War I to Desert Storm* (Lawrence: University Press of Kansas, 2007), 147. The size of the garrison is unclear.

19 Intelligence report quoted in Atkinson, *Army at Dawn*, 125.

20 Frank Greer, "Battle of Oran, Combat Team 18," 19 November 1942, 3, File 301-INF(18)-0.3, Box 5253, Record Group 407, Entry 427, National Archives, College Park, Maryland. Hereinafter cited as RG 407, Entry 427, NA.

were relieved.[21] One platoon leader reflected that "if they had been Germans out there, we'd have been in bad trouble."[22] The men of the Big Red One would have to improve their capabilities if they hoped to push the *Wehrmacht* out of French and German cities, namely by utilizing armor and artillery better. The division's next campaign, the July 1943 invasion of Sicily, saw limited urban combat but the division did improve its coordination with attached armor. Late in the campaign, the division fought to wrest the town of Troina from German control, a key part of the German defenses as Axis forces evacuated from the island. The Germans kept the Americans at bay for a week by defending the heights guarding the approaches to Troina. As the American attack stalled, the division unleashed aerial and artillery bombardments on Troina, knowing that there were noncombatants within. The Americans entered Troina after the Germans retreated and encountered the sickening sights and smells of the Sicilian civilians trapped inside the town. The division might have learned to set aside any qualms to seize towns and cities with fewer casualties among its own men, but there remained a frightful cost.[23]

By November 1943, the division was in England preparing for the anticipated invasion of France. Notably, the 18th Infantry established a facility to sharpen its street-fighting abilities. Regimental records stated that the "memories of Saint Cloud linger in our heads."[24] Using an abandoned, bombed out British neighborhood in Weymouth, the 18th trained its men how to move inside the village and to capture it with as few casualties as possible. Platoons advanced through defended blocks, endured booby traps, and sent its squads as well as teams within the squads to assault and clear the houses. By the end of December, the regiment was satisfied that "a definite operating procedure is gradually evolving."[25] In January, 3/18 did two exercises at Weymouth while individual platoons and squads did more.[26] The next month, 1/18 incorporated

---

21 Marshall, *Proud Americans*, 29.

22 Lieutenant Edward McGregor, quoted in Malcolm Marshall, ed., *Proud Americans: Men of the 32nd Field Artillery Battalion in Action, World War II, As Part of the 18th Regimental Combat Team, 1st U.S. Infantry Division* (New London: self-published, 1994), 29.

23 On the Americans' reactions, see John B. Romeister, ed., *Combat Reporter: Don Whitehead's World War II Diary and Memoir* (New York: Fordham University, 2006), 191; Carlo D'Este, *Bitter Victory: The Battle for Sicily, 1943* (New York: E. P. Dutton, 1988), 468.

24 Captain Edward W. McGregor, "Record of Events for the Period December 1 to 28, 1943," 29 December 1943, 1 in "18th Infantry Historical Report, December 1943," File 301-INF(18)-0.3, Box 5254, RG 407, Entry 427, NA.

25 McGregor, "Record of Events for the Period December 1 to 28, 1943," 1.

26 1st Lieutenant Joseph P. Gurka, "Battalion Journal for the Month of January, 1944," 29 January 1944, 1 in "18th Infantry Historical Report, January, 1944," File 301-INF(18)-0.3, Box 5254, RG 407, Entry 427, NA.

smoke and hand grenades at Weymouth.[27] The training at this abandoned city was imperfect. The 16th Infantry rarely used it, preferring to train for its upcoming amphibious assault. The 26th Infantry used the facility but was disappointed that soldiers could not use live ammunition.[28] Vital organic units, such as the regiments' Cannon and Antitank Companies, did not participate in the training.[29] Nevertheless, the training facility at Weymouth shows the Americans learning to "speak" the grammar of urban combat.

In this regard, the 1st Infantry Division was not alone. By 1943, stateside training for replacements and new divisions had improved with reports that came from the battlefield. Improvements included a village-fighting course with three purposes. The first was to teach draftees about the chaos, confusion, and mayhem of urban fighting. The second purpose was to teach the proper tactics, techniques, and procedures of urban combat, such as assaulting and capturing buildings and houses, moving from roof to roof, and avoiding as well as setting booby traps. The third purpose was to train draftees to perform these skills as a team – whether squad or platoon. The training culminated in a mock village battle where draftees demonstrated their proficiency at cover, mutual support, and teamwork to clear streets, assault houses, and firing at surprise, moving targets under simulated fire and explosions. It remarkably included tank support at the end of, but not during, the exercise.[30] While it taught basic skills, it did not fully prepare most soldiers for the realities of an urban battle.

In January 1944, the U.S. Army published Field Manual (FM) 31-50, *Attack on a Fortified Position and Combat in Towns*. This field manual explained the uniqueness of the urban environment and instructed soldiers how to plan, move, attack, and maintain command and control. What is noteworthy is that FM 31-50 advised officers to make use of supporting weapons but cautioned

---

27 Captain Edward W. McGregor, "S-3 Periodic Report for the Month of February, 1944," 28 February 1944, 2 in "18th Infantry Historical Report, February 1944," File 301-INF(18)-0.3, Box 5254, RG 407, Entry 427, NA.

28 26th Infantry Unit Journal, 22 December 1943 and "Training Notes, no. 53: Period 1 January 1944 to 14 January 1944 Inclusive," 28 December 1943, 3 both in "26th Infantry Historical Report, December 1943," File 301-INF(26)-0.3, Box 5267, RG 407, Entry 427, NA.

29 See, for example, "Report of Activities, G-3 Section, 1 February 1944 to 29 February 1944," 4 March 1944, 5, File 301-3, Box 5104, RG 407, Entry 427, NA.

30 William R. Keast, "The Training of Enlisted Replacements," 338 and Bell I. Wiley, "The Building and Training of Infantry Divisions," 449 in Robert R. Palmer, Bell I. Wiley, and William R. Keast, eds, *The Procurement and Training of Ground Combat Troops* (Washington, D.C.: Historical Division, Department of the Army, 1948). See also Peter R. Mansoor, *The GI Offensive in Europe: The Triumph of American Infantry Divisions, 1941–1945* (Lawrence: University Press of Kansas, 1999), 110 and Lee Kennett, *G.I.: The American Soldier in World War II* (New York: Charles Scribner's Sons, 1987), 42-54.

against the use of tanks and tank destroyers.[31] FM 31-50 demonstrates the United States Army applying the lessons from the battlefield and actively learning the grammar of urban operations. However, the advice against using armor shows that its grasp on this specific grammar was not yet complete, especially as combat units such as the 1st Infantry Division found it necessary to utilize infantry-armor cooperation in towns and cities. Field forces, including the Big Red One, developed more sophisticated methods and integrated armor, artillery, and infantry together in urban fighting more completely in 1944 and 1945 than was prescribed in FM 31-50.

The Weymouth facility proved prescient since the 1st Infantry Division encountered stiff urban combat on the Continent after invading Normandy on 6 June 1944. The Americans learned in France that defeating the German *Wehrmacht* required a level of combined-arms fighting that they did not possess in 1941; the urban environment amplified those lessons. During the grinding fights through the French hedgerows in June and July, as well as the headlong pursuit in August and September, the 1st Infantry Division mastered combined-arms warfare and learned to coordinate infantry, armor, and artillery. Seizing Caumont in Normandy on 12-13 June required coordinating between armor, artillery, and infantry.[32] In assessing the fighting in July and August, division leadership accepted the need to maintain strong tank-infantry coordination, including when fighting in towns and villages.[33] With the victories against German forces in July, the Allies pursued the retreating Germans back toward Germany through August. But as supply lines became overstretched by September and the Allied advanced slowed, the *Wehrmacht* renewed its resistance along the reconstructed belt of fortifications along Germany's western border, oftentimes called the Siegfried Line. As they strengthened the Siegfried Line, German units used their Eastern Front experience to expertly "transform every village into a menacing fortress."[34] To inspire his soldiers to dig in their heels, Adolf Hitler gave the order to "Stand your ground or die! ... Every bunker,

31 *FM 31-50: Attack on a Fortified Position and Combat in Towns* (Washington, D.C., Government Printing Office, 1944), 61.

32 See the G-3 Periodic Report for 12-13 June 1944 as well as the G-3 Journal "G-3 Journal and File, 12-15 June 1944," File 301-3.2, Box 5123, RG 407, Entry 427, NA; 26th Infantry Regiment Journal in "Report After Action, 26th Infantry, 1 June 1944 to 30 June 1944," 51-3, File 301-INF(26)-0.3, RG 407, Entry 427, NA; Sergeant Lawrence P. Manley, "History of the 26th Infantry Regiment," n.d. (Sgt. Manley Mss., 26th Infantry History, McCormick Research Center, First Division Museum, Wheaton, IL. Hereinafter cited as MRC.), 87.

33 Lieutenant Colonel Clarence E. Beck, "G-3 Report of Operations, 1 August to 31 August 1944, Inclusive," 10 September 1944, 61-66, File 301-3, Box 5105, RG 407, Entry 427, NA.

34 Russell F. Weigley, *Eisenhower's Lieutenants: The Campaign of France and Germany, 1944–1945* (Bloomington: Indiana University Press, 1981), 422.

every block of houses in a German city, every German village must become a fortress."[35]

Taking the town of Stolberg, within the Siegfried Line, proved how difficult the urban environment could be for veteran units like the 1st Infantry Division, and the battle from 19 to 22 September foreshadowed the kind of intense urban combat the Americans could expect as they entered Germany. The German defense of Stolberg necessitated house-by-house, room-by-room, and cellar-by-cellar assaults. Cool, rainy weather made a difficult operation more miserable. The fight into the city's edge was challenging enough, and one tanker remembered that the Germans used "every house as a gun emplacement and each street as a line of fire."[36] In contrast to FM 31-50 and Bert Levy's earlier advice, American infantry fought alongside tanks in Stolberg, which proved essential since German tanks helped defend against that American attack. Tiring of German soldiers in the cellars and German tanks inside the city, records show American GIs impatiently crying out for Molotov cocktails made of a concussion grenade and a bottle of gasoline.[37] While 1/16 fought from the northwest, 1st Battalion, 26th U.S. Infantry (1/26) fought from the southeast but the 16th and 26th made no attempt to coordinate their movement and fighting.[38] Nevertheless, the men of the 26th encountered the same difficult, grinding fight that 1/16 faced.[39] An exhausted 1st Infantry Division pulled out of the area and the 104th Infantry Division took credit for seizing Stolberg in November.

The fighting in Stolberg revealed how difficult urban fighting can be even for veteran soldiers. First, the Americans fought motivated and well-equipped German soldiers that slowed the Americans' pace to a crawl. The defenders, the veteran German *12th Infantry Division* refitted and re-equipped after fighting in Russia, were not the demoralized German soldiers fleeing from France. The strong defense of Stolberg is a key reason why the fighting became so ugly. The Germans in Stolberg show that the more motivated a defender and

35 Adolf Hitler quoted in Rick Atkinson, *The Guns at Last Light: The War in Western Europe, 1944–1945* (New York: Henry Holt & Co., 2013), 251.

36 Harold D. Howenstine, *History of the 745th Tank Battalion, August 1942 to June 1945* (Nurnberg, Germany, n.p., n.d.), 57.

37 Red 5 to S-3, 20 September, 19; S-3 to Capt. Murphy, 20 September, 20; S-3 to Capt. Groves, 20 September, 20 in "Journal CT 16, September 1944," File 301-INF(16)-0.7, Box 5239, RG 407, Entry 427, NA.

38 That lack of coordination was partially because 1/26 had been loaned to the 3rd Armored Division during this time.

39 For its part, 1/26 received a Presidential Unit Citation for the heavy fighting and losses incurred from assaulting several pillboxes and bunkers, capturing five towns, and its combat in Stolberg.

the more effective his defense, the more he can prolong and worsen an urban battle. Secondly, 1st Infantry Division soldiers fought alongside tanks from the 3rd Armored Division rather than 745th Tank Battalion, which was usually attached to the Big Red One. Whereas the Americans were relying more heavily upon tank-infantry teamwork, communication problems between the 1st Infantry Division and the 3rd Armored Division limited effectiveness.[40] Third, the Americans struggled against the urban terrain's three-dimensional nature. Alongside forcing the Americans into a slow, attritional, house-to-house fight, the Germans also used underground tunnels to get behind the Americans after they cleared a house and tanks had passed. One American patrol reportedly disappeared in the streets, mostly likely a victim of German soldiers using tunnels.[41] The Big Red One's proficiency in urban combat had improved dramatically by this point but urban fighting remained a difficult "grammar" to master.

In October, the U.S. Army faced its first significant urban challenge: the city of Aachen. The job of taking Aachen fell to the Second and Third Battalions of the 1st Division's 26th Infantry Regiment (2/26 and 3/26). Unlike St. Cloud and its 4,000 residents, Aachen had a wartime population of about 20,000 and a defense of approximately five to six thousand Germans with artillery and armor. The core of the German defenses were the *246th Infantry Division* which also included a reclassified German Air Force and naval personnel, a 150-man SS battalion, a battalion of men in their 50s and 60s, along with 125 city policemen. While the Germans did not enjoy the sort of organizational strength that the Americans had, the urban terrain greatly amplified their defensive strength.[42] Although only a few weeks after the fighting in Stolberg, the battle

40 Red 6 to S-3, 21 September, 3 in "Journal CT 16, September 1944".

41 Major General Gerhard Engel, "First Battle of Aachen, 16 Sept-22 Sept 1944," Foreign Military Studies, MS # A-971 (Karlsruhe, Germany: Historical Division, Headquarters United States Army, Europe, Foreign Military Studies Branch, March 1946), 16; Entry 39 at 1200, 20 September 1944 in "G-3 Journal and File, 17-20 September 1944," File 301-3.2, Box 5132, RG 407, Entry 427, NA. The disappearing patrol: S-3 to G-3, 20 September 1944, 9 and S-2 to Red-2, 20 September 1944, 10 in "Journal CT 16, September 1944". On the use of tunnels, see Lucian Heichler, *The Germans Opposite VII Corps in September 1944* (Washington, D.C.: Office of the Chief of Military History, Department of the Army, 1952), 72.

42 Charles B. MacDonald, *Siegfried Line Campaign* (Washington, D.C.: U.S. Government Printing Office, 1963), 307. The prewar population of Aachen was around 165,000. The five to six thousand German defenders (and this is an approximation) belonged to Colonel Gerhard Wilck's *246th Infantry Division*. For more on this division, see Major Robert E. Price, III, et al., *Aachen: Offensive, Deliberate Attack, MOUT* (Fort Leavenworth, KS: Combat Studies Institute, 1984), 63. Christopher Gabel puts the civilian population as low as 7,000. Christopher Gabel, "Knock 'em All Down: The Reduction of Aachen, October 1944," in *Block by Block: The Challenges of Urban Operations*, eds. William G. Robertson

for Aachen shows the extent to which the Americans had grasped the grammar of urban operations.

In a postwar speech, 2/26's commanding officer, Lieutenant Colonel Derrill Daniel, outlined how his battalion planned the attack on Aachen. Notably, he said that the greatest influence upon his staff's planning was the Allies' failed attempts to take Cassino, Italy in 1943 and 1944.[43] To prevent another Cassino, battalion leadership relied on the application of massive firepower. Mortars and artillery could isolate an area in Aachen; tanks, tank destroyers, and machine guns could pin down the defenders; and infantrymen armed with small arms, bayonets, and grenades could kill or capture the defenders. Second Battalion coined the slogan "Knock 'em all down!" to remind the soldiers "the necessity for keeping up a continuous stream of fire with all available weapons." Each rifle company therefore became a small combined-arms task force that included three tanks or tank destroyers, two 57-mm anti-tank guns, two additional bazooka teams, and two heavy machine guns.[44]

Determined to prevent the enemy from attacking from the rear, officers impressed upon the men to attack every room in every building. The plan also included evacuating all civilians to the rear. The battalion leaders resolved to keep supply dumps near the frontlines because they anticipated a heavier demand on all types of ammunition, especially explosives. Maps marking important intersections and buildings were distributed widely to help maintain command, control, and coordination among the various teams.[45] The attack was designed to push methodically through Aachen, emphasizing firepower as well as command and control rather than speed.

Capturing Aachen was a grueling ten-day battle that tested American urban warfare fluency. To start, the battalions attacked the city from the east, which

---

and Lawrence A. Yates (Fort Leavenworth: U.S. Army Command and General Staff College Press, 2003), 82.

43 Lieutenant Colonel Derrill Daniel, "The Capture of Aachen," n.d., 4, Folder 228.01, HRC Geog. M Germany, 370.2 – Aachen, Center for Military History Archives, Fort McNair, Washington, D.C. This postwar speech affords the best opportunity to glimpse into how American officers planned urban operations in World War II.

44 Daniel, "The Capture of Aachen," 5, 7; "Clearing Area South of the Rail Road Tracks," n.d., 10 in "1st Div., Battle of Aachen, 8-22 Oct. 1944," Box 24012, "European Theater of Operations Combat Interviews, 1944–1945," Record Group 407, Entry 427-A, National Archives, College Park, MD. Hereinafter cited as RG 407, Entry 427-A, NA.

45 Supply: "Clearing Area South of the Rail Road Tracks," 10; Maps: "Aachen: 8-20 October 1944, Second Battalion, 26th Infantry," 5 in the "1st Division WWII Outstanding Combat Achievements by all Rifle Companies Report," MRC; Civilians: Daniel, "The Capture of Aachen," 5-7.

unhinged the German defense plan because it assumed an attack from the west.[46] The combined-arms task forces proved effective: infantry-support weapons, armor, and infantry found different ways to work together; artillery fired into the city from the south; and fighter-bombers received missions to attack targets inside the city. The Americans relied on firepower to pin down, close with, and kill their enemy. Aside from improved tactical effectiveness, tank-infantry teamwork also meant necessary mutual support. American G.I.s protected tanks from German soldiers dropping grenades onto the open tops of tank destroyers, or firing rockets from the rubble, atop buildings, within a cemetery, or after popping up from a cellar door or sewer grate. These elements of the urban environment also proved useful to spot German anti-tank vehicles. For their part, tanks and tank destroyers used machine gun and cannon fire to help the infantry move and assault buildings. Infantrymen and tankers adapted various methods to maximize teamwork.[47] Whenever possible, infantry remained off the streets and advanced through so-called "mouseholes" exploded in the common walls between buildings.[48] Congruent with the "Knock 'em all down!" motto, the division loaned two self-propelled 155-mm artillery pieces that could drop buildings with two shots.[49] Finally, although the U.S. Army struggled to develop adequate close air support procedures throughout the war, division artillery fired red smoke shells into Aachen to mark targets for tactical fighter-bombers to attack. This did not revolutionize American close air support doctrine but the Americans did integrate airpower into the battle as well.[50]

46 Price, *Aachen*, 59-60.

47 Major William R. Campbell, "Tanks with Infantry," (Fort Knox, KY: General Instruction Department, The Armored School, 1947): 6-7; "Employment of Armored Vehicles in Street Warfare as Seen by an Infantryman," n.d., Sgt. Manley Manuscripts, 26th Inf. History, MRC.

48 "Aachen, 8-20 October 1944, Second Battalion, 26th Infantry," 7 in the "1st Division WWII Outstanding Combat Achievements by all Rifle Companies Report," MRC; Daniel, "The Capture of Aachen," 10-11.

49 To define terminology, trucks towed 155 mm cannon and soldiers manhandled them into position where they remained in static positions. A 155 mm "self-propelled" gun was an M2 155 mm cannon mounted atop a tracked vehicle that could, therefore, propel itself. Two shells collapsing a building: Danger 6 to S-3, 14 October 1944 in "S-3 Unit Report for Month of October," 101 in "Report After Action, Month of October, 1944," File 301-INF(26)-0.3, Box 5268, RG 407, Entry 427, NA.

50 Capt. Rennie to S-3, 13 October 1944; Lt. Smith to S-3, 13 October 1944 in "S-3 Unit Report for Month of October," 88, in "Report After Action, Month of October, 1944," File 301-INF(26)-0.3, Box 5268, RG 407, Entry 427, NA. Artillery marking targets: "Unit Report 33rd F.A. Bn. 1 thru 31 October 1944," 1 November 1944, 4-6, 11 in "33rd Field Artillery Battalion

As Stolberg had revealed earlier, the fight to seize Aachen was not easy despite the planning. World War II veteran and historian Charles MacDonald writes that the Americans marked their progress in "buildings, floors, and even rooms" rather than blocks.[51] One veteran recalled that it could take all day to advance one block.[52] Despite accurate maps, the city's destruction caused confusion among the attacking Americans as German soldiers still infiltrated to the rear to attack from behind the troops.[53] Rainy weather added to the misery while German counterattacks dislodged the Americans from hard-won gains and killed valuable veteran small-unit leaders. In one counterattack, 3/26 suffered approximately fifty casualties including a veteran company commander.[54] During the battle, casualties were high enough to force officers to cannibalize mortar crews to fill depleted rifle units, and a stream of inexperienced replacement enlisted men and officers took over for dead and wounded veterans.[55] These green soldiers became casualties at frightful rates despite their stateside training. One veteran of the battle remarked that replacements' training was never sufficient to prepare them for the life and death struggle of an urban battle.[56] Third Battalion recorded an increase in combat fatigue cases as exhaustion sapped the men's strengths.[57]

The two battalions diligently removed all captured Germans, civilian and military, from the area as quickly as possible largely to ensure that their rear remained clear of any Germans. Aachen had several air-raid shelters of various sizes and most civilians sheltered there when the battle began. As the Americans found these shelters, so the people were removed to facilities outside the city, taking with them few possessions. When the regiment's military

Report of Operations, June-December 1944," File 301-FA(33)-0.3, Box 5226, RG 407, Entry 427, NA.

51 MacDonald, *Siegfried Line Campaign*, 311.

52 Leroy Stewart, "Hurry Up & Wait," 1975, 63, unpublished memoir in WWII Veterans Collection, 1st Infantry Division, 26th Infantry Regiment, Box 2, United States Army Military History Institute, Carlisle, PA.

53 Danger 6 to S-3; S-6 to White 6, 13 October 1944 in "S-3 Unit Report for Month of October," 96-7; Stewart, "Hurry Up & Wait," 60.

54 The weather: Drew Middleton, "Battle of Aachen Moving to a Close," *New York Times*, 20 October 1944, 3. Counterattack losses: Blue 6 to S-6, 16 October in "S-3 Unit Report for Month of October," 130.

55 "Clearing Area South of the Rail Road Tracks," 13; Michael D. Runey, "Chaos, Cohesion, and Leadership: An American Infantry Battalion in Europe, October-December 1944," (M.A. Thesis, Pennsylvania State University, 2001), 72.

56 Stewart, "Hurry Up & Wait," 60.

57 Runey, "Chaos, Cohesion, and Leadership," 74-76.

government officer found seven barracks nearby, the civilians were moved there. By the end of October, the barracks were housing over 3,700 individuals. Families remained together and individual leaders were chosen to police and oversee their fellow civilians while supervised by military police and medical professionals. The civilians lived on produce from nearby farms and captured enemy provisions seized elsewhere rather than consume U.S. Army rations. Contrary to the civilians' expectations of harsh treatment exposed to the elements, they were relieved to enjoy the accommodations given to them.[58]

When their last position became untenable on 21 October, the Germans surrendered. The cost was high: the two American battalions lost nearly 500 men killed and wounded, or the equivalent of two rifle companies. Ammunition consumption was also high. Colonel Daniel's battalion had consumed 5,000 mortar rounds, 40,000 .30-caliber machine gun rounds, 4,300 grenades, nearly 27,000 rounds of rifle ammunition, and 50 gallons of flamethrower fuel.[59] In his study of 3/26, Michael Runey argues that twelve days of urban fighting, compounded by physical exhaustion and a long casualty list, had wrecked unit cohesion at the squad, platoon, and company levels.[60] Similarly, the city itself looked like giants had trampled it. After a four-hour tour of the city, an intelligence officer wrote that "burst sewers, broken gas mains and dead animals have raised an almost overpowering smell in many parts of the city. The streets are paved with shattered glass; telephone, electric light and trolley cables are dangling and netted together everywhere, and in many places wrecked cars, trucks, armored vehicles and guns litter the streets."[61] Aachen was knocked down. The 1st Infantry Division applied hard-learned lessons of combined-arms fighting with its understanding of the grammar of urban operations to seize the first major German city in ten days.[62] To be sure, Aachen was not the

58 "Evacuation of Civilians from Aachen," n.d., in "1st Div., Battle of Aachen, 8-22 Oct. 1944".

59 Casualties: the Americans lost 75 killed and 414 wounded. Harry Yeide, *The Longest Battle, September 1944 to February 1945: From Aachen to the Roer and Across* (St. Paul, MN: Zenith Press, 2005, 96. Few German soldiers managed to escape the city and those not killed became prisoners of war. Ammunition consumption: "Clearing Area South of the Rail Road Tracks," 10, 11.

60 Runey, "Chaos, Cohesion, and Leadership," 84.

61 Lieutenant Robert G. Botsford quoted in Office of the Assistant Chief of Staff, G-2, First United States Infantry Division, *Selected Intelligence Reports*, vol. 1, *June 1944–November 1944* (Germany: n.p., 1944), 80.

62 A more complete analysis of the fight for Aachen in the context of the U.S. Army grappling with urban operations can be found in Alec Wahlman, *Storming the City: U.S. Military Performance in Urban Warfare from World War II to Vietnam* (Denton: University of North Texas Press, 2015), 23-69.

division's last urban fight but it marks their understanding and mastery of the environment.

The fighting inside and outside Aachen exhausted the 1st Division. After Wilck surrendered the city, VII Corps allowed the division to rest, refit, and replenish its ranks with new replacements. It is worth noting that by late-1944, the division was a completely different organization from the unit that sailed to England in 1942 to train for the invasion of North Africa. By November, the 16th Infantry's G Company, for example, included six officers and 165 enlisted men, compared to only fifteen men were in the entire company three years prior.[63] An incoming flow of green officers and enlisted men replaced the outgoing stream of veteran casualties. This personnel situation made training all the more important as combat-hardened officers and noncommissioned officers integrated and prepared for combat replacements.

The division's next fight was in the Hürtgen Forest. The densely wooded forest hid deep ravines and included few adequate roads and trails that the Germans either mined or targeted with their artillery and mortars. Units found themselves lost and stumbled into German kill zones with frightening regularity.[64] The forests and insufficient road networks also minimized the effectiveness of American armor, artillery, and airpower, and as a result, tested the Americans' growing dependence on combined-arms fighting.[65] Personnel losses from trench foot as well as battle casualties quickly drained fighting units of combat veterans. Dropping temperatures, snow, freezing rain, and long nights in November and December turned the combat into a nightmare.[66] Veterans regularly portrayed the fighting in the Hürtgen Forest as some of the worst combat they had endured since assaulting Omaha Beach the previous June.

The division's 16th Infantry endured heavy fighting for the town of Hamich while the 18th grappled against the Germans for control of Heistern. What is instructive is the 26th Infantry's fight for Merode at the end of November.

---

63 Major John G.W. Finke, "The Operations of Company 'G', 16th Infantry (1st U.S. Inf. Div.) in the Drive to the Roer River, 17-27 November 1944 (Rhineland Campaign)," (Fort Benning, GA: Advanced Officers Course, 1946–1947), 3-4. Copy at United States Army Military History Institute, Carlisle, PA.

64 Finke, "Operations of Company 'G', 16th Infantry in the Drive to the Roer," 12-4, 17; Miller, *A Dark and Bloody Ground*, 29-30.

65 Weigley, *Eisenhower's Lieutenants*, 364-5; Edward G. Miller, *A Dark and Bloody Ground: The Hürtgen Forest and the Roer River Dams, 1944–1945* (College Station: Texas A&M University Press, 1995), xiv; Robert Sterling Rush, *Hell in Hürtgen Forest: The Ordeal and Triumph of an American Infantry Regiment* (Lawrence: University Press of Kansas, 2001), 23-24.

66 Major Kenneth W. Hechler, "Hürtgen Forest, 16-30 Nov. 1944, 1st Bn., 26th Inf., 1st Div," 24 May 1945, 5 in "1st Inf. Div, Battle of Hamich Ridge (Hürtgen Forest), 16-29 Nov. 44," RG 407, Entry 427-A, NA.

When the attack through the Hürtgen began on 16 November, the 26th's battalions plodded slowly against aggressive German resistance. The division's commanding general, Major General Clarence Huebner pressured the 26th's Colonel John Seitz to make progress that was longer than hundreds of yards.[67] Because the 26th fought mostly within the forest with slick ground and few roads, its armored support was of limited help through much of the fighting.

On 28 November at 1000 hours, Lieutenant Colonel Derrill Daniel's 2/26 attacked the town of Merode, with a promise of artillery support from the division.[68] For many soldiers in the Second Battalion, Merode was their first urban fight. One replacement tanker remembered that Merode was in the open down a gentle slope 600 yards from the woods from which the Americans exited to attack.[69] Combat interviews described Merode as "a strongly fortified village blocking several eastern exits from the forest leading to the Roer River and the [strategic] approaches to the Cologne plain [sic]." The Germans could easily defend the town because it was in the open: approaches to it lacked cover and their artillery had long since "zeroed in" on the woods outside the town.[70] No more than two battalions of German soldiers defended the town.[71]

When 2/26 and the supporting armor left the cover of the woods, a storm of German shells nearly stopped the attack as it began but 2/26 pressed toward Merode.[72] As the Americans methodically captured the area's bunkers, pillboxes, and castle, the Germans pulled out of Merode, abandoning defenses that had concealed machine gun and anti-tank rocket positions.[73] By 1,700, the Americans – Second Battalion's E and F Companies as well as a few tanks and tank destroyers – had secured Merode, but the armor withdrew when the

67 Gerald Astor, *The Bloody Forest: Battle for the Huertgen: September 1944–January 1945* (Novato, CA: Presidio Press, 2000), 196.

68 G-6 to S-6, 28 November, "S-3 Unit Journal," 166 in "Headquarters 26th Infantry, Report After Action, Month of November 1944," File 301-INF(26)-0.3, Box 5268, RG 407, Entry 427, NA.

69 Astor, *Bloody Forest*, 285.

70 Major Kenneth W. Hechler, "Hürtgen Forest, 16-30 November 1944, 2nd Bn., 26th Inf., 1st Div.," 25 May 1945, 3 in "1st Inf. Div, Battle of Hamich Ridge (Hürtgen Forest), 16-29 Nov. 44," RG 407, Entry 427-A, NA.

71 The combat interviews claim one battalion defended Merode: Hechler, "Hürtgen Forest, 16-30 November 1944, 2nd Bn., 26th Inf., 1st Div.," 3-4. But Harry Yeide asserts that it was two battalions: Yeide, *Longest Battle*, 183-4.

72 Yeide, *Longest Battle*, 183-4.

73 Hechler, "Hürtgen Forest, 16-30 November 1944, 2nd Bn., 26th Inf., 1st Div.," 1.

fighting stopped.[74] Most fatefully, communications into Merode were poor and three inoperable tanks blocked the sole road into the town.

German artillery began shelling the Americans in Merode around 1,900 hours, which blocked the western approaches to Merode and prevented the Americans from sending reinforcements. Following this artillery barrage, several tanks and a battalion from the German *5th Parachute Regiment* counterattacked.[75] By 2000 hours, American staff officers became more concerned about Second Battalion's tenuous positions inside Merode. Neither towed nor self-propelled anti-tank weapons could enter the fray, so the battalion rushed in bazooka ammunition to balance the odds.[76] The battalion desperately tried to remove the tanks or create a path around the tanks but the well-laid defenses prevented the Americans from getting armored support into Merode. The poor communication made it difficult for artillery to support the American infantry for lack of observation.[77] Colonel Seitz informed the division of Daniel's inaccessible and precarious position and that the infantry were "going to take a beating."[78] Throughout the twenty-ninth and thirtieth, 2nd Battalion's E and F Companies were effectively isolated.

On the afternoon of 30 November, the 26th Infantry could only account for two men from E Company and fourteen from F Company. German tanks hunted the American infantrymen by firing into every building.[79] Desperate but hopeful, Daniel remained convinced by early evening that knots of survivors were still fighting since German artillery continued to shell the area.[80] Although not clear when, the last radio contact from Merode was a series of messages: "There's a Tiger tank coming down the street now, firing his gun into every house ... He's three houses away, now, and still firing into every house ... Here he comes ..."[81] On 1 December, the division gave up these two compa-

74 Maurice A. Belisle, "The Operations of the 26th Infantry Regiment (1st Infantry Division) in the Attack on the Hürtgen Forest, 16 November-5 December 1944 (Rhineland Campaign)," (Fort Benning, GA, Advanced Infantry Officers Course, 1949–1950), 24-25.

75 Hechler, "Hürtgen Forest, 16-30 November 1944, 2nd Bn., 26th Inf., 1st Div.," 4.

76 Lt Betz to S-3, 29 November 1944, "S-3 Unit Journal," 177.

77 "Unit Report 33rd F.A. Bn. 1 thru 30 November 1944," 1 December 1944, 10 in "33rd Field Artillery Battalion Report of Operations, June-December 1944," File 301-FA(33)-0.3, Box 5226, RG 407, Entry 427, NA.

78 S-6 to G-3, 30 November 1944, "S-3 Unit Journal," 180.

79 Lieutenant Sidney Miller, quoted in Miller, *A Dark and Bloody Ground*, 120; Entry 11, 30 November in "G-3 Journal and File, 28-30 November 1944," File 301-3.2, Box 5138, RG 407, Entry 427, NA.

80 S-6 to White 6, 30 November 1944, "S-3 Unit Journal," 188.

81 Hechler, "Hürtgen Forest, 16-30 November 1944, 2nd Bn., 26th Inf., 1st Div.," 4.

nies and the attached heavy weapons from H Company as lost.[82] Later German prisoners attested that most Americans were captured on 1 December only as they ran out of ammunition.[83]

Although a small battle, the fight at Merode confirmed how important combined-arms fighting had become in an urban battle, even in small towns. Although circumstances prevented the Americans from using armor and artillery to support the defenders, the Germans' infantry-tank-artillery fighting helped assure their recapture of the town. Lastly, many of these soldiers were fighting in their first urban battle, having been added to the regiment after the fighting in Aachen. While there is no indication that the replacements fought worse than veterans, Merode shows that even veteran units with as much experience as the 26th Infantry could still struggle in the urban environment. The constant turnover in personnel was one factor that illustrated how rapidly a unit learned the grammar of urban warfare.

Aachen demonstrates the 1st Infantry Division's mastery of the grammar of urban operations and the attack into Bonn in March 1945 shows how creative and innovative they could be. By early March, the major obstacle slowing down the Allied advance was the Rhine River. By now, the infantrymen, artillerists, and tankers of the 1st Infantry Division had captured towns and villages through hard, costly fighting, within the Hürtgen Forest in November and December, within Belgium in January, and were now taking German towns and cities. As the division approached Bonn, it received orders to seize the bridge over the Rhine within the city. Elements of the 16th and 18th U.S. Infantry Regiments were sent to capture it. As Germans streamed over the Rhine in retreat, their officers knew the value of destroying those bridges before the Allies could take them. Because time was a critical factor, there were only a few hours to plan and the regiments considered the best way to capture a bridge in the heart of a major German city.[84] As the 16th and 18th Infantry Regiments planned their assault on Bonn, the attack showed how adept they had become at combined-arms fighting and how creative the Americans could be.

Speed and surprise were critical because the goal was to take the bridge intact but not provoke a prolonged urban battle. The plan was to forego a preparatory artillery bombardment in order to drive the two regiments' infantrymen

---

82 1st Lieutenant John E. Reynolds, "Activities of 26th Infantry, for December 1944," 1 January 1945, 1 in "26th Infantry Report After Action, Month of December 1944," File 301-INF(26)-0.3, Box 5268, RG 407, Entry 427, NA.

83 Office of the Assistant Chief of Staff, G-2, First United States Infantry Division, *Selected Intelligence Reports*, 103.

84 Entry 121 at 2317 and Entry 122 at 2335, 7 March 1945, 11-12 in "G-3 Journal and File, 5-8 March 1945," File 301-3.2, Box 5146, RG 407, Entry 427, NA.

in tanks and trucks into Bonn before the Germans recognized the attack. The assault forces received orders to avoid firefights in order to speed the penetration into the city. And so, four years into the war and after only four hours of planning, G.I.s mounted tanks and tank destroyers to charge boldly into a major city without any artillery support. The ability to quickly launch a nighttime, combined-arms urban attack with creativity and a degree of "cockiness" was a result of the division's veteran status.[85] While the short fight in Bonn revealed the division's experience, it was also not a flawless attack.

In the attack, other battalions encountered problems but 3/16 managed to enter the city before the Germans could react. Once inside Bonn the Americans were unable to press forward to take the bridge. According to an intelligence officer, the German defense resembled more "the nature of a covering action for a withdrawal" across the bridge rather than a stout defense.[86] The Germans' desperation of keeping the bridge open outweighed the Americans' attempts to capture it, which heavily shaped the urban battle. That is, the Americans were not methodically trying to seize the city but launch a rapid thrust to seize a bridge. As the Germans fought to keep the Americans at bay, American armor fought and destroyed German armor and motorized vehicles within Bonn.

The Americans did not seize Bonn's bridge before the Germans destroyed it. However, the ability to plan and launch their forces rapidly, the understood combined-arms mentality, and the audacity show how far the 1st Infantry Division had come since struggling within St. Cloud in November 1943. At the same time, that the Germans in Bonn's outlying suburbs slowed down elements of the American advance shows that the urban environment remains a combat multiplier for a defending army and can magnify the fog and friction of combat, even if that defender was in the throes of defeat. Just because the Americans had learned and were applying the grammar of urban warfare did not guarantee automatic success every time.

Between the failure at St. Cloud, the training in Weymouth, and the stiff fights at Stolberg, Aachen, Merode, and Bonn, the 1st U.S. Infantry Division learned the grammar of urban operations. The Americans at St. Cloud grappled, as if in the dark, against the town's periphery for three days with little planning and coordination. The training at Weymouth only included riflemen

85 After this battle, Major Albert Smith recalled that the men of K Company, dashing into Bonn, were "feeling a bit cocky." Interview of Major Albert Smith, 7 in "1st Infantry Division Roer River to Bonn, 25 Feb-9 March 1945," RG 407, Entry 427-A, NA.

86 Interview of Captain Fred W. Hall, Jr., S-2 for 16th Infantry Regiment, 15 March 1945, 1-2 in "1st Infantry Division Roer River to Bonn, 25 Feb-9 March 1945," RG 407, Entry 427-A, NA.

but it shows the Americans' realization that urban operations required specific training. Concurrent improvements in stateside training also included many of the fundamentals of fighting within villages and towns. Also, the army's publication of FM 31-50 indicates its realization that urban combat was different enough to warrant its own doctrine. While the training and the doctrine were imperfect, they indicate an army grappling to learn this distinctive grammar.

Field forces, as demonstrated by the Big Red One, learned rapidly through experience. But this learning process was difficult, violent, and costly: although the American division employed combined-arms fighting within Stolberg in September 1944, that battle remained difficult regardless of the Americans' veteran status. The planning for Aachen in October accounted for the unique characteristics of the urban environment. As such, the Americans broke into smaller combined-arms teams, evacuated every civilian encountered, all while maintaining a continual flow of supplies and replacements. Merode confirmed the importance of combined-arms fighting in modern urban battle but also showed that the lesson-learning process was not a constant straight line toward increased effectiveness and battlefield victory. Bonn shows a confident, experienced division moving with near recklessness. As the Americans embraced combined-arms warfare and grasped the uniqueness of urban operations, so they effectively outfought their German enemy in towns. Most importantly, these lessons developed over time and at the cost of many lives lost, both civilian and military.

In some ways, the learning process was unique to the specific context of the U.S. Army in World War II. During World War I and the Interwar Period, the Americans struggled to embrace and indoctrinate a robust combined-arms mindset. The World War II battlefield forced the Americans to achieve proficient combined-arms organization and fighting throughout the combat arms. This wartime process of integration, when applied to the urban environment, allowed the Americans to master the grammar of urban operations. That is, given the strengths and weaknesses of the American military during this time, in order for the Americans to master urban operations required them first to incorporate combined-arms warfare into its doctrine and fighting.

In other ways, this process is not unique to America's World War II army. American infantry doctrine did not "remember" many of these hard-won lessons after World War II. The army revised FM 31-50 in 1952. In the revised edition, the army applied all the lessons from World War II, including the importance of combined-arms coordination in urban operations. But, in his *Storming the City*, Alec Wahlman argues that, despite improved doctrine, American urban operations capabilities atrophied between World War II and the Vietnam War and that the United States failed to maintain its fluency of the "urban grammar."[87] He asserts that the U.S. marines who fought to retake the city of Hue from the North Vietnamese Army in 1968 had to relearn the grammar of urban operations "on the fly" like their fathers had in World War II, at an increased cost in lives lost. The Americans had to rely upon other competencies – such as small-unit leadership, firepower, logistical support, flexibility, and a combined-arms mentality – to overcome the lack of prewar training.[88]

In a comparative analysis of urban warfare in the 1990s, William G. Rosenau concludes that the grammar of urban battle remains a complicated, dangerous, and demanding form of warfare despite dramatic advances in weapons technology. He asserts that attackers consistently lack an advantage in confined urban spaces where civilians and infrastructure can affect the conduct of fighting at the political and strategic levels.[89] Analyst Raphael S. Cohen shows with the Israeli Army that this specific grammar crosses cultural lines, too. Israeli operations against Hamas within Gaza in 2009, 2012, and 2014 have shown the continuities of the grammar of urban operations. Cohen argues that the Israeli experience has shown the limited effectiveness of airpower and that urban battles are won on the ground in savage and brutal fighting. Indeed, Cohen writes that, despite improvements in technology since 1945, "when conventional ground forces meet determined resistance in urban terrain, the result is never a clean, bloodless operation."[90] The Germans in Stolberg and Hamas in Gaza both demonstrate how the well-motivated defender can force a longer and more destructive fight if they so choose.

Because they are manmade, cities pose special challenges to armies that are not present in any other combat environment. Similarly, it imposes rules and restrictions upon technologies that other environments do not. Technologies must be rethought and repurposed: in World War II, the Americans learned how to use tanks and tank destroyers alongside infantry effectively in urban battles. Aachen even showed that airpower can play a role. But satellite technology did not help Iraqi forces to retake Mosul in less than nine months between 2016 and 2017, especially when a defending enemy can burrow through buildings or use underground passageways. Modern technology remains beholden to the nature of urban warfare. As such, armies that do not think

87 Wahlman, *Storming the City*, 120-123.
88 Wahlman, *Storming the City*, 237-243.
89 Rosenau, "Lessons," 384-390.
90 Raphael S. Cohen, "Five Lessons from Israel's Wars in Gaza," *War on the Rocks*, 3 August 2017. https://warontherocks.com/2017/08/five-lessons-from-israels-wars-in-gaza/.

through how its various weapons will work in an urban battle may have to do what the Americans did in World War II: figure it out as they go along at the cost of their own soldiers and civilian dead. The best technology will not save an ill-trained army that is unprepared for an urban fight and all its complex demands and challenges.[91]

As global demographic trends continue to point toward ever-increasing urbanization, modern-day militaries would find it in their best interest to prepare for combat inside cities. Recent statements by senior American military leaders on the importance of preparing to fight inside megacities indicate that they are beginning to reawaken to the realities of urban operations and the challenges that they pose.[92] The urban environment imposes its own grammar that demands military forces' attention and preparation. The experience of the 1st U.S. Infantry Division in World War II shows what happens when a military organization does not understand that grammar but also that it can, with great difficulty, master it.

Works Cited

Archival Material

Center for Military History, Washington, D.C.

Lieutenant Colonel Derrill Daniel, "The Capture of Aachen," n.d., Folder 228.01, HRC Geog. M Germany, 370.2 – Aachen, Center for Military History Archives, Fort McNair, Washington, D.C.

Donovan Research Library, Fort Benning, GA

Robertson, Major General Walter M. "Fighting in the City of Brest," *Twelfth Army Group Battle Experiences* 50 (28 September 1944): 1-2.

Belisle, Maurice A, "The Operations of the 26th Infantry Regiment (1st Infantry Division) in the Attack on the Hürtgen Forest, 16 November-5 December 1944 (Rhineland Campaign)." Fort Benning, GA, Advanced Infantry Officers Course, 1949–1950.

91 John Spencer, "The Army Needs an Urban Warfare School and It Needs It Soon," *The Modern War Institute*, 5 April 2017. https://mwi.usma.edu/army-needs-urban-warfare-school-needs-soon/.

92 Matthew Cox, "Chief: Army Will Need Smaller Units for Megacity Combat," *Military.com*, March 21, 2017. http://www.military.com/daily-news/2017/03/21/chief-army-will-need-smaller-units-for-megacity-combat.html. See also John Spencer, "The City is the Battlefield of the Future," *Wall Street Journal*, July 19, 2017. https://www.wsj.com/articles/the-city-is-the-battlefield-of-the-future-1500500905.

McCormick Research Center, Chicago, IL

"1st Division WWII Outstanding Combat Achievements by all Rifle Companies Report" Sergeant Manley Manuscripts, 26th Infantry History

Fort Knox, Kentucky

Campbell, Major William R. "Tanks with Infantry." Fort Knox, KY: General Instruction Department, The Armored School, 1947.

National Archives, College Park, MD. Record Group 407, Entry 427 (U.S. Army Operations Reports, World War II)

G-3 Report of Operations, File 301-3

Division G-3 Journal and File, File 301-3.2

16th Infantry Journal, File 301-INF(16)-0.7

18th Infantry Report of Operations, File 301-INF(18)-0.3

26th Infantry Report of Operations, File 301-INF(26)-0.3

33rd Field Artillery Battalion Report of Operations, June-December 1944, File 301-FA(33)-0.3

National Archives, College Park, MD. Record Group 407, Entry 427-A ("European Theater of Operations Combat Interviews, 1944–1945")

1st Division, Battle of Aachen, 8-22 Oct. 1944

1st Inf. Div, Battle of Hamich Ridge (Hürtgen Forest), 16-29 Nov. 44

1st Infantry Division Roer River to Bonn, 25 Feb-9 March 1945

United States Army Military History Institute, Carlisle, PA

Howenstine, Harold D. *History of the 745th Tank Battalion, August 1942 to June 1945*. Nurnberg, Germany, n.p., n.d.

Leroy Stewart, "Hurry Up and Wait," 1975, WWII Veterans Collection, 1st Infantry Division

Finke, Major John G.W. "The Operations of Company 'G', 16th Infantry (1st U.S. Inf. Div.) in the Drive to the Roer River, 17-27 November 1944 (Rhineland Campaign)." Fort Benning, GA: Advanced Officers Course, 1946–1947.

Published Material

Adams, John G.B. *Reminiscences of the Nineteenth Massachusetts Regiment*. Boston: Wright & Potter Printing Company, 1899.

Amble, John. "The Battle for Mosul, with Col. Pat Work" (MP3 podcast). *The Modern War Institute Podcast*. Posted 14 February 2018. https://mwi.usma.edu/mwi-podcast-battle-mosul-col-pat-work/.

Astor, Gerald. *The Bloody Forest: Battle for the Huertgen: September 1944–January 1945*. Novato, CA: Presidio Press, 2000.

Atkinson, Rick. *An Army at Dawn: The War in North Africa, 1942–1943*. New York: Henry Holt & Co., 2002.

Atkinson, Rick. *The Guns at Last Light: The War in Western Europe, 1944–1945*. New York: Henry Holt & Co., 2013.

Clausewitz, Carl von. *On War*. Translated by Michael Howard and Peter Paret. Princeton: Princeton University Press, 1984.

Cohen, Ralph S. "Five Lessons from Israel's Wars in Gaza." *War on the Rocks*, 3 August 2017. https://warontherocks.com/2017/08/five-lessons-from-israels-wars-in-gaza/.

Cox, Matthew. "Chief: Army Will Need Smaller Units for Megacity Combat," *Military.com*, 21 March 2017. http://www.military.com/daily-news/2017/03/21/chief-army-will-need-smaller-units-for-megacity-combat.html.

D'Este, Carlo. *Bitter Victory: The Battle for Sicily*, 1943. New York: E. P. Dutton, 1988.

Echevarria II, Antulio J. "Reconsidering War's Logic and Grammar," *Infinity Journal*, Issue No. 2 (Spring 2011): 4-7.

Engel, Major General Gerhard. "First Battle of Aachen, 16 Sept-22 Sept 1944." Foreign Military Studies, MS # A-971. Karlsruhe, Germany: Historical Division, Headquarters United States Army, Europe, Foreign Military Studies Branch, March 1946.

Heichler, Lucian. *The Germans Opposite VII Corps in September 1944*. Washington, D.C.: Office of the Chief of Military History, Department of the Army, 1952.

Hills, Alice. "Continuity and Discontinuity: The Grammar of Urban Military Operations." *In Cities, War, and Terrorism: Towards an Urban Geopolitics*, edited by Stephen Graham, 231-246. Malden, MA: Blackwell Publishing, 2004.

Hills, Alice. *Future War in Cities: Rethinking a Liberal Dilemma*. London: Frank Cass, 2004.

House, Jonathan. M. *Combined Arms Warfare in the Twentieth Century*. Lawrence: University Press of Kansas, 2001.

Howe, George F. *Northwest Africa: Seizing the Initiative in the West*. Washington, D.C.: Office of the Chief of Military History, Department of the Army, 1957.

Johnson, David E. *Fast Tanks and Heavy Bombers: Innovation in the U.S. Army, 1917–1945*. Ithaca, NY: Cornell University Press, 1998.

Kennett, Lee. *G.I.: The American Soldier in World War II*. New York: Charles Scribner's Sons, 1987.

Levy, Bert. "Street Fighting." *Infantry Journal* 51 (September 1942): 22-9.

MacDonald, Charles B. *Siegfried Line Campaign*. Washington, D.C.: U.S. Government Printing Office, 1963.

Mansoor, Peter R. *The GI Offensive in Europe: The Triumph of American Infantry Divisions, 1941–1945*. Lawrence: University Press of Kansas, 1999.

Marshall, Malcolm, ed. *Proud Americans: Men of the 32nd Field Artillery Battalion in Action, World War II, As Part of the 18th Regimental Combat Team, 1st U.S. Infantry Division*. New London: self-published, 1994.

Middleton, Drew. "Battle of Aachen Moving to a Close" *New York Times*, 20 October 1944.

Miller, Edward G. *A Dark and Bloody Ground: The Hürtgen Forest and the Roer River Dams, 1944–1945*. College Station: Texas A&M University Press, 1995.

Office of the Assistant Chief of Staff, G-2, First United States Infantry Division. *Selected Intelligence Reports*. Vol. 1, *June 1944–November 1944*. Germany: n.p., December 1944.

Palmer, Robert R., Bell I. Wiley, and William R. Keast. *The Procurement and Training of Ground Combat Troops*. Washington, D.C.: Historical Division, Department of the Army, 1948.

Price, III, Major Robert E. et al. *Aachen: Offensive, Deliberate Attack, MOUT*. Fort Leavenworth, KS: Combat Studies Institute, 1984.

Reid, jr., Samuel C. *The Scouting Expeditions of McCulloch's Texas Rangers; of The Summer and Fall Campaign of the Army of the United States in Mexico – 1846; Including Skirmishes with the Mexicans, and an Accurate Detail of the Storming of Monterey; also the Daring Scouts at Buena Vista; Together with Anecdotes, Incidents, Descriptions of Country, and Sketches of the Lives of the Celebrated Partisan Chiefs, Hays, McCulloch, and Walker*. Philadelphia: G. B. Zieber and Co., 1848.

Robertson, William G. and Lawrence A. Yates, eds. *Block by Block: The Challenges of Urban Operations*. Fort Leavenworth: U.S. Army Command and General Staff College Press, 2003.

Romeister, John B., ed. *Combat Reporter: Don Whitehead's World War II Diary and Memoir*. New York: Fordham University, 2006.

Rosenau, William G. "'Every Room Is a New Battle': The Lessons of Modern Urban Warfare," *Studies in Conflict and Terrorism* 20, no. 4 (Oct-Dec 1997): 371-394.

Runey, Michael D. "Chaos, Cohesion, and Leadership: An American Infantry Battalion in Europe, October-December 1944." (M.A. Thesis, Pennsylvania State University, 2001.

Rush, Robert Sterling. *Hell in Hürtgen Forest: The Ordeal and Triumph of an American Infantry Regiment*. Lawrence: University Press of Kansas, 2001.

Spencer, John. "The Army Needs an Urban Warfare School and It Needs It Soon." *The Modern War Institute*, 5 April 2017. https://mwi.usma.edu/army-needs-urban-warfare-school-needs-soon/.

Spencer, John. "The City is the Battlefield of the Future." *Wall Street Journal*, July 19, 2017. https://www.wsj.com/articles/the-city-is-the-battlefield-of-the-future-1500500905.

Spencer, John and John Amble. "A Better Approach to Urban Operations: Treat Cities Like Human Bodies," 13 September 2017. https://mwi.usma.edu/better-approach-urban-operations-treat-cities-like-human-bodies/.

U.S. War Department. *Field Manual 100-5: Tentative Field Service Regulations, Operations*. Washington, D.C.: Government Printing Office, 1939.

U.S. War Department. *Field Manual 100-5: Field Service Regulations, Operations*. Washington, D.C.: Government Printing Office, 1941.

U.S. War Department. *Field Manual 31-50: Attack on a Fortified Position and Combat in Towns*. Washington, D.C.: Government Printing Office, 1944.

Wahlman, Alec. *Storming the City: U.S. Military Performance in Urban Warfare from World War II to Vietnam*. Denton: University of North Texas Press, 2015.

Watson, Ben. "What the Largest Battle of the Decade Says About the Future of War." *Defense One*, 28 June 2017. http://www.defenseone.com/feature/mosul-largest-battle-decade-future-of-war/.

Weigley, Russell F. *Eisenhower's Lieutenants: The Campaign of France and Germany, 1944–1945*. Bloomington: Indiana University Press, 1981.

Wheeler, James Scott. *The Big Red One: America's Legendary 1st Infantry Division from World War I to Desert Storm*. Lawrence: University Press of Kansas, 2007.

White, Nathan William. *From Fedala to Berchtesgaden: A History of the Seventh United States Infantry in World War II*. n.p., 1947.

Yeide, Harry. *The Longest Battle, September 1944 to February 1945: From Aachen to the Roer and Across*. St. Paul, MN: Zenith Press, 2005.

CHAPTER 3

Saxon Cities in the Great Northern War (1700–1717)

Alexander Querengässer

To Anglo-Saxon scholars, The Great Northern War is often seen as an epic clash between the young warrior king, Charles XII of Sweden, and the reforming Czar, Peter the Great of Russia. While this is what it eventually became, it began as an ambitious attempt by Augustus the Strong, Elector of Saxony and King of Poland, to regain Polish lands lost to Sweden in the previous century. Had he succeeded, he might have strengthened his position in Poland, bound his two countries closer together, and established a major new power in eastern Europe. Augustus started the war in February 1700 with a surprise attack on Swedish-held Riga. It failed, setting the pattern for the nearly twenty years of warfare that followed. At the commencement of the struggle, Augustus' prestige was at least equal to, and probably greater than that of his Danish and Russian allies, but by the end of it he was very much the junior partner of Peter the Great and held the crown of Poland at the Czar's pleasure.[1]

For the most part, Augustus' war was fought in Poland and Pommerania, far from his ancestral lands in Saxony. Nevertheless it was the Electorate of Saxony that enabled him to maintain his war effort. It was the Saxon army, not the Polish, which fought the decisive battles and this army was raised and nurtured in the Electorate and received its supplies and equipment from Upper Saxony.[2] The Saxon cities were the backbone of the elector-king's military machine. They provided accommodation for thousands of his troops and the

---

* The author wishes to thank Mr. Richard O'Sullivan for his help with the article.

1 The best account the Northern Wars available in English is that by Robert I. Frost, *The Northern Wars: War, State and Society in Northeastern Europe, 1558–1721* (Edinburgh: Routledge 2000). Also helpful is the recently published Steve Kling, ed. *Great Northern War Compendium. A Special Collection of Articles by International Authors on the Great Northern War. 2 Volumes* (St. Louis: LLC dba THGC Publishing 2015).

2 The author wrote his dissertation on the Saxon military in the Great Northern War. It will be published as: Alexander Querengässer, Das kursächsische Militär im Großen Nordischen Krieg 1700–1717 (Paderborn: Schöningh, 2019). For the moment, see Alexander Querengässer, *Die Armee Augusts des Starken im Nordischen Krieg* (Berlin: Zeughaus Verlag 2013). An abridged version can be found in Alexander Querengässer, "The Saxon Army in the Great Northern War," in *Great Northern War Compendium. A Special Collection of Articles by International Authors on the Great Northern War. Volume 1*, ed. Steve Kling, (St. Louis: LLC dba THGC Publishing 2015), 245-254.

 | DOI:10.30965/9783657702787_004

means by which they could be clothed and fed. As we shall see, they were the mainspring of Augustus' ambitions.[3]

German scholarship has not yet fully examined the importance of city economies for the maintenance of the *miles perpetuus* in the late 17th and early 18th century. While military historians have at least started to examine the biletings system, urban historians show no real interest in the military aspects of their respective communes. The early modern age was a unique period in warfare. Urban civilian society was much more integrated into the military than today. The following chapter illustrates the pivotal role Saxon cities had in the maintenance of Augustus' forces during the Great Northern War. It examines how military functions later handled by the state or private contractors, including garrisoning, guarding of POWs, defense, social care system, as well as uniform and weapon production were fulfilled in cities and their citizens in varying capacities. Cities were in this sense a necessary component of the war itself. Saxony was a densly urbanized country, and for the Saxon army, these cities served as fortresses or at least fortified places, prisons, sources for credit, centers of defense production, recruiting areas, garrisons, barracks and even as early modern safe havens for invalid soldiers.

An Urbanized Country

Saxony was one of the most densely urbanized places in Europe. Since medieval times, its ruling dynasty, the Wettins, had encouraged the foundation of towns, as had most of the small princes of the region. The foundation of towns had played as vital a part in the colonisation of the area as the erection of castles and monasteries had in other German territories.[4] This explains why

3 Most of the primary source information used in this article comes from the Hauptstaatsarchiv (Main State Archive) in Dresden and the city archives of Dresden and Leipzig. In many cases these sources have already been quoted in previous articles by the author and the latter are referred to in these notes as they are more accessible to readers from outside Germany. Alexander Querengässer, "'Was nur immer die Kräffte und Vermögen des armen Landes tragen kann'. Das Kurfürstentum Sachsen und der Nordische Krieg 1700–1717," *Neues Lausitzisches Magazin* 137 (2015), 49-80; "Von der Landesdefension zu den Kreisregimentern: Das kursächsische Milizwesen im Großen Nordischen Krieg 1700 bis 1716," *Zeitschrift für Heereskunde* 459 (2016), 2-8; "Leipzig und der Große Nordische Krieg 1700 bis 1721," *Jahrbuch Leipziger Stadtgeschichte* (2015), 67-106.

4 Alexander Querengässer, "Stadtgründungen der Wettiner in der Mark Meißen im Mittelalter," in *Města ve středověku a raném novověku jako. badatelské téma posledních dvou desetiletí (Cities in the Medieval Ages and in Earky Modern Times as Research Topic within the Last*

Upper and Lower Lusatia, which only came under Saxon control at the Peace of Prague in 1635, were less urban than the other parts of the Electorate.

The importance of towns for the colonisation of this area was multifarious. Miltary considerations played a role, because the urban community had to take care for the defense of the towns. So the foundation of towns was the best way to secure the area, because unlike castles, no land and feudal rights had to be given to a knight to maintain just a small group of men of arms. Even a small town was able to provide a much bigger armed force, which could also be used during a campaign.[5] Most Saxon towns were fortified during high and late medieval times. Heinz Müller has concluded that during the 13th century, thirty-five Saxon towns erected walls and twenty more followed suit within the next 150 years.[6] Some of these towns tried to update their fortifications in the 15th century to deal with the new threat of artillery, but few adopted the effective, modern star fortifications developed by military engineers in western Europe during the 16th and 17th centuries.

By the beginning of the 18th century the relative size and importance of Saxon towns differed little from that of today. The two biggest being the capitals Dresden and Leipzig, a center for international trade fairs. Dresden had become the permanent residence of the Wettins around the middle of the 16th century. Between then and 1750 its population grew from 7,693 to 52,052 and during the same period the number of Leipzig's inhabitants increased from 8,481 to 34,730.[7] Apart from these two cities of international importance, the electorate possessed several middle-ranking towns such as Görlitz (11,302), Chemnitz (10,380) and Freiberg (9,885). Even much smaller places, barely villages in terms of population, should be considered as urban, or industrial, communities. On the lower end one can find small foundations not much bigger

Twenty Years) [=*Dokumenta Pragensia 32/2*] (Prag 2015), 511-530 (with an english abstract on 695-697).

5 Otto Mörtzsch, "Das wehrhafte Freiberg im Mittelalter," *Historische Waffen- und Kostümkunde* 7 (1914–1917), 216-224; Herbert Koch, "Wittenberger im Sächsischen Bruderkriege 1446/51," *Historische Waffen- und Kostümkunde* 5 (1909–1911), 126–127; Rainer Groß, "Dresden im 15. Jahrhundert," *Dresden im Mittelalter* (*Dresdner Hefte 65*) (Dresden 2001), 79-82; Enno Bünz, "Eine wehrhafte Stadt? Zur mittelalterlichen Kriegs- und Militärgeschichte Leipzigs," in: *Stadt und Krieg. Leipzig in militärischen Konflikten vom Mittelalter bis ins 20. Jahrhundert*, ed. Ulrich von Hehl (Leipzig: Universitätsverlag 2014), 15-50.

6 Heinz Müller, "Betrachtungen zu den Stadtbefestigungen in Sachsen," *Burgenforschung aus Sachsen 15/16* (2003): 54-55. The problem with Müllers study is that it focus on the territory of the modern free state of Saxony, wich includes Upper Lusatia, wich in medieval times was not part of the Wettin territory, but excludes those parts, wich today belong to the states of Thuringia and Saxony-Anhalt.

7 Karl Czok, *August der Starke und Kursachsen* (Leipzig: Koehler&Ameland 1988), 182.

than modern villages like Liebstadt (436), Rabenau (364), Gottleuba (353), Bärenstein (326), Lauenstein (324) and Krakau near Kamenz (205). It is interesting to note, that except from Krakau all of these smaller towns are not farming towns, like in Prussia, but mining towns in the eastern Erzgebirge. Some of them even declined in population since 1550, like Gottleuba and Liebstadt, both of them losing around forty percent of their former population. This has do to with the diminishing importance of mining in the eastern Erzgebirge. In the western part of these mountains, around Annaberg, Marienberg and Schwarzenberg, nearly fifty percent of the local population lived in towns. In total, the proportion of town population in Saxony grew from thirty to thirty-six percent between 1550 and 1750.[8]

Towns were the economic backbone of the Electorate. Their principal activities were textile production, mining and trade. Leipzig, with its fairs and stock market, was of international importance. The Erzgebirge mining area slowly lost its importance, but at the beginning of the 18th century it was still the third biggest producer in the Holy Roman Empire. Only Styria and Silesia were larger and both of these were under Habsburg control. Saxon mines yielded 4.5 tons of silver a year between 1680 and 1730 in addition to copper, lead, iron, cobalt, bismuth and small amounts of gold.

Augustus the Strong encouraged the growth of factories during his reign and even set up his own arsenal in the small Erzgebirge town of Olbernhau. Nevertheless, the vast majority of products continued to be made by artisans in their own small shops. From late medieval times into the 19th century, Saxony's principal industry was that of textiles. For a long time this put the state in the vanguard of the Industrial Revolution. In 1712, Chemnitz had 187 master cloth makers and 146 journeymen. By 1726 these had increased to 319 and 345 respectively. In 1727 the town also had 305 master linen weavers, 200 of whom had moved there from Silesia, Lusatia and Franconia. In 1700, Oschatz, a town half way between Leipzig and the Elbe river was home to 300 master cloth-makers. In the same year, Görlitz in Upper Lusatia contained 500 master cloth-makers and 400 journeymen. In 1710 the town exported approximately 13,000 pieces, presumably bolts of cloth.[9] Above all else, it was the strength of Saxony's textile industry that enabled Augustus to maintain his impressive mobilization during the Great Northern War.

8 Ibid.

9 Ibid., 126-136.

Saxon Cities as Fortifications

Electoral Saxony only had a handful of fortresses at the beginning of the struggle, and most of these had been neglected for years. Shortly before the war, the military budget was devoted to raising new regiments and preparing the army for offensive operations in far away Poland. Augustus expected a short campaign and never imagined any dangers for his own Electorate. Two of the state fortresses were in fact fortified cities, Wittenberg and the capital Dresden. The Pleißenburg at Leipzig was also a fortress, but separate from the city, which was surrounded with walls. Of the latter the governor, General Hans Rudolf von Minckwitz (1636–1702) painted a glum picture:

> Various suggestions as to how the city might be put into a state of defense during an emergency have been submitted by me to the municipal government, but it has prevaricated, claiming these measures would interfere with trade fairs and discourage foreign visitors.[10]

When Charles XII finally invaded Saxony in 1706 and his advance guard reached the lowlands around Leipzig, the city council begged the local area commander, General Johann Mathias von der Schulenburg, to abandon the city in order to spare it from, "siege, bombardment, storm ... and plunder."[11] In the end, Schulenburg did as he was bid and the city was taken by just two companies of Swedish dragoons. The fortress of Pleißenburg, garrisoned by a few militia units, could have held out, but its commander capitulated after the Swedes convinced him that the elector and the estates had already entered into peace negotiations.[12]

On paper, there was less to be concerned about at Dresden. Its fortifications were more modern and better maintained and the city had a garrison of 5,000 men, the survivors of the debacle at Fraustadt. But here, too, the civil administration was not willing to take on the burden and sacrifice of resistance. After General Zinzenford inspected the suburbs, he deceided to burn most of them, in all 445 houses. The council objected, arguing that the damage would amount to two or three million talers and that the exercise was pointless as the city could not withstand a siege.[13] This was patently untrue as Zinzendorf had

10 Quoted in Querengässer, "Leipzig," 72.

11 Quoted in Ibid., 101.

12 Ibid., 102.

13 SächHStA Dresden 10024 Geheimer Rat, Loc. 9119/1 Der Dreßdenischen Garnison Verpflegung und Unterhalt bet: als der Königl. Schwedischen Armee Einbruch aus Pohlen in Sachsen geschehen ingleichen solcher Residenz Versorgung bet. Anno 1706, fol. 70.

already reported the place fully provisioned, but he gave in and the suburbs were saved. As it turned out, the entire city escaped damage as the Swedes lacked both heavy artillery and the manpower necessary for a siege.

The fact that at both Leipzig and Dresden the civil authorities had successfully defied the Saxon army demonstrates just how badly its reputation had suffered as a result of its repeated defeats. Even allowing for the poor state of their defenses, most of the bigger Saxon towns should have been willing to resist in 1706. The Swedish army lacked the heavy ordnance and the engineering skills necessary to overrun them by force and lacked the manpower to engage in concurrent siege operations. Three years earlier, Charles XII had to wait four months to collect an ordnance train powerful enough to reduce the Polish city of Thorn. Nevertheless, civil authorities in Saxony could hardly have failed to note that despite the opportunity offered, the Saxon army had been unable to intervene and Thorn was now in Swedish hands.

Smaller Saxon fortresses and towns proved equally reluctant to billet troops or make preparations to withstand a Swedish attack. The council at Wittenberg objected to supplying rations for the *Coimsin* batallion of regular infantry because it was already providing for a battalion of militia. Astonishingly, the stadtholder accepted this argument and sent the regulars to the small town of Salmburg, leaving one of Saxony's major fortresses on the Elbe garrisoned solely by militia.[14]

The Elbe was a major obstacle to any army pushing westwards and could only be crossed at half a dozen places. One of these was at the town of Torgau, halfway between Dresden and Wittenberg. Here, a wooden bridge, based on stone pillars, crossed the river. The town council was ordered to destroy it, but chose to disobey, "because at the moment the Elbe is so small and shallow, it can be ridden and driven through at places close to the town and also at Mühlberg and Strehla and because the destruction of the Elbe bridge will not prevent the enemy crossing the river, but will interfere with the town's communications and supplies."[15] The bridge was not dismantled, but it hardly mattered as the Swedes crossed some miles to the south at the town of Meißen, where another bridge was also left intact.[16]

Not all was doom and gloom. The council at Freiberg reported to the elector-king on September 8:

---

14 Querengässer, "Was immer die Kräfte," 69.

15 Quoted in ibid., 72.

16 Ibid., 72-73.

> The local citizens are provided with guns and ammunition and there is a surplus of 3 to 400 matchlock and flintlock muskets available to arm the rural population should it flee here. However, we would need to arm between 1,000 and 1,500 of the latter for them to be effective. For this, we beg your Royal Majesty and electoral Serenity, to graciously provide the arms needed from your arsenal [in Dresden].[17]

One town, at least, was prepared to back the government and obey its orders.

The flight from the countryside described in the letter above was a common occurence during the Swedish invasion. The excesses of Swedish troops during the Thirty Years War were etched deep in the collective memory. Towns and cities seemed to promise safety in numbers and even outdated medieval walls provided some protection for life and property. In Leipzig it was noted that "the flight from the land was widespread. People abandoned their houses, farms and even their livestock, so that in some villages only few people could be found."[18]

The Swedes left Saxony in 1707 to embark upon an invasion of Russia, which ended with Charles XII's crushing defeat at Poltava in 1709. Augustus seized the oportunity offered and, with the help of Czar Peter, regained his Polish kingdom. However, Swedish and rebel Polish forces continued operations for many years to come, so that nearly every summer, the estates and the generals in Dresden feared a new invasion, either fom Poland, Swedish Pommerania or even Hesse-Cassel, whose ruler married a sister of the Swedish king in 1714. With hindsight it seems clear the threat was ephemeral, but at the time it appeared real enough. After recovering from the shock of the 1706 invasion, the Saxons took heart ensuring that if the Swedes came again they would meet with tougher resistence. There were three reasons for this. Firstly, after Poltava, the Swedes were demonstrably weaker. Secondly, the Saxons reorganized their militia; the old "Landesdefension" was disbanded and new formations raised, based on the Saxon "Kreise" (Departments). Thirdly, the Saxons took proper note of the Swedish Army's inability to conduct siege warfare. In 1714 all fortress commanders received the order that "if your exellency's fortress is attacked, you must hold out to the last extremity, which should not be a problem as [...] the enemy lacks the manpower and the means to make a proper assault."[19]

On 23 September 1709, a few days after the elector-king left to renew the war in Poland, the statholder Prince Fürstenberg proclaimed that all Saxon

17 Quoted in ibid., 69.

18 Quoted in Querengässer, "Leipzig," 100.

19 Ibid., 81.

cities "possessing efficient walls and gates [...] must be prepared to defend themselves."[20] The condition of even the major fortified places was still very bad. The commandant of Wittenberg – a state fortress – reported in the summer of 1710 that the city walls had yawning gaps in them, providing unhindered access unless they "be provided with palisades."[21] Indeed the condition of the town's fortifications was so bad, that for a while it was discussed to raze them to the ground, though the proposal was dropped in 1715.

Not only the bigger fortresses, but also the small towns were inspected to see if they could be defended. In 1711 the engineer officer Johann Christoph Naumann was sent into Lower Lusatia to inspect the local town defenses. His findings were worrying. Fürstenberg simply did not have any.[22] The small town of Forst might just stand a siege if its fortified ditches could be repaired and palisaded."[23] The only fortress in this region, Senftenberg, was also in bad shape. A similiar inspection was made by General von Bose in the northern "Kurkreis" (electoral departments).[24] Bose was unhappy about the fortifications at Golzen, Brück and Barut, but thought that Jüterbog might be defended, if a couple of hundred of workers could be found to repair the old walls:

> This city is more than the others provided with high and strong towers, double walls and ditches and also with outer fortifications [...] the towers and inner ring wall are still in good condition, furthermore the ditches and the other fortified works could be repaired within four weeks by 2,000 workers provided they are supplied with sufficient wagons to transport palisades ..., then with the aggressive use of defensive artillery the place should be able to hold out for at least four weeks.[25]

Bose also thought that the 15th century fortress "Eisenhardt" in Belzig would be a suitable garrison for a company of troops. Both, Jüterbog and Eisenhardt could be used as advanced outposts north of the River Elbe. The river would

20 SächsHStA Dresden 11237 Geheimes Kriegsratskollegium, Loc. 464 Gedruckte Mandata de Anno 1682–1709, without fol.

21 SächsHStA Dresden 10024 Geheimer Rat, Loc. 9293/13 Acta Derer Schweden besorgende Invasion aus Pommern in Sachsen, und die dagegen gemachte Veranstaltungen bet. Wie auch was wegen Richtung der Creyß=Regimenter vorgegangen. Anno 1710, fol. 91.

22 SächsHStA Dresden 10024 Geheimer Rat, Loc. 9321/6 Dispositionen gegen Schwedische Invasionen 1701. 1704. 1711. 1714, without fol.

23 Ibid.

24 These are the territories, which originally belonged to the duchy of Saxony-Wittenberg, to which the title of the Saxon elector was bounded. After the ruling dynasty of the Askanians died out in 1422, the duchy was given to the Wettins.

25 SächsHStA Dresden 11237 Geheimes Kriegsratskollegium, Loc. 10925/1 Nachrichten die Landes Defension betr: 1711–1716, witout fol.

form the main line of defence in the event of a Swedish invasion launched from Pommerania.

All these examples show that outdated medieval fortifications could still be brought into play in the defence of Saxony. While in Flanders the Duke of Marlborough was employing his Dutch engineers and huge artillery train to reduce the most modern Vauban fortresses, his counterparts in Saxony could rely on the protection of old town walls in the knowledge that their enemy lacked professional siege technicians and heavy guns.

The City as a Prison

The fortifications sometimes served to keep soldiers in as well as out. In 1715, the *Castelli* Infantry Regiment was sent to Lauban in Lower Lusatia, close to the border with Habsburg Silesia. At first the soldiers were billeted in the suburbs, but it soon became apparent that many were deserting and crossing into Silesia, lured by bounties paid by the Austrian Field Marshal von Häßlinger, who wanted them for his own army. To put a stop to this, the colonel of the *Castelli* Regiment was obliged to restrict his men to the old town of Lauban, which was surrounded by a medieval wall.[26]

Of course, most of the soldiers confined in the towns were Swedish prisoners of war. Wittenberg and Torgau both housed contingents, most of whom had fallen into Augusus' hands when he recaptured Warsaw in 1704. Wittenberg held 213. Initially they were kept in the castle and were not allowed into the town as it was feared students from the university might help them escape (although German, these students were from Swedish controlled Pommerania and Bremen). In December 1704 the military governor, Colonel von Rosen, felt obliged to put 145 of these prisoners into a vault beneath the town hall. There they were denied light and fresh air and were subjected to steam and smoke from the heating system. Forty-eight quickly fell ill.[27] Finally, in January 1705, the prisoners were given permission to exercise in the town, but no more than forty at a time.[28]

26 SächsHStA Dresden 10024 Geheimer Rat, Loc. 9294/2 Acta Die wieder des Königs von Schweden feindl. Desseins in hießigem Lande gemachte Gegenveranstaltungen betr. Ao. 1715. Drittes Buch, fol. 38-39, 79.

27 SächsHStA Dresden 11237 Geheimes Kriegsratskollegium, Loc. 1101 Acta Die Polnisch. und Schwed. Gefangene betreff., without fol.

28 vgl.: SächsHStA Dresden 11237 Geheimes Kriegsratskollegium, Loc. 1102 Gefangene Schweden und Pohlen In dem Königreich Pohlen, welche von dar nach Sachsen in theils Vestungen und Städte in Verwahrung gebracht. Anno 1704 5, without fol.

While this was going on, the council at Torgau was being asked if the prisoners then crammed into Hartenfels Castle might not be distributed among the homes of the townsfolk. Remarkably, the council agreed, and even more remarkably, the arrangement worked out well. In the first instance the enlisted prisoners were answerable to their own NCOs and a few designated Swedish officers; only in the event of serious problems were matters referred to the Saxon guards.[29] Most of the Swedish officers were separated from their men. In October 1704, seventeen were sent to Döbeln, sixteen to Chemnitz and eleven to Rochlitz. Having given their parole, they were allowed to move about freely within these places and in November they even had their swords returned to them. General Horn (the commander of the Warsaw garrison) was permitted to live in comfort in the city of Leipzig and was even given permission to travel freely throughout the electorate on condition that he made no attempt to contact his subordinates.[30]

The City as the Economic Backbone of the Army

The hope that Saxon towns and cities might play a direct part in the defense of the state proved a cruel illusion when put to the test during the Swedish invasion in 1706, but in other respects these communities performed a vital role in keeping the Electorate in the war. As we have seen, Saxony was blessed with an unusually large number of towns and a high level of urban economic activity. Leipzig was particularly important to the war effort. Its biannual trade fairs gave Augustus access to powder and weapons and enabled him to borrow the money needed to pay his troops. At the autumn fair of 1699 he was able to equip his cavalry with 500 pairs of pistols and 500 rifled carbines, purchased from the Maastricht dealer Jacob de La Hay. At the same time he bought 21,000 Talers worth of Dutch ammunition. In 1708, Johann Berg from Solingen contracted to supply 4.000 infantry swords at a cost of 4,333 Talers.[31] Absurd as it may seem, the Swedes also sometimes got away with buying weapons and supplies at the Leipzig fairs. In 1714 they tried to purchase uniforms for their regiments in Stralsund with the help of merchants from Hamburg. On the 23rd of May of that year Augustus felt obliged to remind the city authorities that while providing the Swedes with military equipment and supplies was forbidden, care should also be taken to prevent trade of any sort that "damages our

29 SächsHStA Dresden 11237/1102 Gefangene Schweden und Pohlen, ohne Bl.
30 Ibid.
31 Querengässer, "Leipzig," 92.

interest and helps that of the enemy."[32] The trade fairs were also used to aquire credit and to pay bills. In 1708 the "Generalkriegskasse" (war treasury) borrowed 1 million guilders from the Dutch republic. 300,000 were immediately sent to merchants from Leipzig. For the rest the "court jew" Berend Lehmann gave an advance to the war chest.[33]

In 1710 the swordsmith Johann Brecht from Solingen supplied 700 new swords for the *Seckendorf* Grenadier Batallion, at a cost of one Taler and four Groschen each. The amount due was paid in two installments at the subsequent Michaelis and New Year trade fairs.[34] This batallion, along with three regiments, was hired from the Margrave of Brandenburg-Ansbach. The contract regarding payment for the latter read as follows: "… his Royal Majesty promises to pay to his princely Serenity 6,000 Taler each year for these three regiments, as long as they stay in his service, in two instalments at the Easter and Michaelis trade fairs in Leipzig in the following manner: a banker or merchant living there will be instructed to credit his princely Serenity with the appropriate amount."[35]

The reign of August the Strong in Saxony predated the Industrial Revolution. Although some factories were founded between 1694 and 1733, the army was largely reliant on individual artisans for its uniforms and equipment. The strength of the country's textile industry enabled it to supply the necessary fabrics and uniform kits. In emergencies Augustus was able to increase production by ordering every member of a town guild to work exclusively on the needs of the army. Thus, in 1700 the weavers and apprentices of Grimma and Großenhain were ordered to do nothing but manufacture fabrics for the regiments serving in Poland.[36] Just how important these army contracts were can be gauged by by the example of the elite Chevalier Guard between 1709 and 1712. This unit ordered all of its equipement from the merchant Blechschmieder in Dresden. He in turn employed several sub-contractors within the capital. The embroidered carbine slings and swordbelts were made by the master tailor Michael Wiedmann, the carbine hooks were made by locksmith Johann Cramer from Freiberg, the hats by Johann Philip Hänßelmann, the NCOs' feathers by Peter Schütze, the spurs by Johann Christian Teichern, the saddles by Georg Hencke, the bridles by Johann Daniel Wiegand and Johann Schickedanz, treens of camel hair were made by the loop maker Jonas Teuber,

32 Quoted in ibid., 93.
33 Ibid.
34 Ibid.
35 Ibid., 93-94.
36 Querengässer, *Saxon Army*, 252.

tressels for the trumpets and kettledrums by the loopmaker Christian Thomas from Radeberg (a small town in the northeast of Dresden), the "girdle stuffs" were ordered from the merchant Thomas Weber from Freiberg, who in turn ordered them there from the craftsmen Samuel Süßebach.[37] All these several contracts were worth more than 100 Talers each and it may be assumed that they not only fed the craftsmen mentioned, but several other guild members too. The list provides insight into the various occupations of the time, many of which are lost now. Several others could be added. For example in Leipzig there was a specialist tentmaker named Benjamin Kinder, who in 1702 provided the *Marshall* Infantry Regiment with 852 talers worth of different sized tents. And of course, many tailors earned their money from military contracts. We know of a certain Johann Schwab of Leipzig, who provided the citizen guard with uniforms at a cost of 18 Groschen each.[38] The same sum was paid to the city's tailors in 1710, when they had to make 600 coats for the *Seckendorf* Grenadiers. The lack of urgency displayed by the tailors guild in filling this commission got them into touble. On May 22 the Geheimer Kriegsrat (secret war council) wrote to Leipzig's municipal government: "You will instruct the guild, that they will finish the order of this regiment by puting all other work last."[39]

That the order was not given priority is understandable, because, while army contracts always involved huge amounts of goods and money, payment was far from certain. In 1704 the Leipzig merchant Johann Gerhard Berthold supplied uniforms and other goods worth 30,000 taler to the army. Instead of being paid in coin, he received "Steuerschuldscheine", a kind of tax write-off. Two years later, desperate for cash, he sold the documents to Geheimer Rat Adolph Magnus Count von Hoym for 20,000 talers. Long after the war he was still trying to sue the elector-king for the remaining 10,000.[40]

Other merchants had similar experiences. In 1698 Jonas Parnißke and Andreas Dietrich Apel entered into a contract to supply Lieutenant Colonel von Spiegel of the *Neitschütz* Infantry Regiment with twenty-nine coats, forty-three waistcoats, forty-seven hats with feathers, twelve silver belts, twelve silver embroidered gloves, forty-seven pairs of stocking and fifty-one sashes. These items were for the regiment's officers and the total order was worth 2,682 taler. Payment should have been made by the Easter trade fair. Come September, Apel and Parnißke complained to the general war treasury that

37 SächsHStA Dresden 11237 Geheimes Kriegsratskollegium, Loc. 10928/8 Belege zu der ersten Doppelden Mundirung für die Garde du Corps Ao 1709. 1710. 1711. 1712, fol. 72-132.

38 Querengässer, "Leipzig," 95-96.

39 Quoted in ibid., 95.

40 Ibid., 96.

they had received nothing. As it turned out, the colonel's officers had provided their own uniforms and it also transpired he was being chased by irate craftsmen and merchants from Dresden and Naumburg. In the end the war treasury took responsibility for the debts. Apel and Parnißke must have counted themselves fortunate.[41]

Recruiting Centers

Cities were also important centers for recruiting. The thought of regular food and pay must have been a temptation to those without either. On the other hand, members of guilds and other citizens could not be compelled to join the army. In a country with an economy as highly developed as Saxony, many occupations were exempt from military service.

Occasionally, town councils supported the recruiting effort. In 1704, Leipzig had to provide 140 men for Colonel Nehmitz, who was raising a grenadier battalion. Even then there were complications. Realizing he could not maintain even his present level of mobilization, Augustus halted recruitment of the battalion and ordered the council to send the colonel 6,000 Talers instead.[42] Curiously, Nehmitz reported the city owned him for 104.5 men, implying it already had been sending him money in lieu of troops.

If specific branches of the army required recruits, they would target the towns most likely to produce men with the requisite skills. In 1701, to support its siege operations at Riga, the army went to the town of Freiberg in search of volunteers from its guild of miners.[43] In 1705, Christian Eberhard Rieman, the army's 'Field Baker,' was sent to Leipzig to hire bakers. He was able to get twenty, but still complained that "not only was he impeded by the bakery guild, but he got little help from the town council."[44] The secret war council ordered the municipality to support Rieman in his search for volunteers.

Despite the fact that the haulage of supplies, ammunition, and artillery was vital to all armies in the early 18th century, none of them had established trains. Instead, each spring they went in search of wagons and horses to do the job. Very often these came from towns and districts, which had an obligation to supply them since late medieval times. When in 1705 the pontoons and artillery stored in the arsenal at Dresden were required at the Oder River, it took

41 Ibid., 94.
42 Quoted in ibid., 84.
43 Querengässer, *Saxon Army*, 247.
44 Querengässer, "Leipzig," 84.

62 wagons and 372 horses to get them there. Table 3.1 illustrates how important nearly all oft he Electorate's cities were to the animal and wagon needs of the war.

TABLE 3.1 Pontonier Company and Field Artillery Wagon and Animal Requisitions, 1705

City	Wagons	Haulage animals
Dresden	17	102
Leipzig	18	108
Meißen	3	18
Großenhain	3	18
Wurzen	4	24
Eilenburg	2	12
Freiburg	4	24
Chemnitz	4	24
Zwickau	4	24
Rochlitz	2	12
Colditz	1	6

Source: *SächsHStA Dresden 10024 Geheimer Rat, Loc. 9104/10 Campements derer in Sachßen befindlichen Trouppen und darzu erforderter Magazine Anrichtung bet. Anno 1705, fol. 158.*

As can be seen from the table, the animals and wagons had to be collected from all over the Electorate, so it may be imagined how long it took to prepare the army to move each spring.

The citizens were also subject to an early kind of military draft. Since late medieval times they had been required to arm and send detachments into the field. In the early 17th century this system was converted into the "Landesdefension", or militia.[45] The militia was only supposed to be called out in the event of an invasion, but following Augustus' heavy losses in the Riga campaign of 1700 and 1701 and his need to expand the army, he desperately tried to recuit men from the militia into the regular army. By 1702 his regiments were 6,000 men under strength and he called on the Ämter (districts) and towns to supply troops in proportion to their taxation returns. For instance, in 1702 he asked Leipzig for fifty-three men, and in 1705 he asked the city for

45 Helmut Schnitter, *Volk und Landesdefension* (*Militärhistorische Studien – Neue Folge 18*) ((East-) Berlin: Militärverlag der Deutschen Demokratischen Republik, 1977).

a further eighty-five, of whom only forty-three were furnished.[46] In a report submitted to the elector-king in 1702, General von Flemming noted "that the Dresden and Freyberg contingents of 328 men each are fully recuited and will be distributed among the regiments as ordered. It will require tougher action before anyone from Zwickau reports for duty."[47] This attempt to establish a draft system even confused the members of the War Council. One of them pointed out to Augustus that trying to get enlistments in this fashion was difficult, "because no contracts are entered into with recruiting officers, nor assembly areas assigned ..., nor bounties offered ..."[48]

Most cities and towns decided to meet their quotas, but, initially at least, they avoided the temptation to round up and ship out their poorest and criminal classes. Instead, they went in search of outsiders to fill the ranks. In April 1704, after a new draft was ordered, Jacob Dietrich, the post master of Nossen, complained that his messanger Michael had been kidnapped by the citizens of Dippoldiswalde, a town half way between Dresden and the Bohemian border, and send to the army.[49] They did the same to Christian Krüger from Mühlberg and even packed off one of their own townsmen, a sculptor named Christoph Erbitsch against his will. In Zwickau matters came to a head on May 18 when a desperate mob, led by two members of the town council, tried to take young men out of schools and churches to send them to the army.[50] Finally, a charcoal burner named Andreas Metzen was kidnapped from his home in Mansfield by

46 Querengässer, "Leipzig," 85-86.

47 SächsHStA Dresden 10024 Geheimer Rat, Loc. 9091/2 Completirung derer Regimenter zu Fuss worzu Einige von denen Defensioner auszulesen angeordnet u.s.w. Vol. III, fol. 57.

48 SächsHStA Dresden 10024 Geheimer Rat, Loc. 9091/3 Completirung der Regt. zu Fuß, worzu Einige von denen Defensionern auszulesen; Item Auffbringung der benötigten Artillerie= Proviant= und anderer Pferdte aus Ambtern, Städten und Dörffern; deren Fortmarsch nach Pohlen und Anschaffung nöthigen Geld; auch Was sonst zu Sicherheit des Landes gehörig betr. 1702, fol. 64.

49 Ibid., fol. 53.

50 SächsHStA Dresden 10024 Geheimer Rat, Loc. 9091/7 Acta die von einigen Bürgern wie auch Häschern zu Zwickau u. Werda bey Anschaffung der 1704 neuen Soldaten-Recrut. mit Ober= und Unter=Gewehr visitirten Kirchen=Thürme und andere geistl. Häußer betreffende, gehalten in der Superintendur zu Zwickau 1704, fol. 5-19. Stefan Kroll, too described the problems of cities and rural communities by raising the land recruits. He made use of examples between the years 1730 and 1760, but his results are also valid for the Great Northern War, Stefan Kroll, "Aushandeln von Herrschaft am Beispiel der Landrekrutenstellung in Kursachsen im 18. Jahrhundert," in *Herschaft in der Frühen Neuzeit. Umrisse eines dynamisch-kommunikativen Prozesses* (= *Herrschaft und soziale Systeme in der Frühen Neuzeit* 2), ed. Markus Meumann und Ralf Pröve (Münster: LIT Verlag 2004), 174-177, here 184; Walther Thum, *Die Rekrutierung der sächsischen Armee unter August dem Starken. Inaugural-Dissertation zur Erlangung der Doktorwürde*, Leipzig: Verlagsanstalt Quelle&Meyer 1912, 59.

the citizens of Wittenberg and offered to the army in lieu of one of their own men.[51] Augustus soon realized that getting men in this fashion was counterproductive as they invariably deserted at the first opportunity. In May 1704 he ordered that all men recruited by force should be released from service.[52]

Cities as Garrisons

While the French army of the period was able to garrison a high proportion of its regiments inside Vauban's many fortresses, and the Swedish 'indelningsverk' system provided each of its soldiers with a small farmstead to live on, the Saxon army, like most others in Europe, was billeted in the houses of its citizens. There were a few barracks, as for example the ones at the fortress of Königstein and in Leipzig, but the majority of the soldiers lived cheek by jowl with the people they were defending.

Although the archives are filled with accounts of squabbles between soldiers and their hosts, these tend to give a rather one sided view of the relationship. A recent study by Ralf Pröve reveals that in some ways the towns and cities benefited from having regiments billeted on them.[53] The presence of the soldiers increased demand for bread, meat and beer, while wealthier citizens would pay their "guests" to go and live with less well off residents, putting money in the pockets of both the troops and their new hosts. Less welcome was the fact that off-duty soldiers would hire out their labour. Having already been paid, housed and fed by the army, they could undercut day-workers and journeymen, threatening the latter's livelihoods. This problem was not unique to Saxony. In the 1770s British troops in Boston in colonial Massachusetts were

---

51 SächsHStA Dresden 10024 Geheimer Rat, Loc. 9091/5 Die Aufbringung- und Auslesung 6800 Mann zu Fuß zu recreutirung der alten und Rüstung neuer Regimenter, sowohl formirung einer Landesdefension betreffend. Wie solche des Königs und Churfürst Friedrich August zu Sachsen, Maist. An dero Landschafft beym Ausschuß Tage verlanget, dieses depreciret, selbige aber doch ins Land eingetheilet worden. Anno 1704, fol. 137.

52 Ibid., fol. 58.

53 Ralf Pröve, "Zum Verhältnis von Militär und Gesellschaft im Spiegel gewaltsamer Rekrutierungen (1648–1789)," *Zeitschrift für Historische Forschung* 22 (1995), 191-223; Ralf Pröve, "'Der Soldat in der "guten Bürgerstube.' Das frühneuzeitliche Einquartierungssystem und die sozioökonomischen Folgen," in *Krieg und Frieden: Militär und Gesellschaft in der Frühen Neuzeit*, eds. Bernhard R. Kroener and Ralf Pröve (Paderborn et al.: Ferdinand Schöningh 1996), 191-217.

unpopular not because they were enforcing tyranny, but because they were providing a rival, and cheap, labour force.[54]

Rivalries in the job market were not the only cause of trouble. If a soldier was not economically dependent on his host (for example, because the host was also his employer or at least in the same guild, or because of family relationships in the making), he often thought of himself as belonging to a different and better social class, one distinguished by his uniform. In many cases the host was expected to provide full board and lodging and the soldiers knew what they were entitled to, demanding meat and beer as part of their daily ration. This was bound to cause problems as civilians did not take kindly to continually providing their guests with more and better food than they could afford for themselves.[55]

The comparatively high levels of friction between Saxon civilians and soldiers in the early to mid 18th century can, in part, be explained in terms of teething problems.[56] The army had only come into existence in 1682 and thereafter had spent most of its time fighting the Turks in Austria and Hungary and the French along the Rhine. Following Augustus the Strong's coronation as King of Poland, a large part of the army was sent into that country. Thus, even twenty years after its foundation, the regular army had still not found the need for a codified billeting system. The start of the Great Northern War saw both an expansion of the army and the army being driven out of Poland and back within the borders of Saxony. Between 1704 and 1706 the majority of the infantry and a Russian Auxiliary Corps were permanently stationed in the Electorate, confronting it with a massive and unexpected quartering problem.

From then on, as far as the towns and cities were concerned, the drawbacks to the billeting system seriously outweighed the benefits. None felt this way more than the capital, Dresden. During the Swedish invasion it had had nearly 5,000 troops stationed within its defenses. In 1707 its citizens collected the proud sum of 18,672 Talers for the construction of barracks, a testimony to the lengths they were prepared to go to get the military out of their homes.

54 Michael Stevenson, *Patriot Battles: How the War of Independece was Fought* (New York: Harper Perennial, 2007), 40.

55 Stefan Kroll, *Soldaten im 18. Jahrhundert zwischen Friedensalltag und Kriegserfahung: Lebenswelten und Kultur in der kursächsischen Armee 1728–1796* (Paderborn et al: Schöningh, 2006), 283-289 and 297-298; Bernhard R. Kroener, "Militär in der Gesellschaft: Aspekte einer neuen Militärgeschichte in der Frühen Neuzeit," in *Kriegerische Gewalt und militärische Präsenz in der Neuzeit. Ausgewählte Schriften*, eds. Ralf Pröve and Bruno Thoß (Paderborn et. al: Schöningh, 2008), 72-75.

56 Pröve, "Der Soldat in der guten Bürgerstube," 196-200.

Needless to say, the War Treasury accepted the money gratefully and then spent it on other projects.[57]

Discipline and morale seem to have come close to collapse following the catastrophy of Fraustadt. In March 1706, only three weeks after the battle, the town council of Görlitz on the Oder complained about the behaviour not just of the enlisted men, but also the officers of the *Flemming* Dragoon Regiment. When the clamour continued, the elector-king instructed General von der Schulenburg to ensure that these officers were, "not only cashiered, but also subjected to corporal punishment."[58] Görlitz was not the only city being abused by its garrison. At the end of the month, Augustus was forced to write another letter to von der Schulenburg: "Attached we send you the renewed complaints of the senior civil servant at Leipzig about the mischiefs done by some dragoons on the streets."[59] "Mischiefs" in this context meant the robbing of merchants by soldiers in uniform. This certainly did nothing to undermine the town council's view that having troops stationed in the city was bad for trade.

Wittenberg, too, had its grievances. For several weeks in September 1706 it was garrisoned by the *Coimsin* Battalion. The unit was composed for the most part of Frenchmen who had been persuaded to change sides after being captured at the battle of Höchstädt in 1704. Differences of language and nationality exacerbated by recent defeat led to a rapid breakdown in relations between the townsfolk and the soldiers. Soon the preceptor of the university was reporting, "many excesses have already occurred."[60] Apparently, a woman who had provided two Frenchmen with lodgings, but failed to provide board, had been brutally beaten by one of them with the flat of his sword.[61] Another citizen had been beaten with a pot by three Freenchmen for refusing to put the light out in his parlour.[62]

57 O. von Schimpff, "Heinrich Friedrich Graf von Friesen, königlich polnischer und kurfürstlich sächsischer Geheimer Kabinettsminister und General der Infanterie," *Neues Archiv für Scäshsiche Geschichte* 2 (1881), 180-192 and 170-171.

58 Quoted in Querengässer, "Was immer die Kräfte," 59.

59 Ibid.

60 Ibid.

61 Ibid., 59-60.

62 Ibid., 60.

The Town as a Safe Haven

Little is known about military social care in the Early Modern Times. It was in its infancy, but it did exist. The Saxon Army had something called the 'invalid penny', which was deducted from the soldiers' pay each month and used to provide a form of insurance.[63] However, few men seem to have benefitted from it. In England, Queen Anne ordered that an extra name be added to the roster of each company and the wages of these ghost soldiers be used to create a fund to help the widows of men killed in Flanders.[64]

Measures like these were barely sufficient to provide support in peace time. In times of war, when a single battle produced hundreds if not thousands of permanently maimed men, they were manifestly inadequate. As long as soldiers were men of fortune in the pay of military entrepreneurs, as was the case in the Thirty Years War, princes and states could disclaim responsibility for those disabled in battle, but with the growth of standing armies in the latter part of the 17th century, one might have expected attitudes to change. Eventually they did, but not until after the Great Northern War. In the meantime it fell to the towns and communities to take care of ex-soldiers who were no longer fit for field service. There was both a moral and a practical encouragement for them to do so because men without employment would be likely to become beggars, thieves or disturbers of the peace. As has already been noted, the old medieval requirement that towns and cities should defend themselves was still in force and given that many wealthier citizens were increasingly unwilling to take part in the requisite drill sessions and guard duties, a convenient solution presented itself. The good citizens found the money to enable their communities to hire what were called "Stadtsoldaten" to do the job for them. In most cases the men were ex-soldiers, unfit for field service but not in receipt of the 'invalid penny'. Most large towns maintained a company of such men. That these units had a social as well as military role may be gathered from the fact that in 1716 the Leipzig company of 140 men contained eleven men incapable of performing duty due to age or other infermities. Corporal Michael Schuhmannm (68) "had gout and could no longer attend parade", nor could Melchior Naumann (73), Hans Gäbler (78) and Johann Heinrich Zacharias (70). Jacob Kirchloff (67) was a drinker and "had a stupid face." The 64 years "young" Johann Große had a limp, but begged not to be relieved, because he "would not know what to do, if discharged, having been a soldier since his youth and moreover Capt. Lieut.

---

63 Kroll, *Soldaten*, 490-491.

64 James Falkner, *Marlborough's War Machine* (Barnsley: Pen & Sword, 2014), 181.

Francke [...] had beaten him to a pulp."[65] The 79 years old Gabriel Francke, also asked to be allowed to remain in service, because "if dismissed, he would not be able to earn anything, because once when on guard duty his right arm had been dislocated and he had received a blow to the temple that rendered him unfit for any other kind of work."[66] It may be doubted if any of these men were fit for any sort of duty, but the council was sympathetic and deceided to keep Naumann, Kirchloff, Große and Schuhmann for one or two more years. Sadly, Gäbler. Zacharias and Francke had to be discharged.[67]

Conclusion

In the Early Modern Period, civilian, especially urban, society was much more integrated into the military world than it is today. The principal reason for this was the billeting system, which put residential property to military use and ensured soldiers and civilians were constantly in each others company. This came to an end in the 19th century, when soldiers were rehoused in barracks, thereby separating them from the emerging bourgeoisie. Economically, too, civilians and the military were more closely bound together than today. It was not just tavern keepers, butchers and merchants that benefitted directly from the presence of soldiers; regiments would often order equipment and uniforms from local artisans. Today it would be inconceivable for professional soldiers to hire themselves out as unskilled labour in their free time, but in the early 18th century it was common practice. Furthermore, the transportation system required to move the army's supplies, batteries and pontoons was provided entirely by civilians in accordance with longstanding feudal practice. Overall, many military functions, which are now done either by the state (garrisoning, guarding of POWs, defense, social care system) or private contractors (uniform and weapon production) were fullfilled by cities in early 18th century Saxony. The conclusions reached in this essay regarding the Saxon army would hold good for most armies operating in the first two decades of the 18th century. In many respects military development had atrophied. Despite improvements in procurement, warfare would continue to be conducted with a high dependency on the urban economy and society until the advent of Napoleon.

65 Querengässer, "Leipzig," 90.
66 Ibid., 91.
67 Ibid., 88-92.

Works Cited

Archival Sources

Sächsisches Hauptstaatsarchiv Dresden (SächsHStA Dresden =Saxon Main State Archive Dresden)

SächsHStA Dresden 10024

SächsHStA Dresden 11237

Published Works

Bünz, Enno. "Eine wehrhafte Stadt? Zur mittelalterlichen Kriegs- und Militärgeschichte Leipzigs." In *Stadt und Krieg: Leipzig in militärischen Konflikten vom Mittelalter bis ins 20. Jahrhundert* (*Quellen und Forschungen zur Geschichte der Stadt Leipzig 8*). ed. Ulrich von Hehl, 15-50. Leipzig: Universitätsverlag 2014.

Czok, Karl. *August der Starke und Kursachsen*. Leipzig: Koehler&Ameland, 1988.

Falkner, James. *Marlborough's War Machine*. Barnsley: Pen & Sword, 2014.

Frost, Robert I. *The Northern Wars: War, State and Society in Northeastern Europe, 1558–1721*. Edinburgh: Routledge 2000.

Kling, Steve. Editor. *Great Northern War Compendium. A Special Collection of Articles by International Authors on the Great Northern War. 2 Volumes*. St. Louis: LLC dba THGC Publishing 2015.

Groß, Rainer. "Dresden im 15. Jahrhundert." *Dresden im Mittelalter* (*Dresdner Hefte 65*) (Dresden 2001): 79-82.

Koch, Herbert. "Wittenberger im Sächsischen Bruderkriege 1446/51." *Historische Waffen- und Kostümkunde* V (1909–1911): 126-127.

Kroener, Bernhard R. "Militär in der Gesellschaft. Aspekte einer neuen Militärgeschichte in der Frühen Neuzeit." In *Kriegerische Gewalt und militärische Präsenz in der Neuzeit. Ausgewählte Schriften*, eds. Ralf Pröve and Bruno Thoß, 65-82. Paderborn et. al: Ferdinand Schöningh 2008.

Kroll, Stefan. "Aushandeln von Herrschaft am Beispiel der Landrekrutenstellung in Kursachsen im 18. Jahrhundert." In *Herschaft in der Frühen Neuzeit. Umrisse eines dynamisch-kommunikativen Prozesses* (= *Herrschaft und soziale Systeme in der Frühen Neuzeit* 2), eds. Markus Meumann und Ralf Pröve, 174-177. Münster: LIT Verlag 2004.

Kroll, Stefan. *Soldaten im 18. Jahrhundert zwischen Friedensalltag und Kriegserfahung. Lebenswelten und Kultur in der kursächsischen Armee 1728–1796* (=Krieg in der Geschichte 26), Paderborn et al: Ferdinand Schöningh 2006.

Mörtzsch, Otto. "Das wehrhafte Freiberg im Mittelalter." *Historische Waffen- und Kostümkunde* 7 (1914–1917): 216-224.

Müller, Heinz. "Betrachtungen zu den Stadtbefestigungen in Sachsen." *Burgenforschung aus Sachsen 15/16* (2003): 52-73.

Pröve, Ralf. "Zum Verhältnis von Militär und Gesellschaft im Spiegel gewaltsamer Rekrutierungen (1648–1789)." *Zeitschrift für Historische Forschung* 22 (1995): 191-223.

Pröve, Ralf. "'Der Soldat in der "guten Bürgerstube.' Das frühneuzeitliche Einquartierungssystem und die sozioökonomischen Folgen." In *Krieg und Frieden. Militär und Gesellschaft in der Frühen Neuzeit*, eds. Bernhard R. Kroener and Ralf Pröve, 191-217. Paderborn et al.: Ferdinand Schöningh 1996.

Querengässer, Alexander. *Die Armee Augusts des Starken im Nordischen Krieg* (=*Heere & Waffen 21*), Berlin: Zeughaus Verlag 2013.

Querengässer, Alexander. "'Was nur immer die Kräffte und Vermögen des armen Landes tragen kann'. Das Kurfürstentum Sachsen und der Nordische Krieg 1700–1717." *Neues Lausitzisches Magazin* 137 (2015): 49-80.

Querengässer, Alexander. "Leipzig und der Große Nordische Krieg 1700 bis 1721," *Jahrbuch Leipziger Stadtgeschichte* (2015): 67-106.

Querengässer, Alexander. "Stadtgründungen der Wettiner in der Mark Meißen im Mittelalter." *Města ve středověku a raném novověku jako. badatelské téma posledních dvou desetiletí* [=*Dokumenta Pragensia 32/2*] (Prag 2015): 511-530.

Querengässer, Alexander. "Von der Landesdefension zu den Kreisregimentern: Das kursächsische Milizwesen im Großen Nordischen Krieg 1700 bis 1716." *Zeitschrift für Heereskunde* 459 (2016): 2-8.

O. von Schimpff, "Heinrich Friedrich Graf von Friesen, königlich polnischer und kurfürstlich sächsischer Geheimer Kabinettsminister und General der Infanterie." *Neues Archiv für Scäshsiche Geschichte* 2 (1881): 129-179.

Helmut Schnitter, *Volk und Landesdefension* (*Militärhistorische Studien – Neue Folge 18*). (East-) Berlin: Militärverlag der Deutschen Demokratischen Republik 1977.

Michael Stevenson, *Patriot Battles: How the War of Independece was Fought* (New York: Harper Perennial, 2007).

Walther Thum, *Die Rekrutierung der sächsischen Armee unter August dem Starken. Inaugural- Dissertation zur Erlangung der Doktorwürde*, Leipzig: Verlagsanstalt Quelle&Meyer 1912.

CHAPTER 4

Panic in London? Attitudes of Civilians to Air Attacks in 1917/18 and 1944/45

Linda Parker

On 24 December 1914, a *Friedrichshafen FF29* float plane dropped a high explosive bomb on Dover, Kent. This was the first aerial bomb to be dropped on the United Kingdom, the forerunner of the aerial war that continued throughout the First and Second World Wars.[1] The two world wars of the 20th century introduced the world, and Britain, to the concept of total war, a major aspect of which was the development of air power and the use of aerial bombardment on major cities. In this chapter I would like to take two snap shots of the effects of aerial warfare on London, which was then one of the biggest urban and commercial centres in the world, with a population of over 7 million in 1914 and vast global financial and imperial reach. It could "reasonably lay claim to be the centre of the world."[2]

The bombing attacks on London by German Gotha bombers in 1917 and by V2 Rockets in 1944/45 represent attacks on the City of London which had much in common. They both came as the inhabitants of the city heaved a collective sigh of relief, first at the cessation of zeppelin raids, and during the Second World War when V1 flying bomb campaigns ended. The new raids were done with innovative military technologies, and in the case of V2s, were impossible to counter. The raids of 1917 and 1944/45 then severely strained the morale of Londoners and challenged the capital as a centre for the management of the war effort, both in terms of government, the effective running of the war, and as a hub of production. Most importantly, the reaction to both periods of attack threatened the ability of the British and metropolitan government agencies to retain the confidence of the public and maintain order under renewed attacks on the city, which was high on the list the priorities of the German war machine in both conflicts. The attacks of the Gotha bombers, with their plan to 'set London on fire' and the revenge attacks of the V2 rockets or Vergeltungswaffe (retribution weapon) severely strained the resources of the

1 Nigel Parker, *Gott Strafe England: The German Assault against Great Britain 1914–18*, vol. 1 (Solihull: Helion, 2015), 54.
2 Charles Emmerson, *1913: The World Before the Great War* (London: Vintage, 2013), 15.

 | DOI:10.30965/9783657702787_005

governed and governors in the city of London, showing the effects that total warfare could have on urban morale and physical city landscapes.

World War I

The threat of aerial bombardment by Zeppelin had been present throughout the first stages of the war, but on 31 May 1915, Londoners found themselves in the front line, with an attack of the Zeppelin LZ38, which appeared over the North East suburbs and dropped eighty-nine incendiary bombs and thirty-nine grenades, causing nine fatalities. The further four raids on London in 1915 increased in severity. The attack of L13, on 8-9 September caused damage and casualties in the heart of London: twenty-two died, eighty-seven buildings were damaged and twenty-nine fires were started in the areas around Euston and Liverpool station. They returned in August of 1916, but by that time London's air defences had been strengthened, and despite the appearance of the 'super zeppelin' L31, the raids of August and September were the last, culminating in the spectacular destruction of the L31 in full view of watching Londoners.

By the Spring of 1917, twenty-three Gotha bombers were in service, with more on the production line. The two-engine bi-plane had a wing span of seventy-two feet and a payload of thirteen bombs. The German air force soon worked out that the best results could be achieved from bombing in daylight from a great height. The RNAS (Royal Naval Air Service) and RCF(Royal Flying Corps) planes could not fly high enough to effectively defend against the Gothas. One of the worst raids came on Wednesday 13 June 1917, when a bomb dropped through the roof of the Upper North Street London County Council School which was attended by 600 children. The bomb passed through the girls' department on the top floor, through the boys' department and exploded in the basement, where sixty-four infants were making lanterns. The children in the infants' department formed the majority of the dead and injured. A total of eighteen children were killed and thirty-four injured. In the same raid, at Liverpool station, sixteen died, and nineteen were killed at Fenchurch Street station.

At the inquest on the bombing at the North Street school, *The Times* reported that "much of the evidence given was of the most poignant nature." The coroner paid tribute to the actions of the teachers and the rescuers, witnesses reported that there was no warning of the raid and *The Times* recorded that "the expediency of giving warning when raids were expected was discussed."[3]

3 *The Times*, June 16, 1917, 4.

During the days after the attack, and particularly during the raids of 7 July, parents, bearing in mind the Upper North St incident, besieged schools in order to take their children home, ignoring official advice that the children were safer in school than in the open walking home from school.

The response of the British public was to demand reprisal raids on Germany and to carry out xenophobic attacks on people with German sounding names, however long they had lived in the country. At a meeting at Tower Hill on 15 June strong speeches were made in favour of reprisals, including one by MP William Joynson Hicks (1865–1932). *The Times* reported that "a resolution calling on the government to 'pay back the enemy in the same way as he had treated this country', which was endorsed enthusiastically by the crowd."[4] *The Daily Mail* printed a "Reprisal Map" with its suggestions for German cities which were in reach of allied front line aircraft and could be bombed. There was also increasing public demand for raid warnings. An editorial in *The Times* a few days after the North Street school bombing considered public concern about warnings "not unreasonable and requires prompt action." The Bishop of London, Arthur Foley Winnington Ingram (1858–1946), although he had gained a reputation for being a 'recruiting bishop' at the outset of the war, went against many establishment figures in stating his objection to reprisal bombings. At the burial of fifteen victims of the Upper North Street school, he said that indignation at the incident should not drive thoughts to reprisals: "there was much looseness of thought and phrase about reprisals. He did not believe that the mourners would wish that 16 German babies should lie dead to avenge their dead ... What all demanded was strong deterrent naval and military action."[5] He also voted with the other bishops against reprisals in the parliamentary debates in 1916 and 1917.

A raid on 7 July was a blow to the morale of the population of London, as in broad daylight twenty or more Gothas approached London, undeterred by any air defence. It was only when the anti-aircraft guns in London's parks began to fire that people began to take cover. In that raid 53 people died and 183 were injured. The damage to property had doubled from that of 13 June, being estimated at £200,000.[6] Home Secretary Sir George Cave (1856–1928) announced in Parliament on 28 June that it was "neither practicable or desirable to give warnings," but changed his mind after the July 5th raid.[7] Daytime warnings were to be based on maroons being fired from some fire and police stations with policemen riding around with 'take cover' notices. The confusion and

---

4 *The Times*, June 15, 1917, 3.
5 *The Times*, June 21, 1917, 3.
6 Frank Morrison, *War on Great Cities, A Study of the Facts* (London: Faber and Faber, 1937), 18.
7 *House of Commons Debates, 28 June 1917 Vol 95 cc 512-3; HC Deb 09 July 1917 Vol 95 cc 1627-701.*

inadequacy of night time air raid warnings was particularly resented in the 'Harvest Moon' night time raids from 24 September to 1 October. This had still not been resolved by January 1918 as a letter to *The Times* from a local vicar pleaded: "London has not lost its nerve and all we ask for is a definite clear, audible warning at all hours when a raid is impending."[8] Londoners took shelter increasingly in the tube stations, whether there was a raid or not, and during the week of the 'Harvest Moon' raids many left the city for the night to take shelter in the surrounding countryside. Jerry White has described the decision of Government not to issue comprehensive an effective air raid warnings as arising from class based mistrust of the working people of London, citing "the egregious reluctance to issue public air raid warnings lest the Londoners should panic, riot or use them as an excuse to bunk off war work."[9] A *Times* editorial on June 16 contended that on frequent occasions when alarms proved false, "we should have wholesale interruptions of daily vocations."[10]

The strategy of repeated bombing night after night was a plan to destroy London by fire, according to Neil Hansen.[11] It did not destroy London physically, but the repeated Gotha raids in 1917/1918 went some way to weakening the morale of the people and disrupting city life. The night attacks caused a "tendency of some sections of the population to give way to panic," which added to the chaos caused by physical damage.[12] The total number of deaths throughout the First World War by aerial bombardment was 836, but the psychological impact was large. Between 100,000 and 300,000 people flocked to the tube stations, and another 500,000 took shelter in basements and cellars.[13] And it was estimated that on one occasion in February 1918, one third of a million Londoners went underground.[14] An American engineer, albeit quoted by a Major Freiherr von Bülow (1883–1966), described his impression:

> The air raids ... have aroused extraordinary fear among all sections of the population. Domestic servants have left their employers, the omnibus and tram drivers refuse to go on night duty and abandoned their vehicles as soon as the alarm sounded. The working classes, whose night's rest is

8 *The Times*, January 10, 1918, 3.

9 Jerry White, *Zeppelin Nights: London and the First World War* (London: Vintage, 2015) , 253.

10 *The Times*, June 16, 1917, 7.

11 Neil Hansen, *First Blitz: The Secret Plan to Raze London to the Ground in 1918* (London: Corgi, 2008).

12 Ibid., 299.

13 Edgar Jones, "Air Raids and the Crowd: Citizens at War," *The Psychologist* 29, November 6, 2016.

14 Philip Zeigler, *London at War* (London: Sinclair Stevenson, 1995), 10.

> perpetually broken up, failed to go to work and schoolchildren had to be given permission to sleep in school hours.[15]

However, reports in *The Times*, attempting to minimise the reaction of Londoners claimed that raids caused 'no panic' and reported:

> An extraordinary indication of the futility of the raid as a demonstration of "frightfulness" was the rapidity with which people everywhere settled down to their business when the raiders had disappeared.... Curious scenes were observed in suburban shopping centres when a raid was in progress ... customers would go out into the street to observe progress. It was possible to hear such sentences as "The shrapnel is bursting all around them now. And I shall want two pounds of butter please."[16]

In January 1918 the Riesenflugzeugen, R-Planes or Giants joined in the raids on London attempting once more to drop enough incendiaries to cause serious damage to London and to hinder war production. Due to a lack of supplies of incendiaries and the failure to drop with concentrated precision, this plan failed. The air defences of London had been strengthened by barrage balloons and steel curtains, forcing the attacking planes to an altitude too high to drop the incendiaries with any precision. On the last large Gotha raid at Whitsun, 1918 RAF fighters shot down seven planes and three more were claimed by anti-aircraft guns. German strategic bombing was then halted to support the Spring offensive of the German army in March 1918. It is significant that the breaking of the city's morale was a major aim, as the main targets for the air raids were government buildings, the Admiralty, the Bank of England and Fleet Street. In reality, the poorly built and crowded homes of the East end suffered disproportionately from air raids. Unlike the west end of London where there were many parks and more tube stations, the east enders had a limited choice of shelter in a raid. Neil Hansen has commented that "it was scarcely surprising that many of them tended to panic in the face of air raids."[17]

The Gotha raids of 1917/18 had tested the courage and morale of Londoners severely, but had not resulted in large scale civil disobedience, major strikes or the paralysing of the city's commerce. The nearest London had got to total collapse of morale was in the period of the 'Harvest Moon' raids, but the cessation

15 Freiherr Von Bulow, "Die Angriffe des Bombengeschwader 3 auf England," in *Die Luftwacht* 5 (1927).

16 *The Times*, July 9 1917, 3.

17 Hansen, *First Blitz*, 195.

of those incessant nightly raids as winter approached restored order and confidence to some extent. The German plan to destroy London by fire had failed and although production of war material and industrial products had been hampered by the raids, the aim of causing total panic and chaos in the capital city had not been achieved.

The aerial bombardment of London in the Great War coloured inter-war governments' attitudes to appeasement, rearmament, and the prospect of bombing in a future war. In a speech to the House of Commons on 10 November 1932, Stanley Baldwin (1867–1947), then Lord President of the Council said:

> In the next war you will find that any town within reach of an aerodrome can be bombed within the first five minutes of war to an extent inconceivable in the last war, and the question is, whose morale will be shattered quickest by that preliminary bombing? *I think it is well also for the man in the street to realize that there is no power on earth that can protect him from being bombed, whatever people may tell him. The bomber will always get through.*[18]

Experts on air warfare such as the Italian general Giulio Douhet (1869–1930), author of *The Command of the Air*, predicted that the next war would start with hundreds of thousands of casualties caused by air attack and would be won by the destruction of enemy industry resources and the morale of the population.[19]

Practically, as a result of the bombing raids of the First World War, Londoners and the British government had learned valuable lessons about the necessity for air raid precautions, the organisation of civil defence, and the importance of the maintaining high morale or a "Blitz Spirit." The Committee of Imperial Defence considered the numbers involved in sheltering underground during the Gotha attacks illustrated a lack of resolve which did not bode well for another conflict.[20] It was thought that to avert mass panic in future bombardments, the civilian population must have confidence in the arrangements to protect them. A new body, the *Air Raid Precautions Sub-committee*, which considered the protection of the civilian population from aerial attack, was set up

18 *The Times*, November 12, 1932, 7; emphasis added.

19 Giulio Douhet , *Command of the Air* (1921), translated and republished many times in the 20th century.

20 Edgar Jones, "Air Raids and the Crowd-Citizens at War," *The Psychologist* 29: 6 (2016). Accessed January 30, 2019. https://thepsychologist.bps.org.uk/volume-29/june/air-raids-and-crowd-citizens-war.

in 1924.[21] The air attacks on Spanish cities during the Spanish civil war provided ample evidence of the effects of aerial bombardment and further stimulated the efforts of the government to provide for this eventuality. In January 1938, the Air Raid Precautions Act came into force , which placed responsibility for creating ARP (air raid precautions) services for all local authorities.[22] Winston Churchill (1874–1965), prominent advocate of rearmament, had questioned the slow movement of the act through the House of Commons in 1937. He explained that "the fortitude of the civilian population in the event of sudden air attack would be a vital factor, and the country must be well organised as to make the crime of aerial aggression not worth committing."[23] In January 1938 the parliamentary correspondent of *The Times* reported on the extensive plans that local authorities had put in place. The report also stated "while there can be no question of providing shelters for all the civilian population in the event of an aerial attack, it is believed that local surveys will disclose that there are generally more cellars and other places available then might be at first supposed." The report acknowledged that "London presents the greatest problem and there will be close cooperation between the Home office and London local authorities."[24]

World War II

General Erich Ludendorff (1865–1937) had described the aim of Germany in the bombing of London in the First World War as bringing the actual theatre of war to the capital of the enemy to achieve the "moral intimidation of the British nation and the crippling of the will to fight."[25] This strategy continued into the Second World War with the Blitz in 1940/41 and the attack of the V1 flying bombs the Summer of 1944. During the nine months between September 1940 and May 1941, London was relentlessly bombed, and by the end of the Blitz, around 30,000 Londoners would be left dead, with another 50,000 injured.[26] Much has been written about the "Blitz Spirit," but historians have called into question this interpretation. T.H. O'Brian writing in 1955 and Arthur Marwick writing in 1976 supported the idea that there was no collapse of morale during

21 The National Archives, Cabinet Office, CAB 46, Committee of Imperial Defence.

22 Ibid.

23 *The Times*, November 17, 1937, 7.

24 *The Times*, January 29, 1938, 12.

25 Bulow, "Angriffe," 14-15.

26 BBC History World Wars: The Blitz. Accessed January 31, 2019. http://www.bbc.co.uk/history/worldwars/wwtwo/ff3_blitz.shtml.

the worst hours of the war.[27] However Angus Calder offered "ample evidence, familiar and unfamiliar to indicate widespread fear and paranoia bordering on panic"[28] R. Mackay, in his study of civilian morale in the Second World War concluded that the revisionist analysis had overemphasised the negative features of morale: "The lows did not last for long and were more than outweighed by the highs."[29]

From June 1944 to September 1944 London was subjected to attacks from the V1 (*Vergeltungswaffen or revenge weapon*), the unmanned 'flying bomb'. The arrival of the bomb was heralded by a whining humming noise, a silence as the engine cut out, and the explosion as the bomb descended to earth. The approach of the V1 was very stressful as there was little time to take cover, and on hearing the noise of the engines everyone just hoped that the 'doodlebug' would fly on and land somewhere else. In the first three days of attack by the V1 bombs, 499 people had been killed and 2,000 seriously injured. By 6 July 2,752 people had been killed.[30] Many Londoners left the city, but entering London were 80,000 men recruited to repair the housing stock before winter. Duncan Sandys (1908–1987), the thirty-five year old son-in-law of Winston Churchill, who had seen action in Norway, was placed in charge of handling a response to the V1 threat and was considered to have performed well in this role. The RAF fighter defences had developed swift responses to the pilotless planes. Also, by the end of August 1944 all the V1 rocket launching sites were in Allied hands as the Allied advance in Europe drove forward.

The British government was aware of the threat of rocket attacks on Britain since six photo reconnaissance missions in August 1943 revealed the existence of rocket-like objects at Peenemunde, an island off the north coast of Germany. An air attack on Peenemunde by the RAF only succeeded in delaying production of the new weapon by two months, and further production was moved to the Harz Mountains. Meanwhile in the Autumn of 1942, ski shaped sites thought to be launch pads for pilotless planes were discovered by photo reconnaissance. Home Secretary Herbert Morrison (1888–1965), in a cabinet meeting on 16 November 1943, expressed alarm at the implications for civilians, especially in London. He asked for 2,700 metropolitan police officers to be retained and the cancellation of the release of 3,500 civil defence workers who were to be stood down. He gave as his reason: "The unprecedented

---

27 T.H. O Brien, *Civil Defence* (London: HMSO, 1955); A. Marwick, *The Home Front, The British and the Second World War* (London: Thomas and Hudson, 1976).

28 Angus Calder, The *Myth of the Blitz* (London: Jonathan Cape), 109.

29 R. Mackay, *Half the Battle – Civilian Morale during the Second World War* (Manchester: Manchester University Press 2002), 248.

30 Juliet Gardiner, *Wartime Britain 1939–1945* (London: Headline Books), 644.

strain which a heavy and sustained rocket bombardment would place upon London."[31] In July 1944, while the V1 attacks were still in progress, a committee to consider the expected rocket attacks was set up, called the "The Rocket Consequence Committee," which would be chaired by Herbert Morrison and report back weekly, recommending measures to deal with the effects.[32]

The British press spent much of the summer of 1944 on speculation, some quite wild, of the different types of rocket attacks that could be expected. *The Daily Express* announced "Rocket boats are secret weapon 2," and claimed that speed boats "have been equipped with six barrel devices to shoot six rockets at once."[33] The *Sunday Pictorial* warned: "get ready for rockets."[34] The *Daily Telegraph* reported on "Nazi talk of secret weapons."[35] In June, the *Daily Express* warned, "Strato Bombs are being prepared."[36] The *Sunday Graphic* asked on 30 June "what is the truth behind the German winged Rocket claims?"[37] However, the progress of the Allied armies during the Summer of 1944 into Belgium and France seemed to go some way to negate worries about a new airborne threat.

On 7 September 1944, Duncan Sandys and Brendan Bracken (1901–1958), Minister of Information, held the largest press conference of the war. Duncan Sandys announced "except possibly for a few last shots, the Battle of London is over."[38] During the same press conference he was asked a direct question about the possibilities of a V2 weapon and admitted that "we do know quite a lot about it," but implied that due to the advance of the allies in Europe it was not a significant threat. "In a very few days' time I feel the press will be walking over these places in France and will know a great deal more about it than we do now."[39]

---

31 Roger Hermiston, *All Behind You, Winston: Churchill's Great Coalition 1940–45* (London: Aurum Press, 2016), 311.

32 *Crossbow* was the code name for intelligence operations against all aspects of German long range weapons capability.

33 TNA, Ministry of Home Security Ho 199/375, Press Cuttings, *The Daily Express*, June 28, 1944.

34 The *Sunday Pictorial*, June 2, 1944.

35 *The Daily Telegraph*, July 5, 1944; TNA, Ministry of Home Security Ho 199/375, Press Cuttings.

36 *The Daily Express*, July 17, 1944.

37 The *Sunday Graphic*, June 30, 1944.

38 TNA AIR Ministry papers 20/06/2017 Operation "Crossbow": general papers on retaliation and reprisals, Notes of a press conference on the flying bomb held at the Ministry of Information held on September 7 1944.

39 Ibid.

The day following this remarkable display of hubris, the first ballistic missile in history unleashed death and destruction. The V2 Rocket could not be tracked on radar and no warnings could be given. The rockets were launched from mobile Rocket launchers in and around The Hague, Holland, which was still under German occupation. The V2 Rocket carried 760 kilograms of explosives, was capable of supersonic speed, and could fly at an altitude of over 50 miles. An attack was characterised by a loud double bang, sometimes heard 10 miles away, as the sound of the explosion was followed immediately by a sonic boom. A government report on the rockets stated "that from the sound experienced there was no way of knowing how far away the rocket had landed. People living ten miles away thought the incident was close at hand, but people living close by, within half a mile, often thought that the incident was far away."[40]

The first V2 attack happened at Chiswick in Stavely Road on the evening of 8 September creating a crater thirty feet wide and eight feet deep.[41] A further bomb fell at Epping sixteen seconds later. During the first ten days of attack, twenty-five rockets landed in England, sixteen in London. The assault of bridges on the Rhine, Operation Market Garden gave a ten day let up in rocket attacks, and some hope of finding and disarming the rocket sites, but the operation failed and by 26 September what was left of the Airborne Divisions were evacuated back across the Rhine. The attacks resumed, the aim of the rockets improved and in the week ending 1 November, twenty-six rockets had landed in London, increasingly among the built-up areas.[42] The inner Eastern boroughs of London such as Bethnal Green Hackney, Finsbury Park, and Islington were to have some of the highest number of incidents, but it was believed that the main target was the central London bridges, although the rockets, which were fired from Holland, often fell short and landed on East and North London. As in the Gotha raids of the First World War, the casualties in these areas were made worse by the flimsy and crowded nature of the housing stock.

The government at first imposed a blackout on any information on the rocket attacks, as they did not want the enemy to have any information of whether the rockets had landed or where, leaving the population to speculate on "flying gas mains," although a home intelligence report made it clear that many

40 TNA Ministry of Home Security, HO 186/2299, AIR RAIDS: flying bombs and rocket attacks – "Lessons from Recent Raids – Long Range Rockets."

41 Christy Campbell, *Target London: Under Attack From V-Weapons during WWII* (London: Little Brown , 2012), 382.

42 Basil Collier, *History of the Second World War: The Defence of the Kingdom* (London: HMSO, 1957), 406.

people realised that the explosions were being caused by "a stratospheric shell which could devastate everything within a square mile." On the resumption of attacks after Arnhem on the 25 September, the news blackout continued. In a broadcast on Berlin radio on 6 November Goebbels announced that "the British government has concealed from its people the existence of a long-range rocket."[43] Three days later the press broke their silence. The *Daily Mirror* led the way, with the headline "Nazis go all out on V2 terror in London," and on November 10 Churchill admitted in the house of Commons that the rocket attacks were taking place.[44] The *Times* reported his statement: "A number of rockets have landed, he said, at widely scattered points, but the damage so far had not been heavy. There was however no need to exaggerate the danger, the scale and effects of the attacks have not hitherto been significant."[45] *The Times* was at pains to point out that the press had supported the news blackout for good reason: "There were excellent reasons for withholding all information while the enemy himself was so uncertain about the effects of his attacks. "[46]

An example of a particularly horrific rocket attack was the incident at Woolworths in New Cross Road, Deptford on 25 November, when 168 shoppers and passers-by were killed and 123 seriously injured, twenty-four of the dead were never identified. Shoppers had converged on Woolworths as there was a rumour that saucepans were available for sale and the areas around the store was crowded. Its tea bar was popular with corporation workers, whose HQ was at the Town Hall opposite. The rocket fell at lunch time, and "everyone from four week old babies to adults in their seventies was hurled into the air with the debris."[47] Glass and rubble stretched ankle deep the half mile to New Cross station, which was believed to be the target.

On 6 December in the West End, a rocket fell in Duke Street, off Oxford Street at the side of Selfridges causing much damage. Eight American personnel using a canteen in Selfridges were killed and thirty-two were injured. Ten British civilians died and seven were injured. The blast damaged a basement at the store which had been converted into a secret Bell telephone 'x system' base codenamed *Sigsaly*. In January 1945 the number of Rocket attacks was nearly twice the average for the previous three months. One of the last but most deadly rocket attacks came on 27 March at a five story block of flats in Vallence Road, Stepney. It killed 134 people and injured fifty, decimating the

43 Roger Hermiston, *All Behind You, Winston: Churchill's Great Coalition* (London: Arum Press, 2016) , 322.

44 Ibid.

45 *The Times*, November 11, 1944, 4.

46 Ibid.

47 Maureen Waller, *London 1945* (London: John Murray 2004), 39.

local Jewish community. The attacks, which totalled 1,358 on London, were to last until March 1945. Casualties in the London region were 2,700 dead and 6,500 seriously injured, 1,700 who subsequently died.[48]

Coming at the end of a war that many British people realised was nearly won, and hard on the heels of the V1 bombs, the V2 attacks understandably had a detrimental effect on morale. *The New Yorker* reporter Mollie Panter Downes (1906–1997) wrote that "they arrive so abruptly that you don't have time to get scared – your either dead or simply startled."[49] George Orwell (1903–1950), writing in *The Tribune* on 1 December 1944 described some attitudes to the V2:

> People are complaining of the sudden unexpected wallop with which these things go off. 'It wouldn't be so bad if you got a bit of warning' is the usual formula. There is even a tendency to talk nostalgically about the days of the V1. The good old doodle bug did at least give you time to get under the table.[50]

The approach of the rocket was unseen and unheard until a double bang announced that one had landed. Unlike the V1 rockets, who by the Summer of 1944 were being shot down in large numbers by the RAF fighters, there was no adequate response to the V2 Rockets except destroying them on their launching grounds.[51] The defences carefully built up of fighter aircraft anti-aircraft guns and barrage balloons were all of no help. The rocket could not be tracked or stopped. This apparent helplessness against Hitler's new weapon added to the feelings of uncertainty and fear experienced by the population of London. It was decided that attempts to give specific warnings of the rockets would have led to many false alarms, so there were no official warnings.[52] After the Deptford incident, the Conservative MP for Croydon South wrote to the chief whip saying that "the incident has given rise to a great deal of apprehension. It is suspected, rightly or wrongly, that we are not paying enough attention to the sources of the rockets because of the objections of the Dutch Government in exile."[53] What the people of South Croydon and their MP could not know was

48 Basil Collier, *Defence of the United Kingdom: History of the Second World War – United Kingdom Military Series: Official Campaign History* (HMSO, 1957), 420.

49 Waller, *London 1945*, 43.

50 Campbell, *Target London*, 407.

51 Hawker Tempests, Spitfires and Britain's first jet fighter, the Gloucester Meteor, helped bring down 3,957 of the 7,488 flying bombs that arrived that Summer.

52 Collier, *Defence of the United Kingdom*, 413.

53 TNA, Air Ministry, AIR 20/2652, Papers accumulated by the Air Historical Branch.

the decision of the Chiefs of Staff on 23 December not to bomb the launching sites at the Hague was based on a completely different premise. Their decision was made because such an action "would divert 1,500 Lancaster sorties to counter small scale rocket attacks whose results have no military significance."[54] Christy Campbell comments on this decision in his book *Target London*: "This is how they judged London's peril. And they might be justified, but it did not feel like it."[55] On 3 March 1945, a raid on V2 launching sites at the Hague by direct was attempted, but because of navigational errors, it was a disastrous failure, killing 511 civilians.

Morale would surely have taken a turn for the worse if it had become common knowledge that the government had turned a blind eye to the activities of the intelligence service to deceive the enemy into aiming for south London instead of central London.[56] Colonel Ronald Wingate(1889–1978), the London Controlling Section Deputy Chief,[57] wrote to Brigadier Leslie Hollis (1897–1963), Assistant Secretary at the War Cabinet, and explained that "we have been obliged to adopt a policy ... that is to deceive the enemy that V2s have fallen in the west and southwest with a view to preventing him moving his aim westwards towards central London. During the last fortnight there have been signs of success since V2s have tended to land more to the east and the north of London."[58] The Chiefs of Staff were reluctant to endorse this deception and suggested that by planting a question and answerer in the House of Commons to persuade the enemy that strict censorship still applied to reporting of V2 attacks. Hollis wrote to Churchill's chief military assistant Major General Hastings Ismay (1887–1965): "It would lead to incalculable difficulties if it were to become known that such deception had been the cause of shifting the damage from one part of London to another."[59] However, the Chiefs of Staff were prepared to let the deception continue as long as it did not involve Chiefs of Staff or ministers: Ismay replied to Hollis, "the only possible course is to let the controlling officer do the best he can, referring to the chiefs of staff only when absolutely necessary."[60]

54 TNA, Cabinet Office, CAB 121/215, Special Secret Information Centre.

55 Campbell, *Target London*, 412.

56 TNA, Cabinet Office CAB 154/49, London Controlling Section, Correspondence and papers.

57 An organization within the war cabinet devoted to military deception.

58 TNA CAB 154/49, Ronald Wingate to Leslie Hollis January 25 ,1945. London Controlling Section, Correspondence and papers.

59 TNA Cabinet Office CAB 154/49, Leslie Hollis to Hastings Ismay 26 January ,1945. London Controlling Section. correspondence and papers.

60 TNA Cabinet Papers , CAB 154/49 Ismay to Hollis, 26 January, 1945, London Controlling Section, correspondence and papers.

An interesting insight into the official opinions on morale in the City of London can be seen in a letter from John Drew of the Home Defence Executive to Air Commodore Philip Fullard (1897–1984) in response to Fullard's remarks about horror stories about V2 attacks on London which were circulating in Lisbon. Drew wrote "we get a great deal of backwash of this sort of thing ... our tentative view is that for the greater part it is directly inspired by the enemy to compensate for the relative ineffectiveness of the weapon." Drew admitted that there had been 'bad incidents' but that "these are few in relation to the numbers sent over and there is no doubt that we have been lucky so far." He went on to deal with the reports Fullard had heard of poor morale in the city of London :

> I have had a word with Lucas who runs the war room in the Ministry of Home Security ... He says we have no evidence of any break in morale. In their experience morale is almost a function of casualties per incident. Disregarding the Deptford case and one or two others ... the overall casualty figure is lower than it was for bombs and flying bombs and according to Lucas things would have to get a very great deal worse before any deterioration of public morale takes place.

He ended the letter by commenting once more on the farfetched stories of the enemy: "The best of the bunch is the total destruction of Piccadilly Circus and Leicester Square which the enemy put out some week or two ago. I can assure you that the Café Royal is still there, and I will treat you to lunch when you are next home."[61]

Several aspects of the V2 attacks ensured that morale did not reach unacceptable levels. Mass observation[62] reported the development of a fatalistic attitude to the fact that no warning could be given or precautions taken.[63] As no precautionary measure could be taken, the V2, according to the Home Intelligence reports, inspired "fatalism, nervousness and resignation being about equal."[64] It inspired less nervous apprehension than the V1 , which could

61 TNA, Cabinet Office CAB 154/ 49 John Drew to Phillip Fullard, undated but written in response to a letter from Fullard dated 6 January 1944. London Controlling Section , correspondence and papers.

62 Mass Observation asked people to keep diaries about a range of topics ranging from politics to cooking. the material collected forms a hugely important picture of everyday life, popular culture and ordinary people's actions, attitudes and opinions from the 1930s to the 1950s.

63 Waller, *London 1945*, 40.

64 TNA, Ministry of Information ,Home Intelligence Report, INF1/292, No. 220, 21 December 1944, 3; No. 215, 16 November 1944.

be both seen and heard on its approach. The Incidents of rocket attacks did not deter the increasing numbers of Londoners who were returning to the city, a trend which continued over the winter months of 1944/1945. A sense of solidarity as engendered by the fact the rockets fell on rich and poor alike. Although the effect of the bombs was devastating, the civil defence services did magnificent work in dealing with incidents and saving lives of trapped victims. It was estimated that 20,000 Londoners owed their lives to this rescue work.[65] The organisation of sheltering in the underground tube system was much more organised than in 1917, or even in the blitz of 1940. Deep shelters were opened in July 1944 but their availability did not seem to cause panic in their use, or a lack of morale in their users.

The morale of Londoners under V1 attack was improved by the decision to publish details and diagrams on their capabilities and construction. Although Londoners were tolerant of the government's silence on the V2 rocket, it was nevertheless a relief when Churchill announced their existence, if not their targets. By the time he made his official announcement it was realised that "the absence of warnings and the official silence added to the apprehensions of the nervous."[66] Morale also depended on the ability of individuals to feel that they are actively engaged in the situation, through firefighting, air raid precautions, First Aid, or simply finding the most effective shelter. Apart from the official services there was little that individuals could do to prepare for V2 attacks which although less in number, were unpredictable.

Londoners' anxieties in the Autumn and Winter can perhaps be measured in increased attendance at cinemas and the theatres that had reopened. Zeigler commented: "By early 1945 it was clear that neither the V2 or the occasional air launched V1 was any longer regarded as a deterrent by London audiences."[67] The last V2 was launched on 27 March 1944, and fell near Orpington, killing one and injuring twenty-three. It took a while, but eventually the people of London realised that the threat from air attack was over. Symbolically on 30 April, Big Ben was once more illuminated.

As was discovered by the British War Cabinet when bombing large German cities, devastating aerial attacks do not necessarily cause a significant drop in morale of the civilian population, but the V2 rocket, if it had been ready and utilised earlier than the last months of the war would arguably have driven the long besieged Londoners to protest and unrest, as well as further weakening the physical structure of the capital. The bombings by Gotha aeroplanes were

---

65 J.H. Foreshaw, LCC architect. Quoted in Waller, *London 1945*, 46.

66 TNA, Ministry of Information ,Home Intelligence Report, INF1/292. No. 220, 21 December 1944, 3; No. 215, 16 November 1944.

67 Zeigler, *London at War*, 307.

novel in that they subjected the population of London to direct and planned aerial bombardment for the first time. Although morale in London did not break down entirely, the aerial bombardment of London and the reactions of Londoners to it disturbed the Government enough to take the probability of air attack in a future war very seriously. The attacks by V2 ushered in a new age of aerial warfare, in which it was impossible to defend the population of London by conventional means. On both occasions of new means of air attack, by Gotha bombers in the First World War and by V2 s in the second, it was fortunate that the people of London were protected both by defects in the new technologies and by the sheer size of the metropolis. It is clear that the public's morale and resilience was affected by the percentage killed and wounded and the number made homeless, but in a city of the size of London, those factors never reached a critical mass before the cessation of the attacks. The concentration of the German air force on the Western Front in 1918 and the progress of the Allied forces in Europe in 1945 relieved the pressure on the city before morale deteriorated and criticism of the governments in both wars became more intense. Incidents such as the Upper North Street school in 1917 and the Deptford rocket attack in 1944 may have created shock and horror, but such incidents were isolated enough not to result in widespread panic. This may not have been the case if the attacks had continued and the inability to either defend the city form the V2s or the impossibility of providing adequate protection had been fully revealed to the public.

This chapterr has dealt with the experiences of the effect of specific bombing campaigns on London in two world wars and the problems encountered by the respective governments to maintain the morale its population and the sustain the capital's contribution to the war effort in the face of these attacks It can be seen that sustained aerial bombardment in the First World War led to an appreciation that aerial bombardment would play a major part in future wars, and that preparations for this eventuality were superseded by the development and deployment of the V2. Following the Second World War and the bombing of Japan with nuclear bombs in 1945, the concept of MAD (mutually assured destruction), and most recently the development of drone aircraft, aerial bombardment has become one of the preferred methods of attack throughout the world in the 20th and 21st centuries. Destroying the enemy's cities, damaging civilian morale, destroying vital infrastructure and causing large movement of refugees from cities is still being used as an effective weapon of war, resulting in the deaths of millions of civilians. It can be said to be the main way in which warfare is brought effectively to the urban environment.

Works Cited

Primary Sources

House of Commons Debates
Vol. 95 June and July 1917.

The National Archives
Air Ministry papers, AIR 20/2652.
Air Ministry papers, AIR 20/06/2017.
Cabinet Office, CAB 46, Committee of Imperial Defence.
Cabinet Office, CAB 121/215, Special Secret Information Centre.
Cabinet Office CAB154/49, London Controlling Section.
Ministry of Home Security HO 199/375, Press Cuttings.
Ministry of Home Security, HO 186/2299 Air Raid Precautions Registered Files.
Ministry of Information Home Intelligence INF1/212/3, Reports nos. 220 and 215.

Newspapers
The Daily Express
The Daily Telegraph
The Sunday Pictorial
The Sunday Graphic
The Times

Published Works

Angus Calder. The *Myth of the Blitz*. London: Jonathan Cape, 1989.

Campbell, Christy. *Target London: Under Attack from V-Weapons during WWII*. London: Little Brown, 2012.

Collier, Basil. *History of the Second World War, The Defence of the Kingdom*. London: HMSO, 1957.

Douhet, Giulio. Command of the Air (1921).

Emmerson, Charles. *1913: The World Before the Great War*. London: Vintage, 2013.

Gardiner, Juliet. Wartime *Britain 1939–1945*. London: Headline Books.

Hansen, Neil. First *Blitz: The secret Plan to Raze London to the Ground in 1918*. London: Corgi, 2008.

Hermiston, Roger. *All Behind You, Winston: Churchill's Great Coalition 1940–45*. London: Aurum Press, 2016.

Jones, Edgar. "Air Raids and the Crowd: Citizens at War", *The Psychologist* 29:6 (2016).

Mackay, R. *Half the Battle – Civilian Morale during the Second World War*. Manchester: 2002.

Marwick, Arthur. *The Home Front, The British and the Second World War*. London: Thomas and Hudson, 1976.

Morrison, Frank. *War on Great Cities, A Study of the Facts*. London: Faber and Faber, 1937.

O' Brien T.H. *Civil Defence*. London: HMSO, 1955.

Parker, Nigel. Gott Strafe England: The German Assault against Great Britain 1914–18, Vol 1. Solihull: Helion, 2015.

Waller, Maureen. *London 1945*. London: John Murray, 2004.

White, Jerry. *Zeppelin Nights: London and the First World War*. London: Vintage, 2015.

Zeigler, Philip. *London at War*. London: Sinclair Stevenson, 1995.

Websites

Robinson, Bruce. The Blitz. *BBC*. March 30, 2011. Accessed May 3, 2017. http://www.bbc.co.uk/history/worldwars/wwtwo/ff3_blitz.shtml.

CHAPTER 5

The Death of a City: The Yugoslav Peoples Army Siege of Vukovar, 1991, Refugee Crisis, and Its Aftermath

James Horncastle

The causes for the fragmentation of Yugoslavia are numerous, and an extensive literature on the topic has developed in the past twenty-five years.[1] A factor that has not been adequately accounted for, however, was the Yugoslav People's Army's (JNA) urbicide of the city of Vukovar. The JNA, considered both within Yugoslavia and outside the country as the preserver of the Yugoslav vision, looked on with apathy while its soldiers devastated the picturesque city.[2] Before Vukovar, the general consensus among outside observers was that Yugoslavia's statehood would be maintained. Once the JNA's assault against Vukovar, a fixed, static location largely open to the press, was revealed to the outside world, however, international opinion rapidly turned against the JNA and their primary backer, the Serbian President Slobodan Milosević.

Though the 25 August to 18 November 1991 Siege of Vukovar, and resulting destruction of the city, was a seminal event of the Yugoslav wars, it receives only passing mention in the literature.[3] This oversight is likely due to the fact that the Siege of Dubrovnik, the internationally renowned tourist destination and UNESCO World Heritage Site, occurred concurrently with the Siege of Vukovar.[4] While the Siege of Dubrovnik received much of the international

1 See Sabrina P. Ramet, *Thinking About Yugoslavia: Scholarly Debates About the Yugoslav Breakup and the Wars in Bosnia and Kosovo* (Cambridge: Cambridge UP, 2005), *Passim.*

2 Warren Zimmermann, *Origins of a Catastrophe* (New York: Random House, 1999), 156.

3 For example, Mile Bjelajac and Ozren Žunec recognize Vukovar's importance for shifting international opinion, but do not examine the issue in any detail, leaving the point open to challenge. See Mile Bjelajac and Ozren Žunec, "The War in Croatia, 1991–1995," in *Confronting the Yugoslav Controversies: A Scholars' Initiative* (West Lafayette, IN: Purdue UP, 2010), 250.

4 For examples from the literature see: Mihailo Crnobrnja, The Yugoslav Drama (I.B. Tauris: London, 1996) 173; David Bruce Macdonald, *Balkan Holocausts?: Serbian and Croatian Victim Centred Propaganda and the War in Yugoslavia* (Manchester: Manchester UP, 2003), 104-105; Sabrina P. Ramet, *The Three Yugoslavias: State-Building and Legitimation, 1918–2005* (Bloomington, IN: Indiana UP, 2006), 409. News articles from the period also show how the international community's first focus was upon Dubrovnik, then Vukovar. See: Reuter, "Truce Holds in Beseiged Croatian Town," Toronto Star, 14 November 1991, A3; "16 Killed in Croatia

 | DOI:10.30965/9783657702787_006

press' focus in 1991, and in fact lasted much longer than that of Vukovar, its role as a site of international importance meant that the amount of damage that the JNA forces inflicted upon Dubrovnik was significantly less than that of Vukovar.[5] Instead Vukovar's status as a strategically important city to both the Croatian and Yugoslav/Serb forces, yet lacking the international recognition of Dubrovnik, meant that it and its population were subjected to the full horrors of war.

In order to chart how the destruction of Vukovar became the focal point for changing international opinion, this paper will examine American, Canadian, and International newspapers and agencies from the start of the siege until its conclusion for references to Vukovar, and how the depiction and tone changes over time. Given that North America was geographically remote from Vukovar, and therefore more likely to focus on other matters, the change in perception is demonstrative of what occurred in Europe, but on a greater scale. Prior to the Siege of Vukovar, international opinion was divided on what to do with the crisis in Yugoslavia. Most international actors preferred to keep Yugoslavia intact, whether because of obligations elsewhere, a *realpolitik* outlook, or simply a romanticization of Yugoslavism. The JNA's destruction of Vukovar, however, dramatically altered international opinion. The JNA and Slobodan Milosević, henceforth, were identified as the primary aggressors during the Yugoslav Wars.

Background

Vukovar, a city positioned along the confluence of the Vuka and Danube Rivers, was a significant, but by no means crucial, municipality in the region of Eastern Slavonia in Croatia. A multiethnic and confessional city, Vukovar represented, in many ways, the Yugoslav ideal of different peoples working and living in harmony. Furthermore, the city possessed significance to the Yugoslav state, as Vukovar was the city where the Communist Party of Yugoslavia (KPJ) was officially founded in 1920. For these reasons, Vukovar was held up as an ideal, if slightly small, Yugoslav socialist city. The country's policies during the Cold War, however, would sow the destruction of Vukovar, and transform the

by Army Assaults," *Toronto Star*, 30 October 1991, AP, "Army Halts Shelling of Dubrovnik Trapped Croatians Hope to Flee," ibid., 13 November 1991, Marcus Tanner, "Croatians Launch Attacks against Army," ibid., 16 September, 1991.

5 Central Intelligence Agency Office of Russian and European Analysis, *Balkan Battlegrounds: A Military History of the Yugoslav Conflict, 1990–1995*, vol. 1 (Washington, D.C.: Central Intelligence Agency, 2000), 102.

idea of Vukovar from a symbol of brotherhood and unity to one of excess and destruction.

Understanding Total National Defence, Yugoslavia's defence policy in the Cold War, is crucial to explaining not only the collapse of the country, but why the JNA resorted to urbicide against the city of Vukovar. Total National Defence, formalized in 1969, was a policy whereby the Federal Government of Yugoslavia devolved significant defence powers to the republics and lower forms of government. While this policy made Yugoslavia less vulnerable to the blitzkrieg style its leaders feared, it also posed the problem that Yugoslavia needed a strong ideology to prevent the policy from becoming a liability. Unfortunately the death of Josip Broz Tito in 1980, and the subsequent fragmentation of political power along republican lines, meant that each of the Yugoslav republics possessed the foundations for their own army.[6]

The one entity that embodied the pan-Yugoslav vision, the JNA, recognized the potential threat posed by the TND system should separatist republics seek to leave Yugoslavia. As a result, the JNA managed to successfully lobby for legislation in 1988 that effectively dismantled the TND system, and placed the armed forces throughout the country under their direct control.[7] The short duration between the enactment of this law (1988) and the fragmentation of Yugoslavia (1991) meant, however, that the legacies of the doctrine were still in place. Furthermore, the JNA faced the problem from republics displaying separatist tendencies, most notably Croatia and Slovenia, who encouraged their citizens to avoid enlistment.[8] This had the effect of further Serbianizing the army, and making it more susceptible to appeals of Serb nationalists.

Croatia would not be able to fully capitalize on the legacies of TND to push for independence. One of the primary reasons was that Croatia was not ethnically homogenous: Serbs represented 12.2 percent of Croatia's population.[9] Furthermore, the Serb population was concentrated in the southwest and the northeast of the country (Vukovar's location), making the areas both politically and militarily defensible. In the spring of 1991, the JNA began to

6 James Horncastle, "Croatia's Bitter Harvest – Total National Defence's Role in the Croatian War of Independence," *Small Wars & Insurgencies* 26 (2015): 745-746; Jamie Horncastle, "A House of Cards: The Yugoslav Concept of Total National Defence and Its Critical Weakness," *Macedonian Historical Review* 2:1 (2011), 299-300.

7 James Horncastle, "Reaping the Whirlwind: Total National Defense's Role in Slovenia's Bid for Secession," *The Journal of Slavic Military Studies* 26:3 (2013), 534.

8 General Veljko Kadijević, *Moje Videnje Raspada: Vojska Vez Drzave* (My View of the Collapse: Army without a State) (Belgrade: Politika, 1993), 142.

9 "Population by Ethnicity, 1971–2011 Censuses," Croatian Bureau of Statistics. Accessed January 31, 2019. www.dzs.hr/ENG/censuses/census2011/results/xls/usp_03_EN.xls.

actively supply the Serb residents in these areas with arms and munitions in order to pursue their political objectives; specifically maintaining the unity of Yugoslavia by any means necessary.[10] The growing Serbianization of the JNA, however, meant that it increasingly became a tool of Serbia's demagogue leader, Slobodan Milošević.

Croatia's new nationalist leadership further aggravated the situation. For reasons that remain debated amongst historians, a group of men that included Croatia's Deputy Minister of Defence and key advisor to Franjo Tudjman, Gojko Šušak, fired Armburst rockets into Borovo Selo, a suburb of Vukovar.[11] Although the reasons behind Šušak's choice of Borovo Selo remain speculative, Vukovar's importance to the Yugoslav state and identity cannot be overlooked. These attacks only served to further legitimize the JNA's argument that it conducted peacekeeping operations in the region, even if they were blatant in their support of the local Serb population.[12] Furthermore, on 1 July 1991, Šušak arranged the assassination of Josip Reihl-Kir, the Police Chief of Osijek, who previously had been known for his peacekeeping efforts between the Serbs and Croats of Eastern Slavonia.[13] Šušak and his group's actions provided justification for those individuals that argued in favour of a unified Yugoslavia.[14] In their eyes Croatia was no worse than Serbia or the other republics.

Croatia's leadership was not simply content to separate from Yugoslavia but harbored aspirations of expanding their territorial control into neighboring Bosnia-Herzegovina.[15] Franjo Tudjman, elected in 1990, believed that the Croatian republic represented a truncated portion of the idealized Croatian state. In this regard, he was not that dissimilar from Slobodan Milošević and his pursuit of a Great Serbian State. His belief that Croatia needed to be expanded, however, created severe political and military complications. In the case of the latter, Tudjman initially refused to optimize the TND system as it

10 Laura Silber and Alan Little, *The Death of Yugoslavia* (London: BBC Books, 1993), 110.

11 Macdonald, *Balkan Holocausts?: Serbian and Croatian Victim Centred Propaganda and the War in Yugoslavia*, 104.

12 Little, *The Death of Yugoslavia*, 153-156.

13 Michael Mann, *The Dark Side of Democracy: Explaining Ethnic Cleansing* (Cambridge: Cambridge UP, 2005), 388.

14 Glaurdic correctly identifies that politicians and intellectuals in the West, contrary to the actual development of events, wanted a unified Yugoslavia. See: Josip Glaurdic, *The Hour of Europe: Western Powers and the Breakup of Yugoslavia* (New Haven, CT: Yale UP, 2011), 6.

15 As will be explained in detail later, the JNA and Serbs successfully used the fact that elements of the Croatian government were apologetic about the crimes committed by the Independent State of Croatia (NDH) during the Second World War. See Macdonald, *Balkan Holocausts? Serbian and Croatian Victim Centred Propaganda and the War in Yugoslavia*, 103, 135.

was not designed for offensive operations, which Croatia needed to perform if it were to realize his ambitions. In fact, Tudjman, fearing that the TND could be used against him, made no effort to employ the institutional legacies of the policy. This meant that when Croatia declared independence on 25 June 1991, it did not possess the military means to adequately defend itself against the JNA.

More importantly, Tudjman's naked ambition for territory outside of Croatia alienated the international community. Even a truncated Yugoslavia militarily out-matched Croatia, meaning the latter had to find other means of cementing its claim to independence. Diplomats and politicians from the European Community and the United States during the first half of 1991, however, possessed a decidedly negative view of Tudjman. In particular, details leaked of Tudjman's meeting with Milošević on 25 March 1991, where the two allegedly planned the division of multiethnic Bosnia and Herzegovina.[16] As a result, when the JNA attempted to prevent Croatia's secession, the newly self-declared country did not possess the international support needed to bring pressure that would allow it to overcome its military disadvantage.

The Croatian War of Independence and the Battle for Vukovar

Although Croatia declared independence on the same day as Slovenia, 25 June 1991, it did not immediately rush to implement its sovereignty or support Slovenia. Tudjman failed to do so despite the fact that he and Milan Kučan, the President of Slovenia, had reached an understanding whereby both states would assist one another in their push for independence.[17] Instead, Tudjman delayed responding in force for fear of alienating the international community.[18] Tudjman's refusal to support Slovenia allowed the JNA to rapidly withdraw their forces from Slovenia and focus on Croatia, which possessed a large Serb minority. Borisav Jović, Serbia's representative on Yugoslavia's

16 There is considerable debate over precisely what Milosević and Tudjman agreed to at Karadjordjevo, as the talks took place without witnesses and no written account was provided by either party. That said, it is generally recognized by historians that based on the later actions of both Milosević and Tudjman that they reached an agreement over the future of Bosnia, although the exact nature of that agreement is open for debate. See Ivo Banac, "The Politics of National Homogeneity," in *War and Change in the Balkans*, ed. Brad Blitz (Cambridge: Cambridge UP, 2006); Miroslav Tudjman, *Vrijeme Krivokletnika* (Zagreb: Detecta, 2006), 149.

17 Martin Spegelj, "The First Phase, 1990–1992," in *The War in Croatia and Bosnia-Herzegovina: 1991–1995*, eds. Branka Magas and Ivo Zanic (London: Frank Cass, 2002), 27.

18 Macdonald, *Balkan Holocausts?*, 105; Spegelj, "The First Phase, 1990–1992," 27.

Presidential Council, explained: "Milošević and I resolutely requested the following from Kadijević:"

> 1. Respond to the Slovenes vigorously using all means including the air force, they must absolutely no longer be allowed to disrespect the Yugoslav People's Army. Then withdraw from Slovenia. We shall make a timely decision on that matter. In that way army morale shall be improved, Croatia shall be scared and Serbian people calmed.
> 2. The main YPA forces shall be grouped on Karlovac-Plitvice [Lakes] line to the West; Baranja, Osijek, Vinkovci – Sava [River] to the East and Neretva [River] in the South. In that way all territories inhabited by Serbs shall be covered until the final resolution, that is until the people freely decides in a referendum.[19]

The Serbian government and the JNA believed that they would be able to accomplish this task in short order.[20] Critical to the JNA holding the Karlovac-Plitvice line, and carving up Croatia, was taking the city of Vukovar, which is situated along the Danube and was at that point in the JNA's strategic rear.[21] From the JNA's perspective, this should not have been a difficult task.

Vukovar, at the outset of the conflict, was particularly vulnerable to a rapid attack by the JNA. While the Minister of Defence Martin Špegelj recommended a strategy of placing the JNA's garrisons under siege, Vukovar was isolated. Given its presence in the region the JNA was confident the siege would take two weeks. In terms of regular military forces Croatia possessed only 400 soldiers. Supplementing these soldiers were 300 police officers and 1,100 locals who had previously received military training as part of the Total National Defence system. These forces only possessed limited arms and ammunition. Against this force the JNA placed approximately 36,000 soldiers, with extensive armored and air support.[22] Furthermore, paramilitary units from Serbia

19 Borisav Jović, "Izjava Na Osnovu Pravila 89 (F)," ed. International Criminal Tribunal for the Former Yugoslavia (The Hague2003). Accessed January 31, 2019. http://www.icty.org/x/cases/slobodan_milosevic/proswitness/bcs/mil-wit-jovic.htm.

20 Mario Šebetovsky, "The Battle of Vukovar: The Battle That Saved Croatia" (United States Marine Corps, 2002), 4-5.

21 While scholars, most notably Martin Spegelj, debated the necessity of taking Vukovar, Yugoslavia's Minister of Defence, General Veljko Kadijević, regarded it as a strategic necessity. See Kadijević, *Moje Videnje Raspada*, 135-38.

22 Šebetovsky, "The Battle of Vukovar: The Battle That Saved Croatia," 9-13.

proper – most notably Vojislav Šešelj's *White Eagles* and Arkan's *Tigers*, supplemented the JNA forces.[23] As such, the JNA's expectations of a rapid victory was reasonable.

The JNA's rapid victory, however, did not occur due to several organizational issues. First, and perhaps most telling, was the morale issues suffered by the JNA. It was one thing to fight, and die, for Yugoslavia; it was entirely a different thing to fight for a Greater Serbia. The JNA genuinely believed that it was the embodiment of a multiethnic Yugoslavia. The JNA's attack on Slovenia, however, raised doubts if this was actually the case or, in fact, it was a tool of Greater Serbian ambitions. The Siege of Vukovar and the JNA's 'police' actions in Croatia, however, helped confirm for many that it served Milosević's goals. Misha Glenny, a journalist covering the conflict, interviewed an AWOL Macedonian JNA officer who left his post because "most of the JNA soldiers just wanted to go home alive."[24] Furthermore, Borisav Jović notes that he and Milosević put pressure upon Kadijević to remove non-Serb officers from the JNA.[25] The JNA's decision to remove non-Serb officers meant that due to Yugoslavia's ethnic quota system in federal jobs it lost many of its best commanders, who were replaced by undertrained and underprepared Serbs. The result was that there was poor coordination amongst the JNA forces.

The JNA, unable to take Vukovar through storming the city, relied upon its artillery and air force to batter the city into submission. The JNA, having based its regular forces upon the Soviet model, was a highly mechanized force, and did not want for tanks nor artillery. Furthermore, Croatia did not possess an air force to counter the Yugoslav Air Force (RZ I PZO). Given the limitations of the ground forces in coordinating their attacks, General Zivota Panić explained that the JNA high command, "decided not to fight house to house. We would take Vukovar with heavy weapons."[26] Two problems, from a strictly military standpoint, arose from this strategy. The first, which this paper will explore later, was that the decision to bombard Vukovar into submission, rather than taking the city by storm, meant that it considerably lengthened the battle.

The second problem was tactical and arose from the fact that the bombardment made the city easier to defend by making the JNA's advance more difficult. The JNA's bombardment, the worst a European city faced since the

23 Horncastle, "Croatia's Bitter Harvest – Total National Defence's Role in the Croatian War of Independence," 756-757.

24 Misha Glenny, *The Fall of Yugoslavia: The Third Balkan War* (New York: Penguin Books, 1992), 124.

25 Jović, "Izjava Na Osnovu Pravila 89 (F)."

26 General Zivota Panić, cited in *Wars of Independence, Death of Yugoslavia* (London: BBC, 1995), 43 Minute.

Second World War, leveled homes and scattered debris throughout the town. This debris inadvertently made it easier for the Croatian defenders, as it helped create chokepoints for the advancing JNA armor and provided ready ambush points for its defenders. Given the JNA's inability to coordinate infantry and armored formation, their tanks were incredibly vulnerable to the Croatian defenders, who skillfully exploited the training provided by TND's emphasis upon irregular tactics to inflict severe losses upon the attackers.[27] Thus despite the limited supplies that reached the defenders, the Croatian defenders used them to maximum effect by exploiting the JNA's decision to bombard the city.

The JNA not only faced issues in coordinating its own forces; perhaps most problematically it had to work with the Serbian paramilitaries. Serbian paramilitaries are symbolic of the excesses of the Yugoslav Wars in general. JNA commanders, furthermore, looked upon them with disdain.[28] This, however, was not necessarily true. Serbian paramilitaries received considerable training from the Ministry of the Interior in irregular warfare and possessed effective and charismatic leadership.[29] Furthermore, unlike the JNA, the Serbian paramilitaries were ardent believers in their mission. As Vojislav Šešelj, the commander of the Serbian Volunteer Guard, explained: "[Vukovar is the] key stronghold of the Croatian fascists. When Vukovar falls, the fascists will be finished. My boys are volunteers; they know what they are fighting for."[30] One of the other paramilitary leaders, Dragoslav Bokan, stated that "In wartime, [fighting] was my duty as a Serb nationalist."[31] This contrasted considerably with the morale issues that the JNA's own soldiers faced.[32] As a result, any successful attack on Vukovar required that the JNA employ paramilitaries, although this military necessity would, in many ways, damage the overall JNA/ Serbian war effort due to the irregulars' excesses.

Despite the problems faced by the JNA, their overwhelming material and manpower superiority meant that by October the Croatian defenders were in a perilous position and in desperate need of supplies. Starting on 12 October 1991, and using newly acquired material from the Barracks War, the Croatian forces moved to relieve Vukovar. Just as the Croatian Army was about to make a major breakthrough, however, Franjo Tudjman, against the advice of his military advisers, halted the operation. Tudjman did so in order for a Medicines Sans Frontieres (MSF) convoy that was providing support to both parties might pass

27 Šebetovsky, "The Battle of Vukovar: The Battle That Saved Croatia," 34-36.
28 Horncastle, "Croatia's Bitter Harvest," 757.
29 Ramet, *The Three Yugoslavias*, 428.
30 Vojislav Šešelj in *Wars of Independence*, 26 Min.
31 Dragoslav Bojkin in ibid.
32 Horncastle, "Croatia's Bitter Harvest," 756.

unhindered.[33] The delay, however, allowed the JNA's 252nd Armored Division to maneuver into position to block the Croatian Army's advance, thus dooming the Croatian Army's ability to relieve the city.[34] Vukovar would eventually succumb on 18 November 1991, eliminating the last major obstacle to the JNA's advance into Eastern Slavonia. The political circumstances, however, had shifted considerably from when the JNA began its assault in August.

Vukovar as a Domestic and International Symbol

What is critical to note about Tudjman's policies during this period is that he, unlike the JNA or their Serb benefactors, recognized the importance of the international community in achieving his objectives. The JNA, and to a lesser extent Yugoslavia, benefitted from the fact that outside observers, accustomed to a united Yugoslavia and distracted by the turbulence of the post-Cold War period had a natural constituency of supporters.[35] Media coverage and political opinion in the lead up to and immediate aftermath of Croatia's declaration of independence, therefore, was heavily biased towards a united Yugoslavia. The United States' Deputy Secretary of State James Baker echoed the sentiments of many leading Western European officials when on 21 June 1991 he stated "instability and breakup of Yugoslavia could have some very tragic consequences, not only here, but more broadly in Europe."[36] Both the European Community and Conference on Security and Cooperation in Europe echoed these sentiments, coming out in favour of the "unity and territorial integrity" of Yugoslavia.[37]

Given the disparity of resources between Croatia and even a rump Yugoslavia, Croatia desperately needed to change the international narrative to one that favoured their secession. Tudjman was acutely aware of this fact. As David Bruce MacDonald notes, Franjo Tudjman, upon assuming power in 1990, frequently worked to change the international consensus that a united

---

33 Anton Tus, "The War in Slovenia and Croatia up to the Sarajevo Ceasefire," in *The War in Croatia and Bosnia-Herzegovina: 1991–1995*, eds. Branka Magas and Ivo Zanic (London: Frank Cass, 2002), 56.

34 Ibid.

35 Zimmermann, *Origins of a Catastrophe* 142-48. Some politicians even initially viewed Milosević in a positive light. See Glaurdic, *The Hour of Europe: Western Powers and the Breakup of Yugoslavia*, 6 and 12.

36 James Baker, cited in: Alan Riding, "Europeans Warn on Yugoslav Split," *The New York Times*, June 26, 1991.

37 Ibid.

Yugoslavia was in both the best interests of the peoples of Yugoslavia and the international community.[38] Tudjman went so far as to hire a New York based public relations firm to change his and Croatia's image for the international community.[39] This strategy, however, faced two significant problems.

The first problem that Tudjman encountered in his efforts to portray the Croats as victims of Greater Serbian aggression was the fact that he did not possess a united political party, and segments of his own party undermined his efforts in this regard. Most notably, the Croatian Democratic Union (HDZ) possessed a wing that actively endorsed the Ustaša regime and its methods during the Second World War. Although scholars still debate the number of individuals killed by the Ustaša, there is a general consensus that the regime actively perpetrated a campaign of genocide against Serbs and other minorities of the state.[40] Tudjman, however, needed their support due to their financial connections with the Croatian diaspora. This explains why Tudjman could not dismiss Gojko Šušak in the aftermath of his rocket attacks in Borovo Selo. Šušak, as a prominent member of the diaspora, helped acquire the money needed to finance Tudjman's political campaigns.[41] Thus instead of removing Šušak for undermining his political message, Tudjman soon promoted him to Minister of Defence in September 1991, a position he held until his death in 1998.

The second problem that Tudjman faced was that while not openly identifying with the Ustaša regime, he nevertheless was an ardent believer in a Greater Croatian state. Tudjman, a former JNA General, had fallen afoul with the regime for promoting Croatia's interests above the rest of the federation. Tudjman articulated this point in 1969 when he published *Velike ideje i mali narodi* (Great Ideas and Small Nations), where the ideas he articulated were partially responsible for the regime imprisoning him for two years in 1972.[42] After his imprisonment Tudjman became increasingly radicalized, to the point that he was willing to rehabilitate the genocidal regime of the Independent State of Croatia due to their belief in a greater Croatian state.[43] Given that the Greater Croatian state of the Second World War did not exist in 1991, and

38 Macdonald, *Balkan Holocausts? Serbian and Croatian Victim Centred Propaganda and the War in Yugoslavia*, 105.

39 Ibid.

40 Paul Mojzes, *Balkan Genocides: Holocaust and Ethnic Cleansing in the Twentieth Century* (Lanham, MD: Rowman & Littlefield, 2011), 45-78.

41 Analysis, *Balkan Battlegrounds: A Military History of the Yugoslav Conflict, 1990–1995*, 1, 52.

42 Franjo Tudjman, *Velike Ideje I Mali Narodi* (Zagreb: Matica hrvatska, 1969), *Passim*.

43 For the failures of Yugoslavia to deal with its past during the Second World War see: Tea Sindbæk, *Usable History?: Representations of Yugoslavia's Difficult Past – from 1945–2002* (Copenhagen: Aarhus UP, 2013), *Passim*.

required large swathes of territory from Bosnia to complete, it was difficult for him to present him and the Croatians as victims.

Tudjman also had to confront the fact that Slobodan Milosević skillfully exploited the fact that it was the JNA, and not Serbian forces, at least initially, who were active in Croatia before and during the siege. The JNA, for its part, presented itself as the defender of a united Yugoslavia.[44] Milosević managed to successfully compartmentalize his overt support for the Croatian Serbs through the intervention of the JNA that, as a federal body, he officially did not command. Many diplomats during this period, more notably Warren Zimmerman, saw through this ploy.[45] Nevertheless, given the sympathies of politicians and outside observers for a unified Yugoslavia it was not enough to change their opinion. As Zimmerman noted, "[... the] Croats, for all the euphoria of independence, failed to secure the recognition of any government. However final they considered their separation, their claims to Yugoslavia's assets would still have to be negotiated with the federal government and the hated Milošević."[46]

It was against this background that Tudjman made the fateful decision in August 1991 to make a stand at Vukovar. As Tudjman himself explained, "if we let the Serbs walk into Vukovar, it would have been a disaster for Croatia. So we threw all we had into defending it."[47] Tudjman, however, stated this after the fact, when Vukovar resonated with the international community. The resources Tudjman committed to the siege, however, illustrate that this argument was false.

The Siege of Vukovar had the potential to shift international opinion towards favouring Croatian secession. The ability to relate the violence to a specific city allowed journalists to simplify a complex situation. In his description of the siege on 31 August, Blaine Harden, a reporter for *The Washington Post*, noted: "to the south, roads are sealed off by tanks of the Serb-dominated Yugoslav federal army, which claims to be neutral. But its tanks and jets attacked the city for the first three days of this week – the clearest signal in the war so far that the Serbian guerrillas and the army are working together against Croatian forces."[48] The JNA, contrary to the narrative of them working for a united Yugoslavia, were working with the local Serb forces against the people of Vukovar, who were "packed [in a bomb shelter] today, as it has been for the past week, with

44 Norman Cigar, "The Serbo-Croatian War, 1991: Political and Military Dimensions," *Journal of Strategic Studies* 16:3 (1993), 310.

45 Zimmermann, *Origins of a Catastrophe*, 156–157.

46 Ibid., 142.

47 Franjo Tudjman in *Wars of Independence*, 28 Min.

48 Blaine Harden, "Croats Seek Shelter from Serbian Fire: Residents of City on Danube Huddle Underground During Siege," *The Washington Post*, August 31, 1991, A1.

women, elderly people and squirming children [...]."[49] For Harden, it did not matter so much who was right and who was wrong, because the fault of the conflict was drowned out by the violence he witnessed.

That said, the coverage of the Siege of Vukovar, however, was not immediately pro-Croatian. Instead, the press and politicians' sympathies for a united Yugoslavia affected coverage of the event. Marcus Tanner on 16 September 1991 noted that "Croatia launched a military offensive against the Yugoslav army yesterday, capturing army barracks throughout the republic."[50] Croatia is not the victim in this statement, but rather the aggressor. Likewise, when he mentioned Vukovar, he noted "in Vukovar, eastern Croatia, army tanks raised the siege of the local military base by blasting through Croatian lines."[51] The description of the JNA's breakthrough, and the tone that it takes, creates a neutral impression of the Yugoslav forces. Alan Ferguson, one of the key reporters on developments within Yugoslavia, wrote on 24 September 1991 describing the capture of a Yugoslav Army Base by the Croatian forces. Later reports of the conflict, as we shall see, emphasized the Serbian nature of the aggression. Ferguson, however, did not make that assertion, simply noting that the Croatians faced the "better armed – and increasingly army-backed – Serb insurgents who now control nearly one-fifth of Croatian territory."[52] These two examples are simply two of many from August and September where the media narrative on the Yugoslav Wars was ambiguous.[53]

The ambiguity of the media coverage, and Croatia's need to shift international opinion towards favouring its secession, explains Tudjman's decision to not push the reinforcements forward to Vukovar in the middle of October 1991. Before the convoy was set forth, both sides were receiving blame within the press and by politicians, and efforts were made to maintain neutrality. An 8 October 1991 Associated Press article describing the Siege of Vukovar simply noted "the city occupies a strategic point on the Danube River border with Serbia. Its capture would allow ethnic Serb insurgents, aided by the army, to control a large enclave in Slavonia, a region of eastern Croatia that has been

49 Ibid.

50 Tanner, "Croatians Launch Attacks against Army," A10.

51 Ibid.

52 Alan Ferguson, "Croatian Soldiers Celebrate Surrender of Yugoslav Base," *The Toronto Star*, September 24, 1991, A3.

53 Alan Cowell, "Yugoslavia's Federal Authorities Seem Bent on Widening Control: Yugoslav Army Offensive Batters Eastern Crotian Appeals Go Unanswered," *The New York Times*, 22 September 1991,1; John Tagliabue, "Yugoslav Force Retaliates for Blockade," *The New York Times*, 16 September 1991, A3; "Europeans Arrive in Yugoslavia to Promote Peace Plan," *The New York Times*, 2 September 1991, 3; "Yugoslavia's Ethnic Fighting Begins to Look Like War," *The New York Times*, 1 September 1991, E3.

the scene of much of the fighting since Croatia declared independence in June."[54] The Associated Press, unlike correspondents such as Harden who were actually in Vukovar, were able to take a much more dispassionate perspective on the conflict. Many of the correspondents were not in Vukovar – reporting the developments from either Zagreb or Belgrade – far removed from the fighting. As correspondent Kitty McKinsey noted from Zagreb on 10 October 1991, "European Community monitors today expressed 'deep disappointment' that Croatia and the Yugoslav army were not respecting the latest ceasefire."[55] The European Community apportioned out blamed equally in this instance, rather than identifying the Yugoslavs as the primary culprits.

The protracted campaign in Vukovar, however, not only created pressures on Franjo Tudjman and the Croatians: Slobodan Milošević's status as champion of the Serbs was also at stake. Milošević, having risen to power by promoting Greater Serbia ambitions, could not back down. As a result, on 11 October 1991, the Yugoslav Federal Presidency, now controlled almost exclusively by Serbia, issued a statement that it could not withdraw from Croatia as "this would expose [the Serbs] to physical liquidation."[56] This statement was an example of gas lighting, as Milošević and the Yugoslav Federal Presidency deliberately stroked Serb fears that originated in the Second World War campaign of the Ustaša. As the Associated Press noted, "the statement, coupled with a blunt denial by the army that it had signed any agreement to withdraw from Croatia, deflated hopes that had been raised by a reported peace pact Thursday."[57] Mid-October, in other words, was a period in which the actions of the Yugoslav Peoples Army proved that it did not work for the benefit of all the Yugoslav peoples. It was therefore imperative that Croatia not conduct any action that could jeopardize this shift.

It was against this background of external ambiguity that Tudjman made the critical decision not to exploit the arrival of an aid convoy to lift the Siege of Vukovar. On the same day that Milošević damaged his position as an honest broker in the Yugoslav Crisis, Paul Koring described how the Yugoslav Army halted the aid convoy in a manner very sympathetic to the Croatians. First, he noted how "the shells [...] have turned the cities of Osijek, Vukovar, and

54 AP, "Yugoslavs Open Drive against Croatian Stronghold," *New York Times*, October 8, 1991, A8.

55 Kitty McKinsey, "European Community Monitors Express Exasperation That Neither.," *CanWest News*, October 10, 1991, 1.

56 AP, "Yugoslavia's Army Won't Leave Croatia," *Toronto Star*, October 12, 1991, A14.

57 Ibid.

Vinkovci into living nightmares."[58] Furthermore, in describing how the convoy was halted by the JNA, he recounted how the JNA liaison officer contacted his high command to tell them that "you are shooting at me right now."[59] Koring was not alone in his opinion that the JNA was to blame for this humanitarian crisis in Vukovar. Later news reports on the convoy from the wire services, although more nuanced than Koring's, still imply that for delaying the convoy resided with the JNA.[60] In preventing humanitarian aid from reaching the city, the JNA still practiced the ideology of the Cold War the prioritized military expediency over humanitarian objectives.[61] In the post-Cold War environment, however, the humanitarian aspects of war took on a new significance. The urbicide of Vukovar by the JNA, and the resulting humanitarian crisis, provided a fixed location for the international community to demonstrate this newfound sense of humanitarianism.

The media coverage of the Siege of Vukovar in the aftermath of the failed aid convoy got progressively worse for the JNA, and more favourable to the Croatians. On 18 October 1991, Reuters noted that as a result of the JNA's advance around Vukovar the 8,000 inhabitants of the village of Ilok became refugees under an agreement between the Croatian government and the JNA to evacuate the area.[62] The description of the refugee convoy, and the JNA's response, demonstrates the shift that occurred in coverage of the region after the failed convoy and Milošević's declaration. It noted:

> A convoy of around 500 vehicles – trucks, trailers, tractors and cars – set off from Ilok and passed through the town of Sid toward uncertain new lives away from the front line. Villagers clutched what few belongings they could carry. A convoy of similar length, mostly army support vehicles, afterwards moved up the motorway from Belgrade toward Croatia.[63]

58 Paul Koring, "Dangerous Farce Portrays Yugoslav Ceasefire: Odyssey of Relief Convoy Heading for the Embattled City of Vukovar Is Story of Failing Peace," *The Globe and Mail*, October 12, 1991, A1.

59 Ibid.

60 Reuters, "Ec Convoy Braves Fire to Reach Vukovar," *Toronto Star*, October 14, 1991, A5; Reuter, "Convoy Still Falls Short of Beseiged in Croatia," *The Washington Post*, October 15, 1991, A16.

61 This point is explored in detail in Peter J. Hoffman and Thomas G. Weiss, *Humanitarianism, War, and Politics: Solferino to Syria and Beyond* (Boulder, CO: Rowman & Littlefield, 2017), *Passim*.

62 Reuter, "Yugoslavs Closing in on Key City," *Toronto Star*, October 18, 1991, A10.

63 Ibid.

Reuters clearly identified the Croatians as the victims, whereas the JNA, through their movement of army support vehicles, were the aggressors in the conflict. The JNA were losing the public relations campaign.

The JNA, furthermore, never learned the importance of public relations throughout the siege of Vukovar. While Milosević certainly knew its importance, the JNA officers at the front, let alone their senior commanders, did not have the same appreciation.[64] JNA officers justified the destruction of Vukovar to themselves by believing that they were putting down an Ustaša uprising. These same officers gave the media unfettered access to the city, and described their destructive acts with professional pride.[65] While the JNA's honesty contrasts with the duplicitous actions of the politicians, their willingness to inflict suffering upon a civilian population was therefore in plain view.

As the Siege of Vukovar came to its closing moments in November 1991, the media coverage of its fall demonstrated the decisive shift in international opinion from ambiguity to one of favouring the Croatians. On 4 November the Independent News Service noted that the 10,000 civilians that remained within Vukovar "eked out a hellish existence in freezing cellars."[66] Critically, the article also noted "in the most dramatic battle, the city of Vukovar appeared to be falling to Serbian forces."[67] Milošević's ability to plausibly deny his role in the conflict was now a thing of the past. So desperate were Milošević and his allies to regain the international moral high ground that on 9 November his representatives requested that the United Nations dispatch peacekeepers to the region.[68] It was, however, too late for the JNA to effectively alter international opinion. Reports of the siege and eventual surrender of Vukovar continued to emphasize the nature of Serbian aggression against the city.[69] Chuck Sudetic, in one account, noted the suffering of a 49 year old Serb woman, who had to

---

64 *Wars of Independence.*

65 Glenny, The Fall of Yugoslavia: The Third Balkan War, 102-103.

66 The Independent News Service, "Croatia under Siege as Sanctions Date Looms," *Toronto Star*, November 4, 1991, A11.

67 Ibid.

68 Reuter, "U.S. Joins Canada, Ec in Sanctions against Yugoslavia," *Toronto Star*, November 10, 1991, H4. It is important to note that there was also a military calculus to this move, as the Croatian armed forces were gaining considerable strength during this period, and challenging the JNA's preexisting gains. See: Tus, "The War in Slovenia and Croatia up to the Sarajevo Ceasefire," 41-66.

69 Joseph Fitchett, "In Vukovar, 2 Ways of Fighting a War," *The New York Times*, November 19, 1991; Chuck Sudetic, "Croats Concede Danube Town's Loss," *The New York Times*, November 18, 1991; "Croatia Seeks Surrender in Besieged Vukovar Croatia Concedes Defeat in Battle over Vukovar," *Toronto Star*, November 18, 1991, A1.

live in her basement for 76 days.[70] The JNA, in other words, could not even claim to be fighting for the Serbs of Croatia, as it was also responsible for their suffering.

If the JNA's efforts to take Vukovar marred their and Milošević's efforts to present themselves as the defenders of both Yugoslavia and its people, the aftermath proved even more damning. First, the sheer destruction of the city provided a clear example of JNA/Serbian excess. An article in *The New York Times* noted "To Guernica, Coventry, Stalingrad and Dresden the world may now add Vukovar and Dubrovnik."[71] The destruction of Vukovar (and Dubrovnik) in other words, ranked amongst the worst cases of urbicide of the twentieth century. With the JNA not having a consistent media plan to challenge this narrative, besides playing on racist stereotypes of the Croats, Croatia quickly capitalized on the destroyed city, both in domestic and international media, to create sympathy. Years later, Croatia constantly reemphasized Vukovar to encourage its own people to not give up hope of recapturing national territory, but simultaneously to demonstrate to the world that they were the victims in this conflict.[72]

Croatia was not completely Machiavellian in exploiting this legacy, as doing so also served to provide domestic support. The JNA's annexation of Eastern Slavonia and other sections of Croatia in 1991 displaced 265,000 people within the country itself.[73] Furthermore, an additional 250,000 Croats from Serb-occupied territories ended up as refugees throughout Europe and North America.[74] For those that remained, the Croatian government, regardless of its ideology, could not deemphasize the importance of Vukovar without encouraging potential unrest.[75] Therefore, posters and addresses concerning Vukovar featured prominently in Croatian government addresses from the Siege of Vukovar all the way through its eventual re-conquest in 1995.

Refugees from Vukovar and Eastern Slavonia did not just end up in the remainder of Croatia; a significant number also ended up in Europe and North America. These refugees, while attempting to integrate into their new societies, simultaneously could not detach themselves from the plight of their homeland. In this way, the refugees that the JNA and Serbs created in an effort to

70 "House-to-House Fighting in Croatian City Nears End," *The New York Times*, November 14, 1991, A1.

71 "Listen to the Silence," *New York Times*, November 22, 1991,

72 Catherine Baker, Sounds of the Borderland: Popular Music, War and Nationalism in Coratia since 1991 (Franham, Surrey: Ashgate Publishing, 2010), 22.

73 *Documents (Working Papers) 1993*, (Strasbourg: Council of Europe, 1993), 9.

74 Ibid.

75 Baker, *Sounds of the Borderland*, 22.

construct a racially pure homeland actually served to undermine their claims amongst the international community. Local news coverage from Canada, US, and the UK frequently described the issues faced by the refugees – keeping the Serbs past actions in Vukovar at the forefront.[76] Combined with the ongoing struggles in Bosnia, this provided Croatia with the victim-centered status that it needed for international support. This support came despite the fact Tudjman continued to pursue his Greater Croatian objectives in Bosnia and Hercegovina.

Conclusion

The JNA's destruction of Vukovar played a pivotal role in shifting international opinion in favour of Croatia. The JNA's urbicide of the city, and subsequent creation of a refugee crisis in its aftermath, caused international opinion to shift against Serbia and the JNA. Whereas reporters and international governments were previously ambivalent to Tudjman and the Croatian government's claims, in the aftermath of Vukovar international opinion shifted and subsequently viewed Croatia as a victim. The destruction of Vukovar, in fact, presaged how the devastation of cities in future conflicts, such as Aleppo in the Syrian Civil War, would serve to rally international opinion and lead to more of an activist stance by the international community. Thus, the relationship between a more activist international community and the destruction of cities is a subject that bears further scrutiny and inquiry.

Works Cited

Analysis, Central Intelligence Agency Office of Russian and European. *Balkan Battlegrounds: A Military History of the Yugoslav Conflict, 1990–1995*. Vol. 1, Washington, D.C.: Central Intelligence Agency, 2000.

AP. "Army Halts Shelling of Dubrovnik Trapped Croatians Hope to Flee." *Toronto Star*, 13 November 1991, A3.

AP. "Yugoslavia's Army Won't Leave Croatia." *Toronto Star*, 12 October 1991, A14.

AP. "Yugoslavs Open Drive against Croatian Stronghold." *New York Times*, 8 October 1991.

Baker, Catherine. *Sounds of the Borderland: Popular Music, War and Nationalism in Coratia since 1991*. Franham, Surrey: Ashgate Publishing, 2010.

76 Macdonald, *Balkan Holocausts?*, 204.

Banac, Ivo. "The Politics of National Homogeneity." In *War and Change in the Balkans*, edited by Brad Blitz, 30-43. Cambridge: Cambridge UP, 2006.

Cigar, Norman. "The Serbo-Croatian War, 1991: Political and Military Dimensions." *Journal of Strategic Studies* 16, no. 3 (1993): 297-338.

Cowell, Alan. "Yugoslavia's Federal Authorities Seem Bent on Widening Control: Yugoslav Army Offensive Batters Eastern Crotian Appeals Go Unanswered." *The New York Times*, 22 September 1991.

Crnobrnja, Mihailo. *The Yugoslav Drama*. I.B. Tauris: London, 1996.

"Croatia Seeks Surrender in Besieged Vukovar Croatia Concedes Defeat in Battle over Vukovar." *Toronto Star*, 18 November 1991, A1.

Documents (Working Papers) 1993. Strasbourg: Council of Europe, 1993.

Ferguson, Alan. "Croatian Soldiers Celebrate Surrender of Yugoslav Base." *Toronto Star*, 24 September 1991, A3.

Fitchett, Joseph. "In Vukovar, 2 Ways of Fighting a War." *The New York Times*, 19 November 1991.

Glaurdic, Josip. *The Hour of Europe: Western Powers and the Breakup of Yugoslavia*. New Haven, CT: Yale University Press, 2011.

Glenny, Misha. *The Fall of Yugoslavia: The Third Balkan War*. New York: Penguin Books, 1992.

Harden, Blaine. "Croats Seek Shelter from Serbian Fire: Residents of City on Danube Huddle Underground During Siege." *The Washington Post*, 31 August 1991, A1.

Horncastle, James. "Croatia's Bitter Harvest – Total National Defence's Role in the Croatian War of Independence." *Small Wars & Insurgencies* 26 (2015): 742-61.

Horncastle, James. "Reaping the Whirlwind: Total National Defense's Role in Slovenia's Bid for Secession." *The Journal of Slavic Military Studies* 26, no. 3 (2013): 528-50.

Horncastle, Jamie. "A House of Cards: The Yugoslav Concept of Total National Defence and Its Critical Weakness." *Macedonian Historical Review* 2, no. 1 (2011): 285-302.

Jović, Borisav. "Izjava Na Osnovu Pravila 89 (F)." edited by International Criminal Tribunal for the Former Yugoslavia. The Hague, 2003. http://www.icty.org/x/cases/slobodan_milosevic/proswitness/bcs/mil-wit-jovic.htm.

Kadijević, General Veljko. *Moje Videnje Raspada: Vojska Vez Drzave* (*My View of the Collapse: Army without a State*). Belgrade: Politika, 1993.

Koring, Paul. "Dangerous Farce Portrays Yugoslav Ceasefire: Odyssey of Relief Convoy Heading for the Embattled City of Vukovar Is Story of Failing Peace." *The Globe and Mail*, 12 October 1991, A1.

"Listen to the Silence." *New York Times*, 22 November 1991.

Little, Laura Silber and Alan. *The Death of Yugoslavia*. London: BBC Books, 1993.

Macdonald, David Bruce. *Balkan Holocausts?: Serbian and Croatian Victim Centred Propaganda and the War in Yugoslavia*. Manchester: Manchester UP, 2003.

Mann, Michael. *The Dark Side of Democracy: Explaining Ethnic Cleansing*. Cambridge: Cambridge UP, 2005.

McKinsey, Kitty. "European Community Monitors Express Exasperation That Neither." *CanWest News*, 10 October 1991, 1.

Mojzes, Paul. *Balkan Genocides: Holocaust and Ethnic Cleansing in the Twentieth Century*. Lanham, MD: Rowman & Littlefield, 2011.

"Population by Ethnicity, 1971–2011 Censuses." Croatian Bureau of Statistics, http://www.dzs.hr/ENG/censuses/census2011/results/xls/usp_03_EN.xls.

Ramet, Sabrina P. *Thinking About Yugoslavia: Scholarly Debates About the Yugoslav Breakup and the Wars in Bosnia and Kosovo*. Cambridge: Cambridge UP, 2005.

Ramet, Sabrina P. *The Three Yugoslavias: State-Building and Legitimation, 1918–2005*. Bloomington, IN: Indiana UP, 2006.

Reuter. "16 Killed in Croatia by Army Assaults." *Toronto Star*, 30 October 1991, A18.

Reuter. "Convoy Still Falls Short of Beseiged in Croatia." *The Washington Post*, 15 October 1991, A16.

Reuter. "Truce Holds in Beseiged Croatian Town." *Toronto Star*, 14 November 1991, A3.

Reuter. "U.S. Joins Canada, Ec in Sanctions against Yugoslavia." *Toronto Star*, 10 November 1991.

Reuter. Yugoslavs Closing in on Key City." *Toronto Star*, 18 October 1991.

Reuters. "Ec Convoy Braves Fire to Reach Vukovar." *Toronto Star*, 14 October 1991.

Riding, Alan. "Europeans Warn on Yugoslav Split." *The New York Times*, 26 June 1991.

Šebetovsky, Mario. "The Battle of Vukovar: The Battle That Saved Croatia." United States Marine Corps, 2002.

Service, The Independent News. "Croatia under Siege as Sanctions Date Looms." *Toronto Star*, 4 November 1991, A11.

Sindbæk, Tea. *Usable History?: Representations of Yugoslavia's Difficult Past – from 1945–2002*. Copenhagen: Aarhus UP, 2013.

Spegelj, Martin. "The First Phase, 1990–1992." In *The War in Croatia and Bosnia-Herzegovina: 1991–1995*, edited by Branka Magas and Ivo Zanic, 14-40. London: Frank Cass, 2002.

Sudetic, Chuck. "Croats Concede Danube Town's Loss." *The New York Times*, 18 November 1991.

Sudetic, Chuck. "House-to-House Fighting in Croatian City Nears End." *The New York Times*, 14 November 1991.

Tagliabue, John. "Europeans Arrive in Yugoslavia to Promote Peace Plan." *The New York Times*, 2 September 1991, 3.

Tagliabue, John. "Yugoslav Force Retaliates for Blockade." *The New York Times*, 16 September 1991, A3.

Tanner, Marcus. "Croatians Launch Attacks against Army." *Toronto Star*, 16 September 1991, A10.

Tudjman, Franjo. *Velike Ideje I Mali Narodi*. Zagreb: Matica hrvatska, 1969.

Tudjman, Miroslav. *Vrijeme Krivokletnika*. Zagreb: Detecta, 2006.

Tus, Anton. "The War in Slovenia and Croatia up to the Sarajevo Ceasefire." In *The War in Croatia and Bosnia-Herzegovina: 1991–1995*, edited by Branka Magas and Ivo Zanic, 41-66. London: Frank Cass, 2002.

Wars of Independence. Death of Yugoslavia. London: BBC, 1995.

Weiss, Peter J. Hoffman and Thomas G. *Humanitarianism, War, and Politics: Solferino to Syria and Beyond*. Boulder, CO: Rowman & Littlefield, 2017.

"Yugoslavia's Ethnic Fighting Begins to Look Like War." *The New York Times*, 1 September 1991.

Zimmermann, Warren. *Origins of a Catastrophe*. New York: Random House, 1999.

Žunec, Mile Bjelajac and Ozren. "The War in Croatia, 1991–1995." In *Confronting the Yugoslav Controversies: A Scholars' Initiative*, 232-73. West Lafayette, IN: Purdue UP, 2010.

CHAPTER 6

"Government Forces Dare Not Penetrate": Urban Arab Palestine, No-Go Areas, and the Conflicted Course of British Counter-Insurgency during the Great Rebellion, 1936–1939

Simon Davis

The Great Palestine Arab rebellion against British rule, sometimes termed the first authentic intifada,[1] lasted from April 1936 until summer 1939. The British Mandate's facilitation of Zionist expansion in Palestine had since the 1920s recurrently aroused violent Arab protest, mainly at urban points of interface with Jewish communities. Initially, the great rebellion seemed just such another occurrence, beginning with inter-communal riots in Manshiyeh, the mixed Arab-Jewish workers' suburb separating the Jewish city of Tel Aviv from its mainly Arab neighbor Jaffa. But despite the reinforcement of exhausted Palestine Police with 300 Cameron Highlanders, a quarter of the infantry in Palestine, the disorders metamorphosed into lasting, territory-wide Arab civil disobedience. Coordinated by National Committees in each principal town, elite leaders hurriedly formed the Jerusalem-based Arab Higher Committee, hoping to preserve leadership over qualitatively new levels of nationally conscious activism. Proliferating rural sniping and sabotage, mainly on Jewish settlements, most engaged the British military, predisposed to familiar small-war, anti-banditry traditions, largely derived from experience in India. But urban political violence, mainly in the form of reciprocally escalating Arab and Jewish bombings, shootings and stabbings, was left to the increasingly overwhelmed police. Consequent loss of control over Arab towns forced the British High Commissioner, Sir Arthur Wauchope, to invoke emergency regulations in June 1936. But subsequent military repression, frequently contemptuous of civil political context, merely aggravated Arab resistance, which was transformed, British observers noted, from past patterns of spasmodic anti-Zionist violence into a comprehensive uprising against British Mandatory rule itself.

1 Charles Townshend, "First Intifada: Rebellion in Palestine, 1936–39," *History Today*, 37:7 (1989). Accessed January 31, 2019. http://www.historytoday.com/charles-townshed/first-intifada-rebellion-palestine-1936-39.

 | DOI:10.30965/9783657702787_007

Crushing Arab Palestine therefore became an essential cynosure, in Cabinet and military opinion in London, of British worldwide imperial credibility.[2]

Historians are presently re-examining subsequent brutal campaigning as a prehistory of Britain's post-1945 counter-insurgent "dirty wars," and for Arab Palestine as so destructive and shocking as to render it incapable of self-defense against Zionist expropriation a decade later.[3] But recent studies follow the British army into its comfort-zone of rural pacification, where regular troops were blooded, under career officers jockeying for position prior to the anticipated European war.[4] These forces were doctrinally averse to grueling and tedious urban warfare, as well as effective intelligence and security duties, particularly in labrynthine, sullen, culturally alien Arab old cities. Rather, these were contained as no-go areas, leaving their civil societal and economic provisions to atrophy. Ironically, when under such conditions urban rebel surges followed, military reactions were of an indiscriminate severity which objectified the urban centers concerned as enemy nodes to be reduced, rather than structural hubs of a polity to be recovered.

British military license over, rather than aid to, the Mandatory civil power progressively obliterated the British Colonial Office policy, exercised stealthily by Wauchope since late 1931, of encouraging Arab Palestinian development to cultivate political trust. Wauchope's endeavor had been to reconcile Palestine's Arab and Jewish communities on terms of material and political convergence, proceeding to consensual post-colonial self-government in ways that continued to support British Middle Eastern interests. Towards the Arab side, this was initially manifested in paternalistic concern for distressed Arab peasants, mediated politically with notable elite interlocutors. Only shortly before the rebellion did Wauchope finally attend to urban governance and material reforms. But once disorder erupted, British military destructiveness

2 British National Archives (hereafter TNA) Colonial Office (hereafter CO): CO733/310/1 *Palestine Disturbances*, 1936 April-May.

3 Georgina Sinclair, "'Get Into a Crack Force and Earn Twenty Pounds a Month All Found': The Influence of the Palestine Police on Colonial Policing 1922–1948," *European Review of History* 13:1 (2006), 49-65. Andrew Mumford, *The Counter-Insurgent Myth: The British Experience of Irregular Warfare* (Abingdon: Routledge, 2012), 3-6. Benjamin Grob-Fitzgibbon, "Further Thoughts on the Imperial Endgame and Britain's Dirty Wars," *Journal of Imperial and Commonwealth History* 40:3 (2012), 506, 509. David Lloyd, "Settler Colonialism and the State of Exception: The Example of Palestine/Israel," *Settler Colonial Studies* 2:1 (2012), 59-80.

4 Among his fine contributions, Matthew Hughes, "The Practice and Theory of British Counter-Insurgency: The Histories of the Atrocities at the Palestinian Villages of al-Bassa and Halhul, 1938–1939," *Small Wars & Insurgencies* 20: 3-4 (2009), 528-550, is a key micro-history. Also, Norris, Jacob, "Repression and Rebellion: Britain's Response to the Arab Revolt in Palestine of 1936–39," *Journal of Imperial and Commonwealth History* 36:1 (2008), 25-45.

compounded the prejudicial, antipathetic legacy of earlier British administrative negligence towards the Palestinian Arab city. An exception, to be analyzed closely, was Major General Richard O'Connor, notably in his retaking of Old Jerusalem, Jericho, Hebron, Beersheba and Gaza which rebels had taken over during a crisis of British power in October 1938. As will also be seen, his was a minority position, overshadowed by advocates of unlimited repressive force, including his contemporary Bernard Montgomery, and Air Commodore Arthur Harris, both future successful wartime commanders remembered for totalizing, aggressive operational philosophies. They tested these in Palestine in both rural *and* urban settings, on principles dismissive of political considerations, either for past or future policies of development and reconstruction. Rather than being considered part of the order being defended, such Colonial Office civil strategies became a casualty, never to recover, of British counterinsurgency, along with much of urban Arab Palestine itself.[5]

This as yet overlooked, but nonetheless essential urban context of the great rebellion will be surveyed here. Cultural historians of the Mandatory period have already identified towns and cities in Arab Palestine, despite the British official conceit of its quintessential rusticity, as vital social, cultural and political crucibles of proto-modernity. They moreover served as hubs of emerging urban-rural exchange conducive to increasingly national Palestinian consciousness, manifested for example in fluid, back-and-forth migration patterns and associated cultural evolutions. But in British colonialist framings, urban Arab Palestine, whether for aesthetic or merely parsimonious reasons, was seen as inscrutably lawless, squalid, dirty and dysfunctional. By default these attitudes made no-go areas out of the Palestine Arab city, creating deficits in British legitimacy, authority and intelligence which allowed epicenters of rebellion to develop. Not only were the Mandatory authorities surprised by the great rebellion, they lacked the means of response, beyond abandoning civil order to military license.[6]

As suggested above, British military mentalities objectified Palestine Arab urban centers as enemy nodes to be neutralized, not vital elements of a polity to be reclaimed, seeking to move on quickly to the war they wanted: rural pacification by regular field units. As the rebellion dragged on, within the urban enclaves bypassed and cordoned, rebel authority liquidated British institutions

5 See David French, "Nasty Not Nice: Nasty not Nice: British Counter-Insurgency Doctrine and Practice, 1945–1967," *Small Wars and Insurgencies* 23:4-5 (2012), 744-761.

6 For an enduring model, see Albert Hourani, *A History of the Arab Peoples* (New York: MJF Books, 1991), 295-299, 333-340; Kimmerling, Baruch and Migdal, Joel, *The Palestinian People: A History* (Cambridge, MA: Harvard University Press, 2003), 102-134.

along with the bourgeois and notable-dominated Arab Palestinian order, imposing retributive para-military justice, often religiously inspired. Even when, perforce, British troops were obliged to recover urban centers abandoned to such opponents, rural counter-insurgency priorities remained, leaving war-induced urban depreciation un-redressed, and a new urban-rural divide in effect. In ways to be explored, Arab Palestine's national polity was thereby decapitated and fragmented. Although outside the scope of this study, the rebellion's counter-integrative effect may indeed have negated collective capacities for self-defense during the war of 1948, enabling the State of Israel to emerge.[7]

Yet, as suggested above, hostile British military objectification of urban Arab Palestine was a variation rather than abnegation of previous middling civil British colonialist attitudes. Since the Ottoman defeat little had been done to redress pervasive Great War-era urban depreciation, of housing, infrastructure and economic life, compounded by the severe 1927 earthquake. While urban Arab Palestine was left to local indigenous notable governance, under straitened Ottoman-era fiduciary, legal and revenue-raising terms, the British implicitly looked to Zionist enterprise as a self-financing engine of development, concentrated in Palestine's urban and industrial sectors. They supposed its achievements would collaterally benefit all Palestinians. Instead an ethnically segregated social economy emerged, with Arab urban nodes, particularly old cities or neighborhoods being "othered" in Zionist thinking, as in British, as unregenerate repositories of anti-civilization.[8] Wauchope eventually recognized the dangers of such prejudices. In 1934 – thirteen years after Tel Aviv was granted full incorporation, enabling its expansion as a model, modern

7 May Seikaly, *Haifa: Transformation of a Palestinian Arab Society, 1918–1939* (London: I.B. Tauris, 1995), esp. Chs.4, 6, 8 and 10; Ann Mosely Lesch, *Arab Politics in Palestine, 1917–1939: Frustration of a Nationalist Movement*, (Ithaca, NY: Cornell University Press, 1979), 55-75, 102-122; Mustafa Kabha, *The Palestinian Press as Shaper of Public Opinion, 1928–1939: Writing Up a Storm* (London: Valentine Mitchell, 2007); Weldon C. Mathews, *Confronting an Empire, Constructing a Nation: Arab Nationalists and Popular Politics in Mandate Palestine*, (London: I.B. Tauris, 2006), 56-100; Adnan Abu Ghazaleh, "Arab Cultural Nationalism in Palestine during the British Mandate," *Journal of Palestine Studies*, 1:3 (1972), 41-44, 55-60; George Mansur, "The Arab Worker under the Palestine Mandate (1937)," *Settler Colonial Studies*, 2, 1 (2012), 192-204; CO733/370/9 *Notes on Leaders of Armed Gangs*, Deputy Inspector-General A.J. Kingsley-Heath, CID, October 14, 1938.

8 Mark LeVine, *Overthrowing Geography: Jaffa, Tel Aviv and the Struggle for Palestine, 1880–1946* (Berkeley: University of California Press, 2005); Sharon Rotbard, *White City, Black City – Architecture and War in Tel Aviv and Jaffa*, (Cambridge, MA: MIT Press, 2015); On Zionist segregationism, Tamir Goren, "Efforts to Establish an Arab Workers' Neighbourhood in British Mandatory Palestine," *Middle Eastern Studies* 42:6 (2009), 917, 919-921; CO733/297/2, *Political Situation*, 1936 April-June, Chaim Weizmann to the First World Congress of Jewish Physicians, Tel Aviv, April 23.

Jewish metropolis – franchise and governance reforms were extended to Arab towns and cities. Mixed-ethnic Haifa had also been boosted by its confirmation after 1925 as the hub of region-wide British petroleum refining and transportation operations. These became the main reasons for Britain retaining a stake in Palestine, based in the long-term on a unitary, bi-communal state. Arab Palestinian confidence in the latter was sought via colonial development and welfare projects facilitating convergence with high, privately-capitalized Zionist living standards.[9]

But as Jacob Norris has recently shown, concomitant development policy emphasized integrative infrastructure but circumvented Arab cities themselves.[10] Government of Palestine support-services, town planning, water-surveys, policing, some education, partial hospital funding, post and telecommunications, provided little actual capital. Funds went into village micro-projects or roads, railways and ports, leaving urban essentials largely untouched. Likewise, Wauchope's reforms were less material than a political experiment in Arab civil inclusion, leading he hoped to an eventual bi-communal Palestine Legislative Council and then to power-sharing self-government. Colonial Office capital grants, acknowledging the "sense of grievance" under which Arab municipalities worked, came only in 1935. A Town Planning Department opened in 1936, complementing the hitherto rurally-orientated Development Department, itself only four years old. Ironically in the week the great rebellion erupted, Wauchope optimistically praised Arab municipal efficiency, responsibility and leaders' sobriety on "racial" issues. His efforts provided too little, too late.[11]

Wider British attitudes, most pronounced in the Jerusalem Secretariat, stood aloof from demands urban Arab Palestine presented. Most British officials lived apart from Palestinians, in physical and cultural simulacra of English suburbs, collectively resentful of this dead-end posting.[12] At best, Arab cities were accorded antiquarian value. In Old Jerusalem this prohibited the installation of piped water, sewers and electricity. Significant public

---

9 On attempted reform, CO733/223/18 1932 *Local Government Bill*; 410/11 *Strategic Importance of Palestine*, 12 April 1939.

10 Jacob Norris, *Land of Progress: Palestine in the Age of Colonial Development* (Oxford: Oxford University Press, 2013), esp. 99-138; TNA/Cabinet Papers (hereafter CAB) CAB23: 1928 Conclusions, 23/60/12, 23/60/21: *Haifa Baghdad Pipeline and Terminus* summarizes discussions on the port's importance and policy implications.

11 Dov Gavish, *A Survey of Palestine under the British Mandate, 1920–1948* (London: Routledge, 2005), 143-146; CO733/269/7 *Municipalities: Grants in Aid*, 6 March-15 July 1935; 302/4 *Municipal Corporations Ordinances*, Wauchope to SofS Thomas, April 26, 1936.

12 On British mentalities, A.J. Sherman, *Mandate Days: British Lives in Palestine, 1918–1948* (New York: Thames and Hudson, 1997), 48-61; Naomi Shepherd, *Ploughing Sand: British Rule in Palestine* (New Brunswick, NJ: Rutgers University Press, 2000), 74-178.

building monumentalized colonial authority, chiefly in Jerusalem: modernist-Orientalist offices, Wauchope's residence, museums, the Jerusalem Arab College producing future teachers and administrators, were built in suburbs or scenic locations framing old cities as distantly picturesque. Meanwhile, continuing late Ottoman patterns of bourgeois Palestinian outmigration left older Arab quarters to a new urban poor.[13]

Their straits were compounded by Zionist developmental and labor segregation, which made Haifa and Jaffa flashpoints in 1936. British failures to re-capacitate agrarian society faster than its population grew forced peasants into the urban labor force. But Arab workers were widely excluded from higher-skilled training and better paying Jewish firms, entering lower-paid seasonal, manual, or public employment. Even here, higher Jewish immigration during the depressed 1930s raised Zionist demands for minimum Jewish employment quotas in hitherto mainly Arab spheres, notably railways and ports, at higher wages sustaining European-level Jewish (versus Asiatic Arab) socio-economic differentials.[14]

Arab urban resentments were aggravated by Mandatory reliance on private enterprise for key aspects of development, invariably favoring better-resourced Jewish contractors, notably for electrification. Needing paying subscribers, the latter favored the well-monetized Zionist sphere but under-served cash and

---

13 Roberto Mazza, *Jerusalem: From the Ottomans to the British* (London: I.B. Tauris, 2009); Ilana Feldman, *Governing Gaza: Bureaucracy, Authority and the Work of Rule* (Durham: Duke University Press, 2008), 21, 48-49, 126-145, 161; Ruth Kark, *Jaffa: A City in Evolution, 1799–1917* (Jerusalem: Itzhak Ben Zvi Press, 1990); Ron Fuchs and Gilbert Herbert, "Representing Mandatory Palestine: Austen St. Barbe Harrison and the Representational Buildings of the British Mandate in Palestine, 1922-37," *Architectural History*, 43 (2000): 281-333; Ylana Miller, *Government and Society in Rural Palestine, 1920–1948* (Austin; University of Texas Press, 1985), esp. "Part II: Government and Society, 1920–1936." CO733/194/9, 1930 *Development Scheme*; Also, Rosa El-Aini, *Mandated Landscape: British Imperial Rule in Palestine, 1929–1948* (London: Routledge, 2004); Israel State Archives (hereafter ISA) Record Group (hereafter RG) 12 5138/2m, *Colonial Development Fund*, 21 August 1929–June 1937: RG2 486/1m, *Report on Improvements at Jaffa Port: Vol.1 1934*, and 486-2m *Vol. 2 1935*; For British projects around, not in cities, CO733/213/3 1932 *Capital Works Program*. ISA RG2 486-29m, *1934: Site for Government Offices, Jaffa*.

14 Nahum T. Gross, "The Economic Policy of the Mandatory Government in Palestine," *Research in Economic History*, 9:1 (1984), 145-150, 166-171; Barbara Smith, *The Roots of Separation in Palestine: British Economic Policy, 1920–1929* (Syracuse: Syracuse University Press, 1993), 3-16; Zachary Lockman, *Comrades and Enemies: Arab and Jewish Workers in Palestine, 1906–1948* (Berkeley: University of California Press, 1996), 50-56, 180-198, 222-262; CO733/703/6 1936 *Public Works: Allocation between Jewish and Arab Labour*. ISA: RG28/01 1951/8-m, *Arab Lightermen's Cooperative, Jaffa*; 1951/9-m and 1951/33-m: *Employment of Jewish Labour at Jaffa Port*. 1934–1937.

credit-poor Arab Palestine.[15] Haifa's housing and social conditions were neglected during its industrial expansion. Arab workers crowded into the deteriorating "old town" and, on nearby waste land into "buyuut al-tanak" – tin houses, where the radical cleric 'Izz al-Din al-Qassam's welfare and ideological programs, including para-military training, attracted many.[16] Jaffa was worse-off: Government help came in 1933 for citrus sheds, a crane, rail sidings and a breakwater but the residents of the old city still depended on one well, had no electricity grid or main sewer. Waste leaks into the port created "disgraceful conditions" blamed solely on incorrigible Arab filthiness rather than British penny-pinching and underlying racial contempt.[17]

Similarly, British surveyors and statisticians confidently recorded Palestine's inanimate phenomena, but covered the human sphere in perfunctory, residential head-counts noting religious identity only.[18] Conscientious District Commissioners were absorbed by rural touring, leaving standing duties, and most urban interface to Palestinian subordinates.[19] Political intelligence was police business, without a Criminal Intelligence Department (CID) until 1931, thereafter the "Cinderella of the force," challenging Foucauldian notions of pervasive surveillance. Indeed, a systemic British colonial knowledge deficit preceded the rebellion. Wauchope's elevation of civil-investigative over para-military policing was resisted by British cadres, many being ex-Black and Tans, nursing resentments of defeat in Ireland. Most urban policing was by Jewish and Arab personnel serving and identifying first with their own communities.[20]

---

15 Ronen Shamir, *Current Flow: The Electrification of Palestine*, (Stanford: Stanford University Press, 2013).

16 Shai Lachman, "Arab Rebellion and Terrorism in Palestine, 1929–39: The Case of Sheikh Izz al-Din al-Qassam," in *Zionism and Arabism in Palestine and Israel*, eds. Elie Kedourie and S.G. Haim (London; Frank Cass, 1982), 52-84; Schleifer, Abdullah, "Izz al-Din al-Qassam: Preacher and Mujahid," in *Struggle and Survival in the Modern Middle East*, ed. Edmund Burke et al. (London: I.B. Tauris 1992).

17 TNA: Treasury Records (hereafater T) T161/864: *Jaffa: Creation of Port and Land Reclamation Scheme*, 31 July 1933. ISA RG 28/01 *Railway and Ports Administration: Port of Jaffa*, 1949/5m, 2/1936-2/1929, Cleaning of Customs Area; 16m 4/1937-11/1930, New Port Offices: RG2 489-5m, 1941-1933 *Jaffa Water Supply.*

18 Gavish, *Survey*, 23, 36-50, 60-89, 143-146. Also, *Census of Palestine 1931: Population of Villages, Towns and Administrative Areas*, (Jerusalem: Greek Convent and Goldberg Presses, 1932).

19 Indicative memoirs include, Edward Keith-Roach, *Pasha of Jerusalem: Memoirs of a District Commissioner under the British Mandate* (London: Radcliffe Press, 1994), 96-133 and Hugh Foot, *A Start in Freedom* (New York: Harper and Row, 1964), 18-46.

20 St. Anthony's College, Oxford: Middle East Center (hereafter MEC), Charles Tegart Papers, Box 2, File 2: Report on Palestine policing, December 1937; For a Foucauldian view, Martin Thomas, *Empires of Intelligence: Security Services and Colonial Disorder after 1914*, (Berkeley: University of California Press, 2008); Then, Geoffrey Morton, *Just the Job:*

British intelligence failings were compounded by Royal Air Force Special Service leanings to adventurous swagger over banal work.[21]

Instead, British order in urban Arab Palestine relied on civil consent and consensus with Palestinian notables, middling and junior state servants, and the passivity of what remained largely featureless masses. Wauchope's hopes for ethno-demographically representative self-governance materialized in plans for a Legislative Council, finally announced in 1935. Zionist opposition to its implicit de-privileging of the Jewish National Home pushed Arab Palestine towards rebellion, with urban confrontations being catalytic. In November 1935, Arab port workers at Jaffa, antagonized by attempted Zionist labor penetration, stumbled on a large clandestine arms shipment bound for Tel Aviv, exposing Jewish para-military preparations to resist the Legislative Council.[22] Evident British unwillingness to investigate and repress Jewish gunrunning inspired 'Izz al-Din al-Qassam, in Haifa, to declare a war of Muslim self-defense: he was soon killed by police.[23] Resulting popular unease was aggravated in March 1936 when after pro-Zionist lobbying in London, Parliament voted down Wauchope's proposals and the Cabinet snubbed an expectant Palestine Arab delegation. In these tense circumstances, three Jewish travelers were murdered by Qassamite hold-outs on the road between Nablus and Jenin in April. Angry Jewish demonstrations followed in Tel Aviv, followed by retaliatory murders and lynching of Arabs. These in turn sparked off intercommunal street battles in Manshiyeh. That the British took repressive action against Arabs before Jews resulted in a Palestine Arab general strike, called by Nablus's radical national committee. A hastily-formed Arab Higher Committee (AHC) of leading urban notables, led by the Grand Mufti of Jerusalem, Haj

Some Experiences of a Colonial Policeman (London: Hodder and Stoughton, 1957), 25-28; Gad Kroizer, "From Dowbiggin to Tegart: Revolutionary Change in the Colonial Police in Palestine during the 1930s," *Journal of Imperial and Commonwealth History* 32:2 (2004), 115-128; John Knight, "The Successful Failure of Reform: Police Legitimacy in British Palestine," in *The Routledge Handbook of the History of the Middle East Mandates*, eds. Cyrus Schayegh and Andrew Arsan (London: Routledge, 2016), 198-211.

21 TNA Air Ministry Records (hereafter AIR) AIR 5/1246, 1247 and 1248 *Palestine Monthly Summaries, 1931–1939*; AIR 23/765 *RAF Palestine and Transjordan, 1938 – April-December*, Harris to HQ Cairo, August 16, 1938 is exemplary on SSOs' wishes for the latest German MP 38 "gangster guns," and fast cars, for roving against rebel "hold ups," while filing routine reports spiced with Haganah chickenfeed on Arab affairs.

22 CO733/293/3 *Legislative Council for Palestine: Proposals for Such a Body*, January-March 1936; 293/4, January-April 1936; 304/7 *Arms Smuggling*, October 1935–January 1936.

23 Lachman, "al-Qassam," 80-84.

Amin al-Husseini, sought to preserve credible leadership by endorsing and affecting to direct these populist initiatives.[24]

What followed was internecine jockeying for supremacy by Arab Palestinian factions and sub-constituencies. Wauchope, the majority of his local British officials, and Colonial Office mandarins worked to preserve what subaltern scholar Ranajit Guha called: "Improvement as the means of political persuasion."[25] The British military, intuitively supported by the metropolitan Cabinet, advocated repression, suggesting Joseph Schumpeter's contemporaneous theories on imperialism as atavistic reactionism by pre-modern martial elites "without definite, utilitarian limits" or political-economic rationality.[26] Military logic held that by crushing Arab Palestine, recent humiliations, notably in Ireland, Egypt and India, endangering the empire's authority over proliferating nationalist and rival-power threats, would be powerfully reversed.[27] Moreover, repression's high-political advocates, including the newly installed, personally pro-Zionist Colonial Secretary William Ormsby-Gore, who had earlier in his career helped draft the Balfour Declaration, the Secretary of State for War Duff Cooper, Neville Chamberlain and Sir John Simon, eagerly cited counter-insurgent doctrines advanced in the 1934 manual, "Notes on Imperial Policing." This remarkable primer barely refers to policing but demanded the early assertion of military over civil power and decisive force at the first sign of trouble, dehistoricizing its case-studies, from Sudan, Egypt, to India and Shanghai, into military-operational situations, where restive colonial subjects feature invariably as counter-rational primitives responsive only to superior armed will. In Palestine, these principles eventually displaced the British civil-colonial order supposedly being defended.[28]

---

24 CO733/293/3 *Legislative Council for Palestine: Proposals for Such a Body*, January-March 1936; 293/4, January-April 1936; 304/7, 1936 Jan-Oct. *Arms Smuggling*. AIR2/1840, *Palestine Emergency: Appreciation by AOC British Forces, 1936*, "Summary of Phases," June 29, 1936; On elite versus popular dynamics, Philip Mattar, *Al-Hajj Amin al-Husseini and the Palestinian National Movement* (New York: Columbia University Press, 1988), 58-72; Baruch Kimmerling, "The Formation of Palestinian Collective Identities: the Ottoman and Mandatory Periods," *Middle Eastern Studies* 30:2 (2000), 54-68. Lesch, *Frustration*, 55-75, 102-122.

25 Ranajit Guha, *Dominance without Hegemony: History and Power in Colonial India* (Cambridge: Harvard University Press, 1997), 32-33.

26 Joseph Schumpeter, *The Sociology of Imperialisms*, (1918) (New York: Meridian Books, 1955), 3-7, 22, 64-70.

27 CO733/315/6, 1936 September: GOC-designate Lt-Gen. Sir John Dill, "The Future". CAB104/7 1936–1938, *Palestine: Arab Revolt*, September 3 and 18, 1936.

28 TNA War Office records (hereafter WO) WO32/4176, 1936–1938 *Palestine Disturbances: Policy Adopted* for the full process. T172/1847, *Palestine 1936*, Simon to Chamberlain,

While Wauchope entreated with the AHC to observe shared civil principles, the military commander, Air Vice-Marshal Richard Peirce, objectified Arab Palestine as an enemy to be defeated. His violent handling of early civil disobedience was prophetically self-fulfilling by precipitating mass armed resistance.[29] Wauchope and the AHC, whose members were familiar, cooperative interlocutors,[30] worked towards a deal involving a Royal Commission on Arab grievances, pending which Jewish immigration (as during the Shaw inquiry of 1929) would be suspended. But Britain's Cabinet, receptive to Zionist claims of exclusive victimhood at Arab hands, ordered "no surrender" to "the gunmen" and "complete rebel submission."[31]

Arab Palestine's urban nodes, in being the earliest flashpoints of mass dissent, were on the front-line of the British military impositions which followed, with old cities cordoned-off as political quarantine spaces, reinforcing their pre-existing ethnic and social segregation.[32] On 29 April protestors at Jerusalem's Damascus Gate were driven behind the city walls which troops then picketed. Shortly afterwards, remembering past Arab violence, the British evacuated old Hebron's orthodox Jewish community to the Jewish Quarter of old Jerusalem. But Zionist shootings and grenade attacks on neighboring Arab residents raised fears of retaliation and old Jerusalem's Jewish Quarter was evacuated too.[33] Anti-immigration picketing in Jaffa, inspired by rumors that Jewish employment quotas were to be a condition of British port development grants, spilled over into attacks on remaining Jewish residents who were evacuated to Tel Aviv.[34]

British troops broke Arab anti-immigration picket-lines at Haifa's docks. In response, on May Day, the local Transport Strike Committee ordered a

---

September 3; See the 1934 manual published as Major General Sir Charles W. Gwynn, *Imperial Policing*, (London: Macmillan, 1939).

29 CO733/292/2, Wauchope to SofS Thomas, May 14, 1936; 307/9, *Arab Delegation*: April 23, 1936; 307/10, May 5, 1936; AHC to Chief Secretary, Hathorn-Hall, May 7, 1936.

30 Zeina Ghandour, *A Discourse on Domination in Mandate Palestine: Imperialism, Property and Insurgency* (London: Routledge, 2009), 15-41 and 123-165.

31 CO733/297/2, Thomas to Wauchope 12 May 1936; Cabinet Minutes, 12 May 1936; Correspondence, May 13, 1936.

32 For British operations WO191/70 *Military Lessons of the Arab Rebellion in Palestine, 1936*, GHQ British Forces Palestine, February 1938; AIR2/3300 *Operations in Palestine and Transjordan: Report by GOC Sir Archibald Wavell*, GHQ British Forces Palestine, August 7, 1938; WO191/8, *History and Notes of Operations: Disturbances in Palestine*, Lt. Gen. Michael Barker, December 12, 1939.

33 CO733/311/3, *Relief Measures: maintenance and rehabilitation of refugees*, Wauchope to Thomas, May 8, 1936.

34 CO733/297/2, Wauchope to Thomas, April 29, 1936. *Palestine* (Peel) *Royal Commission Report, Cmd. 5479*, (London: HMSO, 1937), 96-98; CO733/292/2 *Jaffa Port*, 1936–1937.

counter-demonstration at the District Commissioner's house. It was dispersed *en route* by police baton charges. Crowds spilled into Haifa's new, modernist central thoroughfare, Kingsway. Police gunfire panicked them back into old town which troops and sailors closed-off, under the guns and searchlights of the Royal Navy's third cruiser squadron. But while this perimeter contained demonstrations, within its bounds armed strike-enforcement and monetary levies thrived. Moreover, to police derision, inexperienced military sentries failed to prevent assailants slipping through for gun and bomb attacks on government buildings. Wauchope appealed to Arab notables to curb these "worst excesses" of self-injuring nihilism, fanned by "extremists" among the "poorest classes of the floating Arab population." The AHC replied that "the people no longer follow leadership, leadership follows the people."[35]

Popular rebelliousness spread to sub-district towns. Convoys to Tulkarm's "unruly neighborhood" suffered pot-shots and a truck set ablaze. Here, as in Nablus, crowds of "mostly schoolboys and youths" stoned police. Some from Jaffa tried marching on nearby Jewish settlements; the mostly Arab police nonetheless held firm, as throughout subsequent months, against such demonstrations. Peaceful marches in Jenin and Gaza proceeded, although crowds were fired on in Nazareth after a failed baton charge.[36] Students were prominent in urban civil disobedience, notably anti-Jewish boycott enforcement. In retaliation Wauchope shut Palestine's six government secondary schools and Jerusalem's Arab College, turning them to military use, or as refugee shelters.[37] This was an early indication of punitive disruption rather than defensive maintenance of the urban-based civil institutions hitherto sustaining the Mandate's progressive pretensions. Under zero-sum military-operational imperatives, the AHC's constitutional nationalism, shared by many pro-British Arab notables and civil servants, was indistinguishable from the collective "enemy," a term first applied to the Mandate's Arab citizens by Peirse during planning sessions in July 1936.

Meanwhile, Arab-Jewish violence escalated via a pattern of hit-and-run attacks on Zionist rural settlements reciprocated by bombings and shootings on sitting Arab urban targets, notably market-places in Haifa, Jerusalem and

35 CO733/297/2, Wauchope to Thomas, April 29, 1936; 310/1, *Disturbances (General File)*, Minutes of Wauchope interview with Arab notables, April 21, 1936; WO32/4177 1936 Peirse on Palestine Disturbances; CO733/307/9 and 10, 1936 April-May, *Arab Delegation: Meetings with High Commissioner*.

36 AIR2/1759, *Disturbances in Palestine: Telegrams 1936*; CO733 310/1 *Palestine: Disturbances: General File, 1936*, April 17-21. MEC: John A.M. Faraday Papers, Box 1; Morton, *Just the Job*, 1.

37 ISR RG2.5/126/4m, 1940–1936, *Reopening of Government Schools and Evacuation by Army of Government School Buildings.*

Jaffa. Mainstream Zionist leaders, including David Ben Gurion, blamed rogue Revisionist or anarchist elements but added: "When Jaffa falls into Hell I will not be among the mourners." In Zionist discourse, Jews were the only victims and all Arabs terrorists, demanding Arab police be replaced throughout Palestine by armed Jewish "supernumeraries." Settlement defensive units were created, over Wauchope's objections, to release British troops for rural sweeps. Urban Arab Palestine therefore remained largely undefended from Zionist counter-terrorism, while also subject to slower-working tactics including boycotts of Arab goods, services and workers intended to punish and provoke.[38]

In Jaffa on 15 May, about a thousand Arab protesters blocking the inner-suburban orbital road, King George Street, were driven into the old city by police gunfire and batons. They set up defensive barricades and armed themselves. This, and the shooting in West Jerusalem of three Jewish cinema patrons, greeted Wauchope's unilateral announcement of a Royal Commission, subject to the restoration of peace, without mention of Jewish immigration. Nonetheless, Haj Amin, the AHC president, urged "patience" and passive resistance, not insurrection, when touring the country.[39] Wauchope was encouraged by strikes unraveling in Haifa, and urban calm everywhere but Jaffa, restored by occupation or aerial patrolling, most recently in Gaza by the 11th Hussars' light tanks directly after disembarkation. His hopes were shattered on 25 May when, after RAF aircraft machine-gunned demonstrators in Tulkarm, Peirse issued general orders permitting British forces to initiate fire. This and "punitive searches" to intimidate "bad areas," drew mayoral and clerical protests that uncontrollable popular militancy was now inevitable.[40]

Wauchope advised London however that forces more than doubled by three extra infantry battalions, tanks from Malta, and two scratch RAF squadrons from Egypt and Iraq had averted "complete revolution." The countryside was quiet; most towns were "in hand." Only Jaffa's "lawless and unsanitary" old city, defended by port workers, whom Peirse reported as "the toughest among the strikers," remained an undeniable embarrassment where "Government forces dare not penetrate." Retaking this hitherto neglected and derided old enclave

---

38 Adam LeBor, *City of Oranges: Arabs and Jews in Jaffa* (London: Bloomsbury, 2005), 61. CO733/338/11, *Jewish Agency Memorandum to League of Nations*, Weizmann to Ormsby-Gore, July 18, 1937.

39 CO733/292/2, Mufti to High Commissioner, 27 April, 1936; Wauchope to Thomas, 14 May 1936; 307/9, *Arab Delegation*, Wauchope to Thomas, 23 April 1936; 307/10, Idem., May 5, 1936; AHC to Chief Secretary, Hathorn-Hall, May 7, 1936.

40 CO733/297/2, Wauchope to Thomas, 5 May 1936; Cabinet Minute 12 May; Correspondence, May 13, 1936; Wauchope to Thomas, May 16, 1936. WO32/4177 Peirse dispatch. WO191/70 *Military Lessons of the Arab Rebellion in Palestine*, February 1938.

thereby assumed central significance, where the general futility of rebellion would be demonstrated, precipitating, Wauchope hoped, a collective Arab return to civility.[41]

Peirse acknowledged no such subtleties. He conceptualized Jaffa as "a citadel from whence (sic) bombing and sniping was continually directed," neutralizing the port and main police barracks below. Its "tortuous and narrow covered streets … blind alleys and *culs de sac*" formed an "impenetrable warren." It was "necessary to reduce the place" which was in effect "an exceedingly complicated trench system with vertical sides 30 to 40 feet high." He wanted it stormed, "quarter by quarter, house by house." Wauchope vetoed this "drastic action" as politically disastrous. So Peirse deployed around the objective, drew fire to identify hostile areas then laid a "retaliatory shoot" on them with Vickers guns and rifle-grenades "until all opposition was silenced." Troops would then enter, demolish offending houses and blast paths into the port for two military roads, enabling Jewish black-legs to be convoyed there, breaking the strike. Peirse also suggested using local forced labor to clear old Jaffa's "indescribable filth." Wauchope finessed this quasi-utilitarian aside into representing "Operation Anchor," without irony, as a long-desired town-planning exercise, helped by the Royal Engineers, to demolish "congested and unsanitary" buildings, "opening up and improving the old city."[42]

This fig leaf was blown away however, and the politically crucial action delayed, when one householder, George Mikhail al-Qasimi, urbanely sought a court injunction staying anonymous air-dropped eviction notices of punitive demolitions wherever occupants did not flee. Palestine's Chief Justice, Sir Michael McDonnell, was indeed curious to know which town-planning laws permitted machine-gunning civilians and blowing up their houses. The Government finally admitted to acting under defense regulations, incurring McDonnell's public scorn, and a sequence of judgments against further acts of repression. This encouraged the AHC, Arab mayors and mainly Arab senior civil servants to appeal to "justice" lest a desperate populace turn irreversibly violent. But Ormsby-Gore sacked McDonnell and turned on Arab Palestine's urban elite leaders, in and out of British service, as apologists and secret

41 CO733/297/3 *Worsening Situation*: Cabinet Conference, May 12, 1936, and Cabinet Paper (CP) 138 (36) with conclusions, May 13 and 15, 1936; 310/2, Disturbances, Wauchope memorandum, June 1, 1936 and to Ormsby-Gore, June 16, 1936.

42 WO32/4177 1936 Peirse on Jaffa Operation; CO733/310/1 *Palestine Disturbances*, 1936 April-May for Wauchope's views; 297/2, *Palestine Disturbances*, Wauchope to Ormsby-Gore, June 7, 1936.

orchestrators of violence. This British abnegation of civil norms and dialogue was the first step towards a *de facto* military takeover in Palestine in late 1937.[43]

Wauchope nonetheless tried to sustain "the normal rather than the abnormal" in his reports from reconquered old Jaffa where "nothing of aesthetic value" was damaged. The black-leg scheme was dropped, leaving its people industriously tranquil. Peirse exultantly differed: they had "replied hotly with a considerable volume of fire from a variety of weapons" in eighteen days' fighting which destroyed 222 houses, an important vegetable oil factory, damaging the port itself, but leaving British power triumphant.[44] Moreover, before the political effects of Jaffa's occupation could be evaluated, Peirse declared the "urban phase" over and began rural pacification. Nablus, with its hinterlands in the forefront, declared a civil boycott of the Mandate which Arab mayors threatened to extend nationally. Arab police in Nablus and Jaffa demurred over "repugnant" orders to harry their own communities. Meanwhile, punitive operations elicited responses in kind, moving civil disobedience into incipient guerilla warfare.[45]

Towns remained in the front line: under new emergency powers, the army countered a mass curfew-violation in Acre in early June by blowing up offices at its Jazzar mosque. This action made permanent enemies, and rebels, of the local mufti's family, hitherto hostile to Haj Amin. Tulkarm, Nablus and Jenin, demarcating what soldiers called the "triangle of terror," were attacked recurrently; intelligence suggested urban-resident guerrillas emerging by night to attack rural Jewish and British assets.[46] With British troops "overworked," this "enemy" town was subjected to air-delivered RAF punishment. Peirse also declared Nablus so "completely out of control" as to require "area bombing."

---

43 *Law Reports of Palestine*, vol. 3 (Jerusalem: Government Printing Office, 1938), 122-129; CO733/313/7 July-Aug 1936: *Demolitions in Old City of Jaffa*; 313/1 *Disturbances: Position of Chief Justice: His Eventual Early Retirement*, 1936 June–1937 May. ISA: RG2.11/1 294-16, February 1936–April 1939: *Employment of Arabs in Government Service*. CO733/313/9, *Memorial to High Commissioner by Senior Arab Government Officials*, July 30, 1936.

44 WO32/4177 1936 Peirse on Jaffa Operation: CO733/310/1 *Palestine Disturbances*, 1936 April-May for Wauchope's views; 297/2, *Palestine Disturbances*, Wauchope to Ormsby-Gore, 7 June 1936 and 311/14, July 6, 1936; ISA RG12 Department of Public Works: 414/16-m, *Municipal Services: Property Demolition Old Jaffa: Disturbances 1936*: RG3 736/11m, *Public Security: Disturbances, 1936-Compensation, Damages*, July 29, 1936.

45 AIR2/1840, *Palestine Emergency: Appreciation by AOC British Forces, 1936*, "Summary of Phases," June 29, 1936; 2066 *Disturbances in Palestine: Tactical Lessons*, AOC Palestine, March 1, 1937.

46 CO733/313/7, 1936 July-Aug, *Demolition in the Old City of Jaffa*; 310/4 *Disturbances (General File)*, Acre operation, June 14-15, 1936 and 310/5 Wauchope to Sir Cosmo Parkinson CO, July 28, 1936.

The Colonial Office banned targets within 1,000 yards of any building and helped Wauchope reinstate police precedence because of troops' coarseness to Muslims. Peirse protested these "disgraceful strictures," extolling "Turkish methods" of mass collective punishment, supported by Cabinet-level disciples of "Notes on Imperial Policing."[47]

Ironically, the latter need arose from Peirse's disdain for deploying "troops as police" in towns. Yet he had interned municipal notables, imposed debilitating collective fines, and building demolitions, punitively suspended civil authority and services, all in punishment for nearby rebel incidences. His measures merely created urban authority vacuums. Popular radicalization followed. Notables unmolested by the British were deemed collaborators, most prominently Hebron's mayor Nasr al-Din Nasr who was assassinated on 8 August. Largely unpunished Jewish terrorism meanwhile aggravated urban violence-cycles: Arab demonstrators in Manshiyeh were bombed and shot on 5 August; ten days later two Jewish nurses at Jaffa's city hospital were shot dead. Despite condemnation by Jaffa's National Committee, reprisal murders of Arabs followed in Jaffa, old Jerusalem and Haifa. Reciprocal boycotts paralyzed economic activity; Jaffa's port, when open, worked at half capacity while Tel Aviv, on security grounds, lobbied for a separate port, to complete its long-sought disaggregation from its Arab neighbor.[48]

Rather than protect Palestine Arab civil functionaries, British commanders dismissed them as so weak or disloyal that only "frightfulness" could cow their unmoored constituents. Success was recorded in numbers killed, often tallying all Arab dead as rebels. But resistance continued. Soldiers initially found Haifa "a marvellous place compared to Cairo" joking about "enormous amount(s) of ammunition ... used without effect." Then "bitterness set in", with one officer decrying "the weakness of our present democratic government (I am NOT a blackshirt!)." On 8 August, after the army ignored police intelligence, a "complete strike" at Haifa's port "took everyone by surprise." Two weeks before, British forces began evicting a hundred residents daily from the "unsanitary"

47 AIR2/1840 *Palestine Emergency: Appreciation by AOC British Forces-1936*, June 29. CO733/297/3, *Political Situation*, Wauchope to Ormsby-Gore, July 11, 1936, Peirse to Wauchope, August 20, 1936; 315/6 *1936 Sep: Retaliatory Bombing Action by RAF*; WO32/4177, Peirse Dispatch, Part III, May-June 1936 entries, King's College, London; Liddell-Hart Military History Archive (hereafter LHA), Robert Brooke-Popham Papers, Peirse to Chief of the Air Staff, July 10, 1936; WO191/70 1938 *Military Lessons of the Arab Rebellion in Palestine, 1936*, 32-35 and Ch. 13. CAB 104/7 1936–1938, *Palestine: Arab Revolt*, September 3 and 18, 1936.

48 WO191/70 1938 *Military Lessons*, Ch.4; CO733/303/3 *Collective Punishments (Amendment) Ordinances: Found Necessary After Incidents in the Towns of Safad, Beisan, Nazareth*, May 14-26, 1936; CO733/311/1, Jaffa reports, August 18-20, 1936; 292/2 1936 Jan-Nov. *Jaffa Port.*

tin-town. Qassamite "toughs" used "intensive intimidation" to prevent collaboration by Arab officials and port managers. An "epidemic" of bombings and three days of "critical" disorder were finally recognized as a rising of the urban poor beyond AHC control. Naval shore parties tried to restore order, beginning with a shooting-spree by motorized columns in the old town, which was then cordoned and curfewed. This pattern, of pro-rural asset diversion permitting unexpected urban guerilla and political surges, returned nationally in autumn 1938. In 1936 Peirse blandly dismissed the Haifa surge as a spasmodic, desperate rebel reaction to key rural defeats and that final victory was now obtainable by "area bombing" urban holdouts.[49]

Indeed, the Haifa strike was the last urban outbreak of 1936. In late August Iraqi and Syrian formations under the ex-Ottoman Arab nationalist officer Fawzi al-Quwuqji were detected alongside rebel bands in Galilee. This portended the quasi-regular field phase the British hoped for. The army assumed command from the RAF, appointing a new General Officer Commanding (GOC), Lieutenant General John Dill. The AHC was also warned that Dill, with a further division of troops, would exercise full punitive authority throughout Palestine until all disorder ceased. Wauchope despaired of "bloody soldiers," hoping pathetically to return as "kindly father" once they had finished.[50] Summary capital justice was applied, invariably to Arab arrestees only. Two-hundred notables were interned without trial in roughshod camps at the Sarafand army depot, near Haifa. "(W)ell-known agitators," meaning almost any political persons were arrested and their houses demolished in towns near any violent incident.[51] Facing over 1,200 Arabs dead, urban hardships mounting, unbridled village repression and the financially indispensable citrus harvest jeopardized, the AHC sought face-saving terms. Neighboring Arab rulers

49 WO32/4177 *Palestine Disturbances*: Peirse Dispatch, Part VI, August-September 1936; MEC: Frederick Scrivener Papers, Chief Engineer, Haifa: Box 1, August 19, 1936; CO733/297/3, Peirse to Wauchope, August 20, 1936; Brooke-Popham Papers, Peirse to SofS for Air, August 20, 1936; Imperial War Museum, London, Archives (hereafter IWM): Napier Crookenden Papers, Cheshire Regiment: Palestine, 1936-letters to parents; CO733/312/2, *1936 June-October: Loan of Naval and Military Personnel to the Civil Administration*, Wauchope to Rear-Adm. D'Oyly-Lyon, 3rd Cruiser Squadron, September 3, 1936.

50 CO733/315/2, 1936 *Martial Law*; WO32/4174, *Army Council Instructions to Lt-General Dill Regarding Command of Palestine Armed Forces*, September 3 and 9, 1936; LHA, John Dill papers, Dill to CIGS Cyril Deverell, September 18, 1936.

51 CO733/310/5, *Disturbances*, Wauchope to Ormsby-Gore, Complaint from Sarafand #2, July 23, 1936.

brokered a ceasefire in mid-October, which British hard-liners attributed to the intimidating prospect of Dill's arrival.[52]

This mood was sustained by subsequent military assertions that "Palestine (was) too small for two kings" with Colonial Office resistance to force encouraging rebellion.[53] In July 1937 the Peel Royal Commission, under intimate Zionist influence, recommended Palestine's partition into a Jewish state, for an "intensely democratic and highly organized modern community," leaving a rump to the Arabs – a barely cultured people "virtually dropped out of history," their urban life "still indomitably Asiatic" and resistance merely self-destructive of general, Jewish-created prosperity. The report mocked Wauchope for "government by arithmetic" and Palestinian civil-status as "a legal formula devoid of moral meaning."[54] Arab Palestine was dismayed. Experienced British observers noted "from that moment the revolution really started."[55]

Wauchope's civil system was meanwhile buckling under Treasury orders to fund Dill's 20,000 troops: eight times more than pre-rebellion. Dill also demanded that Palestine provide desert, mountain and general training facilities free-of-charge. Yet he exacted payment for military services such as phone-line repair and checkpoint security. Palestine's budget surplus became a deficit, half-exceeding income. Resulting urban austerity, "starving the social services and discontinuing building," mortgaged public assets and caused "serious unemployment and distress" in Arab municipalities, which had budgeted for more assistance under the 1934 reforms, ironically for actual slum clearance. While some Jaffa residents were paid for their blown-up houses, troops began to demolish Haifa's tin-town in ways observed as "good practice for the tank corps." But overall Wauchope prioritized Arab peasant needs, directing urban grants, under Arab notable protest, to Jewish projects, notably the Tel Aviv port.[56]

52 CO733/297/3-5 *Political Situation*, esp. Cabinet minutes, correspondence September 3-9, 1936: 314/1 *April-December 1936: Mediation: Offers and Attempts by the Arab Kings*, esp Wauchope with AHC, September 12, 1936.

53 LHA: Brooke-Popham Papers, 4/6 AOC Middle East Command to Air Ministry, September 6, 1936.

54 *Peel Commission* 120, 139, 116-124, 5-6, 114, 131-132.

55 Keith-Roach, *Pasha*, 190.

56 CO733/825/1 *Estimates 1937–8: Advance Approval-Public Works Extraordinary*; 334/2, *Costs of Garrison, 1937, Unemployment*, 1937 Jan-Mar; 325/10 *Grants in Aid to Municipalities*, January-July 1937; 339/10 *Loan for Tel Aviv*, May-December 1937. LHA: Dill Papers, Dill to CIGS Deverell, 24 April 1937. CO733/341/14, *Disturbances: Demolition of Old Jaffa City*, 1937 July-Aug; 351/1, *Insanitary Hutments on the Outskirts of Haifa: Evacuation of Inhabitants*, August 17, 1937; IWM: Syd Burr Papers, letter home on tin-town, probably July 1937.

Jaffa port-workers organized to protect their livelihoods. Yet despite their militancy the local British commander declined to disarm Jaffa's population; its weapons were old and poor and would be replaced by smuggling in better, which the police could not prevent.[57] His decision revived Zionist demands for Jewish self-defense including maritime units, to interdict Arabs picketing Tel Aviv from the sea and expel Arab fishermen from the nearby Auja River which the city sought to use for water and hydro-electricity. Rumors spread to the northern lakeside town of Tiberias that Arab fishermen's licenses were to be transferred to Jewish companies. In nearby Safad, the Arab old city was partly demolished to create a Jewish security zone. Finally, Jewish porters, hired at Haifa in January 1937, refused heavy work without mechanical assistance, eventually provided by the Zionist Histadrut union. Its members became "a permanent corps d'élite" but "casualization of the Arab porters" followed Histadrut's banning them from the new machinery. Unrest resumed when their Jewish replacements began arriving in armed convoys.[58]

An ominous urban "murder campaign" of reciprocal shootings and bombings followed. Police control nonetheless held during major crisis-points, notably religious festivals, helped by AHC appeals for Arab community discipline. In July British police ranks were reinforced, with Arab personnel reportedly loyal and efficient, enabling troop-levels to be reduced. But after the Peel report, rebel enforcers within the cordoned old cities resumed the elimination of undercover police informants and effective Arab officers. Community spokesmen also protested British inaction after Zionist shootings and bombings at Arab markets, work-places and bus stations in Jaffa, Jerusalem, and Haifa, asking why state protection was being prejudicially withheld.[59] Indeed only the Mufti's intervention averted a riot in old Jerusalem in May, when three Jewish men in a car trailed him to St. Stephen's Gate. He calmed a mob converging on the vehicle, which escaped before police arrived. Zionist claims of exclusive

57 CO733/292/2 1937: *Jaffa Port*, and 292/3, *Labour Relations*; 334/13 *Tel Aviv Harbour: Protests from Arab Lightermen of Jaffa*, January 29, 1937: 330/3, *Jaffa Port and Tel Aviv Harbour*, August 3-21, 1937. LHA: Laurence Carr Papers, Box 2: memorandum on Jaffa, October 25, 1936.

58 ISA RG12 4/1937, *Municipal Service: Galilee and Nazareth District*, April-June: RG28/01/1951/8-m, *Arab Lightermen's Cooperative, Jaffa*, report on picketing, May 1936: 1953/4-m, February 1937–July 1936, *Aggression Against Jaffa Fishermen by Inhabitants of Tel Aviv*. CO733/311/2 1937 Jan-Jun: *Disturbances*, Wauchope to Ormsby-Gore, April 6, 1937; Haifa CID report, May 22, 1937: 328/9 *Haifa Harbour: Employment of Jewish Labour*, Manager's report, June 18, 1937.

59 CO733/311/12, *Disturbances* (*General File*), for incidents and currents; 25/11, *Police: Appointment of Officers*; 333/7, *Representations from Palestine*, September 29-November 15, 1937.

victimhood at Arab hands and the concomitant demand for arming by Britain meanwhile continued unabated.[60]

Wauchope resisted by insisting that Arab urban crime was "more due to unemployment and to poverty than it was about politics." He cited a "building slump" in Haifa, poor harvests, food shortages and Jewish businesses not rehiring Arabs, which impelled an "unstable and dissatisfied element" back to village life, prone to trouble without the "distraction of the town."[61] But a surge in extortion and killings of urban Arab businessmen and notables suggested a targeting of less militant Nashashibi family supporters. British investigators could not determine whether to blame Jewish provocateurs or pro-Husseini assassins. But Ormsby-Gore, influenced by Zionist and War Office characterizations, declared Haj Amin a "black hearted villain" bent on murdering "moderate" opponents. To Wauchope, the Mufti reflected rather than originated the spirit of rebellion but agreed to deport him if ever he "clearly" broke the law.[62]

Ormsby-Gore ordered him deported on 19 July for denouncing the Peel report. But he evaded arrest, absconding into the sacred precincts of old Jerusalem's Haram al-Sharif. Fear of "considerable bloodshed" precluded further action, even by Arab police. A stand-off followed. To Dill and his supporters this was the final debacle of civil authority. He persuaded the Cabinet to draft unrestricted emergency military powers[63] for which each subsequent incident was minutely scrutinized as a trigger. This came with the assassination in Nazareth on 26 September 1937 of District Commissioner Lewis Andrews by a Qassamite hit-team. Wauchope decried the resulting cascade of emergency decrees as "cracking a nut with a sledgehammer." National committees were banned and two hundred members interned. Political prisoners

60 LHA: Carr papers, Box 2, memorandum, August 30, 1937; IWM: Syd Burr Papers, letter April 29, 1937; CO733/338/11, *Jewish Agency Memorandum to League of Nations*, Weizmann to Ormsby-Gore, July 18, 1937: 332/2 *Public Security*, Wauchope to Ormsby-Gore, March 27, 1937 and April 19, 1937 interview with Dill: 311/2 *Disturbances*, February 6, 1937, Wauchope with AHC and May 31, 1937, St. Stephen's Gate incident.

61 CO733/339/6 *Relief to Counter Unemployment*, September 7, 1937.

62 AIR5/1247 *Palestine: Monthly Summaries, Vol.3, 1934–1937*, June 1937. CO733/352/1 *Cabinet Extracts*, July 14, 1937: 341/26, *Disturbances of 1936: Crimes Committed*, Ormsby-Gore to Government of Palestine, September 8, 1937: 326/4 *Supreme Muslim Council – Movements of President*, February-July 1937. WO191/75, *Preliminary Notes on Lessons of Palestine Rebellion*, Wauchope to Dill, July 15, 1937.

63 CO733/352/3 *Deportation of Arabs*, July 14-September 26, 1937. WO32/4178: 1937 *Palestine: Respective Functions of High Commissioner and General Officer Commanding the Forces*: WO191/89 April 1939. *Report on Military Control in Palestine*, Ch. 2 shows plans originating in December 1936: 191/75, Dill to CIGS, July 16, 1937, Dill to WO July 21, 1937. LHA: Dill Papers, Dill to CIGS, April 24, 1937; Carr Papers, Memorandum October 25, 1936.

further doubled by November. When the AHC remonstrated, it too was outlawed. Its members were deported or fled. Urban notable deportees, such as Jerusalem's mayor Hussein Khalidi and Palestine Arab Bank director Rashid al-Haj Ibrahim, had worked with Britain, generally restraining violent radicalism. But to Dill, decapitating Arab civil society was attacking "terrorism at its roots." A Jewish Mayor of Jerusalem, Daniel Auster, was appointed by decree. An Arab municipal boycott followed, with no substitute functionaries ready. Haj Amin slipped away on 14 October to exile in French Syria. To Wauchope this was *de facto* expulsion. Dill was furious, despite local commanders also advising against "going in to ferret him out." An official audit of the Mufti's accounts followed which found no trace of his funding terror.[64]

Dill's successor, Archibald Wavell, campaigned to formula after January 1938: an initial punitive investment of Arab towns, arrest of nationalist leaders, counter-fire and demolitions whenever resisted, then a "cordon phase" before a "village occupation phase." As before, this aggravated cycles of resistance and retribution. In Lydda, after troops shot pro-Mufti demonstrators, an arson attack destroyed its recently refurbished RAF base. Alleging "masterly inactivity" by Arab police, the army demolished a quarter of the town's houses. Elsewhere, barricades in Hebron's old city impeded arrest sweeps. British house demolitions followed, then a withdrawal with prisoners. Remaining, mainly Arab, police faced predictable reprisals. Civil leaders, mostly pro-Nashashibi, fled, as did *bourgeois* Arabs subject to rebel kidnap, extortion and other forms of revolutionary justice including banning urban debt-collectors from villages, of municipal revenue collection, urban rent payments and use of "Jewish" electricity.[65]

British police withdrew to protect government buildings and British officials, leaving Arab officials unprotected. Government offices moved from old to East Jerusalem in November 1937 and higher functionaries in 1938 to military

64 AIR/5 *Palestine: Monthly Summaries* vol. 3, September 1937; CO733/352/3 *Deportation of Arabs*; Alec Kirkbride, *A Crackle of Thorns: Experiences in the Middle East* (London: John Murray, 1956), 100-101; LHA: Carr Papers, Box 2, memorandum Sarafand camp, October 2, 1937; CO733/326/5 *Supreme Muslim Council Finances*, Wauchope to CO, December 21, 1937.

65 AIR2/3300, *Operations in Palestine and Trans-Jordan: General A.P. Wavell*, September 12, 1937–March 31, 1938; LHA Carr Papers: Diary, October 3-16, 1937; IWM: Burr Papers, letter, early October 1937-'hunt for the Mufti'; CO733/332/10 *Political Situation*, October 19, 1937: 371/10 *Intimidation of Arab Debt Collectors*, August 25-October 4, 1938; Hillel Cohen, *Army of Shadows: Palestinian Collaboration with Zionism, 1917–1948* (Berkeley: University of California Press, 2008), Part II "Rebels and Traitors."

office-suites in West Jerusalem's King David Hotel.[66] Police Inspector-General Roy Spicer was replaced, supposedly too vulnerable in Haifa to assassins, by the more pro-paramilitary Alan Saunders, from Nigeria. Similarly, Sir Charles Tegart, with years of experience in India, arrived as a police anti-terrorist consultant. Although the CID was strengthened, rural frontier fences, road and rail strong-points, patrols, village touring and a new British mounted rural force were prioritized. Police in Arab towns retreated to barracks, notably in Beersheba, Hebron and Tulkarm where activities were increasingly limited to guiding troops on village counter-raids.[67]

In the urban spaces Britain had conceded by default, guerrilla leaders established a revenue system to support their wider operations of tax-levies and charitable collections by clerics, supplemented by bank robberies and ransom. Rebel injunctions against bourgeois red tarbush-wearing, enforcing the cloth peasant *keffiyeh* headscarf, and full Muslim women's dress, attempted to eliminate distinctions at British checkpoints between townspeople and rural operatives.[68] In being "out of bounds" older Arab enclaves were also liable to officially unobservable British retribution: Haifa's police targeted its old town wherever they were attacked; soldiers' revenge-seeking proliferated in and around old Jerusalem; a probable police death-squad operated in Jaffa; attacks on brothels, looting in searches and swindling of local creditors became a quasi-sport. The authorities ridiculed witness-reports, even by well-respected British civilians, often clergymen and educators. In effect, illicit retaliation was condoned as a supplement to legal collective punishments. Both vented the frustrations of guerilla warfare onto hapless "town Arabs" scorned and victimized for their inability to resist.[69]

66 MEC: Colonel Patrick Rice Papers, November 9, 1937, *Protection of Government Officials*. CO733/326/2 *Police Quarters*. September 1937–August 1938. ISA: RG2.23/1 490-14m, *1938–1936, Transfer of Government Offices to Ex-Palace Hotel*. CO733/377/7 *Government Offices at Jerusalem*, November 26, 1938.

67 CO733/366/4, *Situation in Palestine: 1938 Internal Political* diarizes occurrences; MEC: Tegart Papers, Box 1, CID bulletins, December 1937–June 1938; File 3c, *Terrorism, 1936–1937*; Box 2, File 3, *Palestine Internal Security, Dec. 1937–May 1938*. IWM: Burr Papers, letter, January 1938 and April 22, 1938. Ted Swedenburg, *Memories of Revolt: The 1936–39 Rebellion and the Palestinian National Past* (Minneapolis: University of Minnesota Press, 1995). 33. Foot, *Freedom*, 49-52. Keith-Roach, *Pasha*, 191.

68 CO733/372/4 *Rebel Propaganda*, August 18-September 14, 1938; MEC: Tegart Papers, Box 1, File 3c, *Terrorism, 1936–1937*. CO733/370/9, *Notes on Leaders of Armed Gangs*, Deputy I-G of Police, A.J. Kingsley-Heath, May 4, 1938. IWM: Burr Papers, diary entry September 9, 1938.

69 Foot, *Freedom*, 49-53; IWM: Burr Papers, diary entry, September 9-17, 1937 and Alex Morrison Papers, m/s "On the Road to – Anywhere," 21-34. Also, Papers of B.A. Pond, Quartermaster 2/Royal West Kents; CO733/371/2, *Conduct of British Troops and Police*, October-November 1938: 379/3 *Disturbances: Appreciation by GOC Military Forces*,

Ormsby-Gore meanwhile continued to remove long-serving civil officials widely upset by "clumsy and misdirected" military methods. Sir Harold MacMichael, ex-Tanganyika, replaced Wauchope in February 1938, acceding in all but name to the GOC, with the ex-Cyprus Chief Secretary Denis Battershill as bureaucratic caretaker. In April 1938 Lieutenant General Sir Robert Haining of the War Office intelligence staff succeeded Wavell. He was a counter-insurgency enthusiast fixated on the panacea of "village occupation," ignoring urban control. New dock facilities at Jaffa, completed in March 1938, were denied a ceremonial opening for lack of protective forces. More broadly, development officers recorded pervasive urban industrial and commercial stagnation in a climate of violence-prone insecurity.[70]

Major urban disorders returned in June 1938 when the British, unusually, hanged a Revisionist Zionist bus-shooter, Shlomo Ben Yusef. A "general street fight" ensued in Manshiyeh. Jewish mobs attacked police barring their way into Arab old Jerusalem. Serial bombings of Arab markets, buses and taxis in Jaffa, Haifa, Safad and Jerusalem followed. British inaction caused Arab riots and mass police resignations. In response, Haining had battleships, HMS *Malaya* and *Repulse*, shell the Haifa hinterland which he felt calmed the city. Soon after, Zionist bombings killed forty-five Arabs in the old town *suq* and in August twenty-six in old Jaffa. Haining took over the police in September, naming Tegart his deputy, but ignored these incidences. Instead, he disarmed and confined Arab personnel, most of his force, to routine duty. British police joined troops in a new rural offensive intended to end the rebellion in a month. Military safe-areas encompassing public buildings and central spaces in major Arab provincial towns sustained these outward sweeps, leaving other neighborhoods to the rebels.[71]

But before Haining could proceed, forces were diverted to Egypt or kept home during the European war-scare of September 1938. This heralded a

(Wavell), April 7, 1938. LHA: General Sir Richard O'Connor Papers, letters to wife, November 2 and 6, 1938; Roger Courtney, *Palestine Policeman: An Account of Eighteen Dramatic Months in the Palestine Police Force during the Great Jew-Arab Troubles* (London: Herbert Jenkins, 1939), 175-181, on a mooted death-squad. CO733/413/5 *Shooting of Hospital Patient*, June 23-August 3, 1939, suggests implementation.

70 Keith-Roach, *Pasha*, 192-201. MEC: Lt- Gen. Sir Robert Haining papers, 'Despatches on Operations Carried Out by British Forces in Palestine': WO32/9497 *Palestine: War Diary*, 20 May-31 July 1938, and 9498, August 1-October 31, 1938. ISA RG 5/1455/11m *Factories (Arab) Information Relative Thereto*, July-August 1938.

71 CO733/327/8 *Delegation of Powers to GOC in Respect of Defence Considerations*, September 23-October 18, 1938; IWM: Burr Papers, diary entry 9 September 1938; CO733/383/8, *Police Reorganization*, April 12-October 9, 1938: WO191/88 *History/Notes on Operations: Palestine Disturbances*, V and VI, May-August 1938.

startling urban insurrectionary upsurge, taking advantage of Haining's reduction of active policing. Guerrillas emptied Barclay's bank in Hebron, raided banks in Nablus and Jaffa, as well as government offices in Bethlehem which, with the new telephone exchange, were burned down. Inter-communal shootings in Tiberias suggested "trouble brewing" to British civil officers, who took no action. In Jerusalem, clerics serving in Haj Amin's place were assassinated. In September, more Jaffa civic and business notables fled abroad, abandoning their civil-societal functions. Haj Amin's exiled executive had little control over para-military leaders who, having delineated spheres of action locally and noted British troop withdrawals, launched a cascading urban offensive in late September 1938.[72]

Tegart had warned Haining of "deplorable" urban security lapses, hurrying to fortify town-center British police barracks in time. In the interim, Inspector-General Saunders recommended Arab officers, albeit with British "stiffening," should resume active duty, particularly intelligence work. But Haining kept them disarmed and desk-bound: only 107 British policemen covered Jerusalem, backed by sixty-nine Jewish constables and 222 British and Jewish emergency specials. Haifa's old town was ringed by 324 Jewish police and British sailors, but was internally unpoliced. Jenin's thirty malaria-stricken Arab police were effectively besieged; after the town's chief clerk, the Christian Arab Wadi el-Khoury was murdered in the old market, rebels razed the city's customs house and veterinary quarantine station. British officials abandoned Gaza, whose public records and post office were sacked, leaving skeleton forces besieged in the government school and hospital. In Jaffa daytime curfews collapsed when the Irish Guards left for Egypt. After attacks on officials and disarmed Arab police, the Government evacuated. Deployments by Jewish supernumeraries to guard key assets merely aroused mass, spontaneous riot: Mayor Assem Said and most pro-Nashashibi notables fled, yielding to clerically-endorsed rebel justice. Port and municipal offices were looted and revenue went uncollected. Food ran out. In the southern desert town of Beersheba, rebels pillaged the police barracks and destroyed the post office, telegraph station and prison. In early October, Tiberias was seized for four hours; its police arsenal was stripped, twenty-one Jews murdered and their synagogue destroyed. Finally

72 WO191/88 *History/Notes on Operations: Palestine Disturbances*, VIII, September-October 1938; LHA: O'Connor Papers 3/1/1, WO to O'Connor, September 13, 1938, 3/1/2, September 17, 1938; CO733/379/3, *Disturbances: Appreciation by GOC*; 366/4, *Situation in Palestine: 1938 Internal Political*, narrates events. IWM: Lt. R. King-Clark Papers, m/s "Some Experiences in Palestine," September 9, 1938; Keith-Roach, *Pasha*, 196; Swedenburg, *Memories*, 33, 84, 88, 120; Yuval Arnon-Ohanna, "'The Bands in the Palestinian Arab Revolt, 1936–1939: Structure and Organization," *Asian and African Studies* 15:2 (1981), 237-243.

in old Jerusalem on 10 October, seizing on British inaction after an explosion at a secret rebel armory, some 400 fighters seized the Haram. They closed the city gates, leaving two Haram guards' heads under the walls, where they raised their flags. Haining's staff reported "no European could safely go inside" after police and officials fled; rumors abounded of 1,000 guerrillas ready to move on Jewish West Jerusalem.[73]

The Munich accords, postponing war in Europe, came to the Mandate's relief. Chief of the Imperial General Staff Field Marshal Sir Edmund Ironside rushed to Palestine. He exonerated Haining, citing the unexpected "intensity of the opposition," and blamed the crisis on "the failure of the civil government." Two full divisions, under Major-Generals Bernard Montgomery in Haifa, Richard O'Connor at Jerusalem, and air units under Air Vice-Marshal Arthur Harris, all-told about 24,000 men, arrived to reconquer the country.

O'Connor's 7th Division had the cynosure task of retaking old Jerusalem. Yet he differed from his military contemporaries in consulting Saunders and District Commissioner Edward Keith-Roach on how to proceed. Nor did he accept the inevitability of a bloodbath; control was established around old Jerusalem by Arab police checkpoints, keeping troops in the background. Arab police also guided a relatively light two-battalion force into the old city on 19 October, without heavy weapons, beyond a Vickers covering snipers in the Haram's main minaret. Arab police intelligence, from frightened clerics inside the Haram, revealed rebel positions, in return for which O'Connor agreed to an armed observation rather than assault the holy site. Careful reconnaissance showed which city gates were booby-trapped. So O'Connor's entry units, re-equipped with soft hats and gym-shoes, observing discretion to Muslim persons and property, infiltrated via the unguarded Jewish Quarter which, with the Armenian Quarter, they protectively secured. The city-gates, cleared by rebel prisoners, were then opened from inside. Convergent small detachments approached the Haram, which was encircled in ninety minutes. Small-arms exchanges killed one British soldier and nineteen rebels.[74]

---

73 ISA: RG7 Agriculture and Fisheries: 628/8m, *Arming and Safety of Government Officials*, DSP Southern District to Government Offices, 7-18 September 1938; RG1 Executive Council Minutes, Statement by Saunders, August 3, 1938. MEC: Tegart Papers, Box 2. File 2, *Public Security in Urban Areas*, October 6 and 13, 1938; Situation Reports, Aug 1938–April 1939. Box 3, File 4, Inspector-General to Chief Secretary, September 20, 1938; CO733/372/2 *Security of Banks*, September 10-October 28, 1938: 366/4 *Situation in Palestine: 1938*. ISA RG2 336/16m, *1938: Measures for Protection of Jewish Government Officials*. MEC: Papers of Ivan Lloyd-Philips, Southern District Commissioner, Jaffa: Political, 8 October 1938. WO32/9498 *Notes on Operations*: August 1-October 31, 1938.

74 LHA: O'Connor Papers, 3/1/5 and 3/1/6, October 18 and 22, 1936; IWM: Lt. David A. Kennard Papers, Coldstream, Palestine notes, October 1939–April 1939. CO733/366/4, 1938 *Situation in Palestine*.

Besieged rebels exfiltrated that night via tunnels under the city-walls, undetected by O'Connor's force, which lacked searchlights. But old Jerusalem was in British hands. A four-day house search followed under general curfew, accompanied by trucked-in food relief. MacMichael rubber-stamped O'Connor's appointment as Governor of Jerusalem. But the general retained Keith-Roach as political adviser, ordered searches by troops under police supervision to prevent "unnecessary violence" or "un-British" looting. Despite reported *police* looting, O'Connor was determined to restore the force's prestige, appealing to Haining to reconcile with the much-alienated Tegart. O'Connor also toured the city on foot with Keith-Roach, reporting a friendly public, with troops fraternizing with local children to redress past brutal impressions. More practically, O'Connor had Arab CID officers review records from the semi-abandoned old city police barracks. They suggested a rebel cell based in the city bathhouse. O'Connor had the bath-keeper detained: Arab interrogators extracted current names and command structures which he rolled up in quickly-prosecuted re-occupations of Jericho, Hebron, Beersheba and Gaza, whose compromised mayor Fahmi al-Husseini and several Arab district officers he removed.[75]

The arbitrary significance of command personality is highlighted by contrasting events in Montgomery's 8th Divisional area. While O'Connor almost bloodlessly recovered old Jerusalem, Montgomery's troops rounded up 3,000 Arab men in Haifa's *suq* of whom only seventy-five could be criminally charged. This provoked a general strike met with gunfire and house demolitions. Blasting for a military road through old town was halted only by troops' sudden diversion to attack Nazareth. Montgomery subsequently drafted the men of Acre's old city into road labor after a nearby bank raid. Acre itself was "invested" on 5 December by two battalions in an area a fifth the size of old Jerusalem; Harris ordered the RAF to strafe any boats trying to leave. Male inhabitants were paraded before an armored car concealing an informant. Those denounced as "town bandits and assassins" were summarily tried and hanged. Montgomery insisted to O'Connor that rebellion must entail death. Harris concurred, bombing neighborhoods which had displayed rebel flags or were said to house guerrillas.[76]

Haining meanwhile continued to prioritize rural sweeps, aggressively supported by Harris's fighter-bombers. He derided burnt-out town centers as an affront to British prestige but did nothing restorative. O'Connor wished

75 CO733/366/4, 1938 *Situation in Palestine*, MacMichael to Colonial Secretary Macdonald, November 28, 1938; LHA: O'Connor Papers, 3/1/5, 6 November and 3/1/6, late November 1938; MEC: Tegart Papers, Box 1. File 3c, *Terrorism, 1936–1937*.

76 LHA: O'Connor Papers, 3/4/4 Montgomery letter, November 26, 1938. AIR2/3312, *1938: Disturbances in Palestine: Appreciation by High Commissioner*, Palforce to Air Ministry, October 3, 1938.

to reoccupy Jaffa but was limited to a reconnaissance in strength between 31 October and 3 November 1938, from which Haining permitted local commanders to remove troops for guerrilla field-pursuits. O'Connor arrested sixty wanted rebels, with intelligence reporting the citizens friendly. But police were too few to hold on: a general strike followed O'Connor's withdrawal. Tegart contained the strike by enclosing the Arab city with double wire and checkpoints, reinforcing a Mandate-wide road-travel pass system intended to sever urban-rural guerilla links. Staple Arab economic activity was also stifled. Jaffa's hardships were aggravated by a local army embargo on citrus movement, justified as punishment for Arab workers' boycotting Jewish trade. Exports shifted to the otherwise "entirely futile" Tel Aviv port while mercantile credit in Jaffa collapsed. Army tit-for-tat extended to Nablus whose central area served as a fortified safe-zone sustaining district operations. Outside the wire, Nablus was left to the rebels, whose sniping incurred mass retaliatory mortar and machine-gun barrages. Finally, the nationalist Mayor Suleiman Tuqan was kept hostage for a month on the British headquarters' roof until rebel firing ceased.[77]

In Palestine's rural battle-space, body counts increased in early 1939, extraneous to the political context being reconstructed by the new Colonial Secretary Malcolm MacDonald. MacDonald visited Palestine in August 1938, indulging Haining's assurances of victory while preparing a parallel track. The Woodhead Commission on how to implement the Peel report confidentially indicated that in requiring mass Arab expulsions from the proposed Jewish state's territory, partition was impossible. So MacDonald began to contact Palestinian notables with a view to broaching an alternative. Overtures were suspended during the unexpected rebel offensive. Yet once Jerusalem was retaken, MacDonald published Woodhead's report, to Arab Palestinian "jubilation." He then canvassed interned, exiled and refugee leaders. Haj Amin was excluded but his cousin, Jamal Husseini, convened with rivals including Ragheb Nashashibi at the St. James' Conference in early 1939. Their refusal to meet Zionist delegates presaged inevitable failure. But this still cleared the way for a unilateral British White Paper in May reviving proportionally representative Arab and Jewish participation in governance measures intended

77 CO733/327/18, January 5, 1939, *Palestine: District Commissioners' Reports 1938*; Kirkbride, *Thorns*, 106; Keith-Roach, *Pasha*, 210-202; LHA: O'Connor Papers: 3/2/1 O'Connor to GSO1 Jerusalem, November 12, 1938; 3/2/5 Haining to Battershill, November 21, 1938. 404/2 *1939: Disturbances: Appreciation by GOC Military Forces*, April 24, 1939; ISA: RG12 Public Works 4142/6 Cordons and Fortifications, 1938. ISA RG5 1453/13m, *Economic Adviser: Port of Tel Aviv: General Correspondence*, December 13, 1938. IWM: W. Carden-Roe Papers: Palestine May 1938–March 1939; CO733/366/4, *Situation in Palestine*, Incident Reports November 23, 1938.

to prepare Palestine for independence in ten years, with interim limits on immigration and Jewish land purchases and guaranteed Jewish protections but no separate state.[78]

This process diffused Arab Palestine's defiance. Pragmatic factions, including diminished urban elites and impoverished workers, welcomed terms resembling those Arabs largely accepted under Wauchope before the rebellion.[79] Nashashibi supporters helped form "peace bands" to fight pro-Husseini guerillas. Their success, especially in recovering large quantities of arms, enabled urban civil officials and refugee notables to return. But an urban-rural divide opened-up with militant villagers accusing fatigued townsmen of failing the national cause. They raided recently-reconciled Hebron. Internecine score-settling was also manifested by police assassinations of prominent ex-rebels in Jaffa. Haining insisted on destroying all remaining rebel groups within rural killing zones troops delimited for the RAF. British urban re-occupation meanwhile progressed, welcomed by the leading citizens of Gaza and Jaffa in February 1939, then throughout the Mandate.[80] Tarbush wearing was a yardstick, with quasi-ceremonial hat-days declared in Jaffa, Nablus and Jenin between March and May. The restoration of Arab police was particularly welcomed. Work schemes, mainly on roads and public buildings, recouped legitimacy among urban workers: by June the rebellion was over. Even Haining, before leaving in July 1939, made the staggeringly blithe admission that "adherence without equivocation to the White Paper is (the) real solution. The Arabs are beginning to trust us."[81] If the crisis had always been political, was Britain's intervening counter-insurgent war anything more than destructive military-authoritarian caprice?

---

78 CAB24/278, CP 193 (38) Jerusalem Talks, August 6-7, 1938; CO733/386/13, *Policy: Inter-Departmental Discussion on Palestine*, October 7-12, 1938: 386/17, *Sir John Woodhead's Statement*, October 30-November 3, 1938; 387/9 *Political Settlement*, Macdonald to MacMichael, December 12, 1938. CAB104/6 and 8: *Palestine: Arab Revolt*, Ministerial Minutes, October 7, 1938–June 19, 1939.

79 CO377/406/12, *London Conference: Reactions in Palestine*, February-July 1939.

80 CO733/386/22, *Reactions in Palestine*, November 10-19, 1938; WO32/9499, *Operations in Palestine*, November 1, 1938–March 31, 1939; 84/15, *Military Intelligence Summaries 13 January-22 December 1939*: GSO1 HQ British Forces Palestine, esp. January 13, 1939; CO733/327/18, January 5, 1939, *District Commissioners' Reports 1938*; Keith-Roach, *Pasha*, 210-220; LeBor, *Oranges*, 74. Swedenburg, *Memories*, 28, 89-92, 115, 155-159.

81 CO733/398/10, *District Commissioners' Reports*, January-August 1939: 84/15, *Military Intelligence Summaries*, 21 April 1939; LHA: O'Connor Papers, Box 3: correspondence January-April 1939. CO733/406/6, *Policy: Law and Order*, MacMichael to Macdonald, April 13, 1939; 404/2 *1939: Disturbances: Appreciation by GOC Military Forces*, January 7-July 30, 1939, citation from July 7, 1939.

Second World War Palestine remained an armed camp. Urban recovery languished under what became a near-decade under siege. Moreover, Zionist urban shootings and bombings surged in spring and summer 1939, reflecting implacable hostility to the White Paper.[82] But British security policy remained rurally-orientated and anti-Arab. Little consideration was given to protecting hitherto hostile Arab urban centers from outward attack, nor to Arab self-defense. By contrast, Jewish forces partly developed with British help were dedicated enemies of Mandatory policy and Arab Palestine. The latter never fully recovered from the disintegrative shock of British counter-insurgency during the great rebellion. Nor did supportive British civil development principles like those Wauchope had advanced.[83] Revisionist Zionist elements had already crossed permissive thresholds of violence against urban Arab objectives in 1936–1939, conditioning its cadres for extensive ethnic cleansing in the decisive conflict to come.[84]

To recapitulate, during the British Mandate's formative years, the Arab Palestinian town had been parsimoniously deprived, amid Orientalist idealizations of peasant Arab life, of public capital, administrative modernization, or collateral benefits from segregated and hostile Zionist development. Nonetheless, urban Arab Palestine was not time-trapped but evolving into a proto-modern nexus of social change and national political realization: bourgeois, radical and religious revolutionary. In parallel, established urban elites and Arab Mandatory officials, frequently seeking to preserve leadership status, responded to Colonial Office overtures in the 1930s, via High Commissioner Sir Arthur Wauchope, for greater civil inclusion. Britain sought to foster a unitary bi-communal Palestinian state within its regional strategic and economic system. Even here however, rural peasant Palestine enjoyed greater attention, perpetuating a colonial knowledge deficit which Wauchope's belated urban reforms, including shifts in policing favoring intelligence-gathering, were either too late or negated by ingrained lower-level British resistance.

Previous outbreaks of anti-Zionist Arab violence arose in urban interfaces between Jewish and Arab Palestine. So did the great rebellion of 1936–1939. What proved transformative were metropolitan British predispositions, crucially encouraged by Zionist opponents of Wauchope's policies, to see a rebellion to be crushed, rather than civil dissenters with whom to negotiate –

82 CO733/415/4 *Irgun Zvai Leumi*, August 10, 1939.

83 CO733/398/18, *Capture of Jewish Armed Group*, October 10-30, 1939.

84 CO733/398/8, *Setting Up Internal Security Organization to Preserve the Peace*, August 14, 1939; 408/3, *Policy: Jewish Reactions*, Wing Cdr A.P. Ritchie, RAF Intelligence, March 10, 1939. LeBor, *Oranges*, 96-110.

as Arab Palestine's leaders were desperate to do. Emerging scholarship has concentrated on rural aspects of Britain's subsequent "dirty war" against Arab Palestine; this study has detailed hitherto neglected urban counter-insurgency. This reductively identified Arab Palestinian urban centers as "enemy": dangerous, alien and incorrigible, to be forcibly broken and punished by politically indiscriminate means including RAF "area bombing." The military thought little of post-operational reconstruction, while simultaneously scorning British civil authority, and its more nuanced viewpoints, as impeding victory. Urban centers were easy targets for collective punishment, especially when rural counter-insurgency, which British commanders saw as their real war, proved relatively fruitless. But rather than engage with urban Arab Palestine, having liquidated civilian structures as tainted with weakness and disloyalty, British commanders imposed siege-like conditions which exacerbated rather than defended against rebel authority in the no-go areas created. Arab urban centers moreover remained vulnerable to Zionist counter-terrorist attacks, which the British seemed invariably unwilling or unable to prevent.

This undid even the slender progress Wauchope had initiated in Arab Palestine's cities, aggravating their already stark segregation and institutionalized disadvantages in relation to Jewish urban Palestine. Indeed the latter was re-privileged during the Arab rebellion, notably via British strategic endorsement of the Tel Aviv port, water schemes, and labor preference in Haifa. Meanwhile, Britain's rural-operational dogmatism and European-orientated distractions unwittingly facilitated dramatic urban rebel coups in 1938. Innovative techniques under Richard O'Connor, integrating civil with military resources, making quick use of Arab police intelligence assets and deploying light forces, partly recovered the situation. But persisting rural counter-insurgent orthodoxy under GOC Robert Haining and almost fetishistic violence under politically more assertive commanders Montgomery and Harris left Arab Palestine's cities brutalized, beleaguered but still out of control. Behind British wire and checkpoints they remained internally riven between committed, usually working class or ex-peasant migrant rebels, and bourgeois élites eager for peace and the restoration of their social authority and economic prosperity.

Partial material recovery during the Second World War, patching-up burnt-out public buildings or sabotaged infrastructure in support of Allied forces, seems not to have healed these internecine political shocks and cleavages. Lasting urban-rural dis-articulation decapitated and fragmented what had been a cohering national polity, depriving it of self-defense potential, along with integrative national leadership, whether urban notable or radical vanguard, reaching an energetic zenith in the mid-1930s. Arab urban centers, especially in territories demarcated for Jewish statehood by the United Nations in 1947, remained rather than vibrant national epicenters isolated, depreciated and ultimately indefensible enclaves, with Jaffa, Arab Haifa, Acre and Lydda notably yielding to Zionist ethnic cleansing during the *nakba* of 1948–1949.[85]

Works Cited

Archival Sources

British National Archives (TNA), Kew, London:
Air Ministry Records (AIR):
Disturbances in Palestine, AIR 2.
Correspondence: Palestine and Transjordan, AIR 5.
RAF Palestine and Transjordan, AIR 23.
Cabinet Records (CAB):
Cabinet Minutes , CAB 23.
Cabinet Office files, CAB 104.
Colonial Office Records (CO):
Palestine Original Correspondence, CO 733.
Military Intelligence Summaries from Plaestine Transjordan and Iraq, CO 732.
Correspondence Between Permanent Undersecretaries and High Commissioners, CO 907
Treasury Records (T):
Supply Department (Palestine), T161.
Chancellor of the Exchequer's Office, T172.
War Office Records (WO):
Palestine Disturbances, WO 32.
Headquarters, British Forces in Palestine, WO 191.

Israel State Archives, Jerusalem:
Records of the Government of Palestine:
Executive Council Minutes, RG 1.

85 See, Issa Khalaf, *Politics in Palestine: Arab Factionalism and Social Disintegration, 1939–1946*. (Albany: SUNY Press, 1991); Roger Owen, "Economic Development in Mandatory Palestine, 1918–1948," in *The Palestinian Economy, ed.* George T. Abed (London; Routledge, 1988); Deborah Bernstein, "Contested Contact: Proximity and Social in Pre-1948 Jaffa and Tel Aviv," in *Mixed Towns, Trapped Communities*, eds. Daniel Monterescu and Dan Rabinowitz (Farnham; Ashgate Publishers, 2007); Tamir Goren, "Efforts to Establish and Arab Workers' Neighbourhood in British Mandatory Palestine," *Middle Eastern Studies* 42:6 (2007); Mustafa Abbasi, "The Fall of Acre in the 1948 Palestine War," *Journal of Palestine Studies* 39:4 (2010), 6-27.

Chief Secretary's File, RG 2.
Attorney General's File RG 3.
Office of the Economic Adviser, RG 5.
Department of Agriculture and Fisheres, RG 7.
Department of Police and Prisons, RG 8.
Department of Public Works RG 12.
Railways and Port Administration, RG 28.

Imperial War Museuem Archives, London:
Syd Burr Papers.
W. Carden-Roe Papers.
Laurene Carr Papers.
Napier Crookenden Papers.
David A. Kennard Papers.
Alex Morison Papers.
B.A. Pond Papers.

King's College, London; Liddell-Hart Military History Archive (LHA):
Robert Brooke-Popham Papers,
John Dill Papers,
R. King-Clark Papers,
Richard O'Connor Papers.

St. Anthony's College, Oxford: Middle East Center Archive (MEC):
John A.M. Faraday Papers,
Robert Haining Papers,
Ivan Lloyd-Philips Papers,
Patrick Rice Papers,
Frederick Scrivener Papers
Sir Charles Tegart Papers,

Published Works

Abbasi, Mustafa. "The Fall of Acre in the 1948 Palestine War," *Journal of Palestine Studies* 39, Vol. 4 (Fall 2010).

Abu Ghazaleh, Adnan. "Arab Cultural Nationalism in Palestine During the British Mandate," *Journal of Palestine Studies*, 1, no.3 (Spring 1972): 37-63.

Aini, Rosa, El-. *Mandated Landscape: British Imperial Rule in Palestine, 1929–1948.* London: Routledge, 2004.

Arnon-Ohanna, Yuval. "The Bands in the Palestinian Arab Revolt, 1936–1939: Structure and Organization," *Asian and African Studies*. 51, no.2 (July 1981): 237-243.

Bernstein, Deborah. "Contested Contact: Proximity and Social in Pre-1948 Jaffa and Tel Aviv." In *Mixed Towns, Trapped Communities*. Edited by D. Monterescu, D. and D. Dabinowitz, D. Farnham: Ashgate Publishers, 2007.

Cohen, Hillel. *Army of Shadows: Palestinian Collaboration with Zionism, 1917–1948*. Berkeley: University of California Press, 2008.

Courtney, Roger. *Palestine Policeman: An Account of Eighteen Dramatic Months in the Palestine Police Force during the Great Jew-Arab Troubles*. London: Herbert Jenkins, 1939.

Feldman, Ilana. *Governing Gaza: Bureaucracy, Authority and the Work of Rule*. Durham: Duke University Press, 2008.

Foot, Hugh. *A Start in Freedom*. New York: Harper and Row, 1964.

French, David. "Nasty Not Nice: Nasty not Nice: British Counter-Insurgency Doctrine and Practice, 1945–1967." *Small Wars and Insurgencies*, 23, No. 4-5 (2012): 744-761.

Fuchs, Ron and Gilbert Herbert. "Representing Mandatory Palestine: Austen St. Barbe Harrison and the Representational Buildings of the British Mandate in Palestine, 1922–37." *Architectural History*, 43 (2000): 281-333.

Gavish, Dov. *A Survey of Palestine under the British Mandate, 1920–1948*. London: Routledge, 2005.

Ghandour, Zeina. *A Discourse on Domination in Mandate Palestine: Imperialism, Property and Insurgency*. London: Routledge, 2009.

Goren, Tamir. "Efforts to Establish an Arab Workers' Neighbourhood in British Mandatory Palestine," *Middle Eastern Studies*, 42, 6 (November 2009): 917-933.

Grob-Fitzgibbon, Benjamin. "Further Thoughts on the Imperial Endgame and Britain's Dirty Wars," *Journal of Imperial and Commonwealth History* 40, 3 (2012): 503-514.

Gross, Nahum T. "The Economic Policy of the Mandatory Government in Palestine," *Research in Economic History* 9, Vol. 1 (1984), 145-172.

Hourani, Albert. *A History of the Arab Peoples*. New York: MJF Books, 1991.

Goren, Tamir. "Efforts to Establish and Arab Workers' Neighbourhood in British Mandatory Palestine." *Middle Eastern Studies* 42, Vol. 6 (November 2007).

Guha, Ranajit. *Dominance without Hegemony: History and Power in Colonial India*. Cambridge: Harvard University Press, 1997.

Gwynn, Major General Sir Charles W. *Imperial Policing*. London: Macmillan, 1939.

Hughes, Matthew. "The Practice and Theory of British Counter-Insurgency: The Histories of the Atrocities at the Palestinian Villages of al-Bassa and Halhul, 1938–1939." *Small Wars & Insurgencies* 20, no. 3-4 September-December 2009: 528-552.

Kabha, Mustafa. *The Palestinian Press as Shaper of Public Opinion, 1928–1939: Writing Up a Storm*. London: Valentine Mitchell, 2007.

Kark, Ruth. *Jaffa: A City in Evolution, 1799–1917*. Jerusalem: Itzhak Ben Zvi Press, 1990.

Keith-Roach, Edward. *Pasha of Jerusalem: Memoirs of a District Commissioner under the British Mandate*. London: Radcliffe Press, 1994.

Khalaf, Issa. *Politics in Palestine: Arab Factionalism and Social Disintegration, 1939–1946*. Albany: SUNY Press, 1991.

Kimmerling, Baruch and Joel Migdal. *The Palestinian People: A History*. Cambridge: Harvard University Press, 2003.

Kimmerling, Baruch. "The Formation of Palestinian Collective Identities: the Ottoman and Mandatory Periods." *Middle Eastern Studies* 30, no. 2 (July 2000): 54-68.

Knight, John. "The Successful Failure of Reform: Police Legitimacy in British Palestine." In *The Routledge Handbook of the History of the Middle East Mandates*. Edited by Schayegh, Cyrus and Andrew Arsan. London; Routledge, 2016.

Kirkbride, Alec S. *A Crackle of Thorns: Experiences in the Middle East*. London: John Murray, 1956.

Kroizer, Gad. "From Dowbiggin to Tegart: Revolutionary Change in the Colonial Police in Palestine during the 1930s," *Journal of Imperial and Commonwealth History* 32, no. 2 (May 2004): 115-133.

Lachman, Shai. "Arab Rebellion and Terrorism in Palestine, 1929–39: The Case of Sheikh Izz al-Din al-Qassam." In *Zionism and Arabism in Palestine and Israel*. Edited by Kedourie, Elie and S.G. Haim. London: Frank Cass, 1982).

LeBor, Adam. *City of Oranges: Arabs and Jews in Jaffa*. London: Bloomsbury, 2005).

Lesch, Ann Mosely. *Arab Politics in Palestine, 1917–1939: Frustration of a Nationalist Movement*. Ithaca: Cornell University Press, 1979.

LeVine, Mark. *Overthrowing Geography: Jaffa, Tel Aviv and the Struggle for Palestine, 1880–1946*. Berkeley: University of California Press, 2005.

Lloyd, David. "Settler Colonialism and the State of Exception: The Example of Palestine/Israel." *Settler Colonial Studies* 2, no. 1 (2012): 59-80.

Lockman, Zachary. *Comrades and Enemies: Arab and Jewish Workers in Palestine, 1906–1948'* Berkeley: University of California Press, 1996.

Mansur, George. "The Arab Worker Under the Palestine Mandate (1937)," *Settler Colonial Studies*, 2, no. 1 (2012): 192-204.

Mathews, Weldon C. *Confronting an Empire, Constructing a Nation: Arab Nationalists and Popular Politics in Mandate Palestine*. London: I.B. Tauris, 2006.

Mattar, Philip. Al-*Hajj Amin al-Husseini and the Palestinian National Movement*. New York: Columbia University Press, 1988.

Mazza, Roberto. *Jerusalem: From the Ottomans to the British*. London: I.B. Tauris, 2009.

Miller, Ylana. *Government and Society in Rural Palestine, 1920–1948*. Austin: University of Texas Press, 1985.

Morton, Geoffrey. *Just the Job: Some Experiences of a Colonial Policeman*. London: Hodder and Stoughton, 1957.

Mumford, Andrew. *The Counter-Insurgent Myth: The British Experience of Irregular Warfare*. Abingdon: Routledge, 2012.

Norris, Jacob. "Repression and Rebellion: Britain's Response to the Arab Revolt in Palestine of 1936–39." *Journal of Imperial and Commonwealth History* 36, no. 1 (March 2008): 25-45.

Norris, Jacob. *Land of Progress: Palestine in the Age of Colonial Development*. Oxford: Oxford University Press, 2013.

Owen, Roger. "Economic Development in Mandatory Palestine, 1918–1948." In *The Palestinian Economy*, Edited by George T Abed. London: Routledge, 1988.

Rotbard, Sharon. *White City, Black City – Architecture and War in Tel Aviv and Jaffa*. Cambridge: MIT Press, 2015).

Schleifer, Abdullah. "Izz al-Din al-Qassam: Preacher and Mujahid." In *Struggle and Survival in the Modern Middle East*. Edited by Edmund Burke, et al. London; I.B. Tauris, 1992.

Schumpeter, Joseph. *The Sociology of Imperialisms*, (1918). New York; Meridian Books, 1955.

Shamir, Ronen. *Current Flow: The Electrification of Palestine*. Stanford: Stanford University Press, 2013.

Seikaly, May. *Haifa: Transformation of a Palestinian Arab Society, 1918–1939*. London: I.B. Tauris, 1995.

Shepherd, Naomi. *Ploughing Sand: British Rule in Palestine*. New Brunswick: Rutgers University Press, 2000.

Sherman, A.J. *Mandate Days: British Lives in Palestine, 1918–1948*. New York: Thames and Hudson, 1997.

Sinclair, Georgina. "'Get Into a Crack Force and Earn Twenty Pounds a Month All Found': The Influence of the Palestine Police on Colonial Policing 1922–1948." *European Review of History* 13, No. 1, (March 2006): 49-65.

Smith, Barbara. *The Roots of Separation in Palestine: British Economic Policy, 1920–1929*. Syracuse: Syracuse University Press, 1993.

Swedenburg, Ted. *Memories of Revolt: The 1936–39 Rebellion and the Palestinian National Past*. Minneapolis: University of Minnesota Press, 1995.

Thomas, Martin. *Empires of Intelligence: Security Services and Colonial Disorder after 1914*. Berkeley: University of California Press, 2008.

Townshend, Charles. "First Intifada: Rebellion in Palestine, 1936–39." *History Today* 37, No. 7, (July 1989). http://www.historytoday.com/charles-townshed/first-intifada-rebellion-palestine-1936-39.

CHAPTER 7

Occupied Naples and the Politics of Food in World War II

Stefan Laffin

When Colonel Edgar E. Hume, who commanded the Allied Military Government (AMG) in the United States 5th Army's Italian sector, entered Naples on 1 October 1943, he soon faced tasks already familiar from the Allied arrival in Sicily roughly three months earlier. This entailed first and foremost ferreting out food stocks and restoring the water supply destroyed by the German *Wehrmacht*. Though the predominant tasks of the initial phase of Allied Military Government – prevention of unrest and securing the Army communication lines – were still crucial, equally vital was the provision and supply of food. As a painful lesson learned from Sicily, the supply of food was naturally tied closest to the prevention of unrest.[1] By February 1944, Naples entered a new phase of military government and Charles Poletti would take over as Regional Commissioner for Naples and the Campania Region, a position he would hold until the Allied advance to Rome in June.[2] This phase of military governance permits us to closely examine the occupational procedures by consulting the personal papers of military government personnel like Poletti, Maurice F. Neufeld, Poletti's closest collaborator, or Ellery W. Stone, whose papers can provide useful insights through the lens of the Vice-President of the Allied Control Commission (ACC) for Italy.[3]

In spite of its major political and military consequences, such as the downfall of the first Axis nation, the initial fighting of US-American troops in the European theater of war, and the opening of a second front in Europe, the Italian Campaign has been neglected for the most part by both historical scholarship and public memory. With few exceptions, the accounts have been produced by

1 Manoela Patti, "Il Pane Americano. La Politica Alleata degli Ammassi in Sicilia (1943–1945)," *Zapruder* 25 (2011), 34-36.

2 Poletti's biographical file, 26 October 1944, Charles Poletti papers; Box 12; Rare Book and Manuscript Library, Columbia University Library.

3 Ellery Stone was in Italy since September 12, 1943, as part of the Allied Military Mission to the Italian Government and from November 10, 1944 onwards Chief Commissioner of the Allied Commission for Italy. See Ellery W. Stone Papers, Box 1, Hoover Institution Archives, Memorandum from May 7, 1945.

 | DOI:10.30965/9783657702787_008

participants involved. This is particularly true for the Allied soldiers – both officers and rank and file – and the Italian partisans. The scholarly accounts pale in comparison, though some important studies have been published.[4] So when the Italian Campaign itself is under-researched, especially if juxtaposed to the Eastern Front or the invasion of Normandy, one can logically infer that the concomitant and subsequent occupation of Italian territory is even more understudied.[5] Only recently have studies emerged that shed light on the implications of the Allied occupation of Italy by focusing on social and everyday aspects.[6] While the impetus to research the Allied occupation of Italy in World War II has largely come from within Italy herself, US-American scholarship has also developed an increased interest in the general state of occupation. Invasions in Afghanistan and Iraq have instigated research inquiring into the legal status of occupation for one; on the other hand, the rather ingenuous treatment of Allied occupations in the context of World War II which allegedly served both as prologue and blueprint for the economic and political rehabilitation of West Germany, in particular, has been challenged.[7]

Besides contributing to research concerned with occupations, and here most notably the case of Naples in World War II, the chapter also seeks to add to scholarship on the politics of food in times of crisis or conflict.[8] Food was

---

4 Carlo D'Este, *Lo sbarco in Sicilia* (Milan: Mondadori, 1988); Rick Atkinson, *The Day of Battle. The War in Sicily and Italy, 1943–1944* (New York: Holt, 2007) which marks the second volume of the author's liberation trilogy, a written account of the US Army's participation in the Mediterranean theater of war. See also the military history studies by Martin Blumenson who has published extensively about the Italian Campaign.

5 For countries under German occupation, there is an emerging and ongoing debate: Tatjana Tönsmeier, "Besatzungsgesellschaften. Begriffliche und konzeptionelle Überlegungen zur Erfahrungsgeschichte des Alltags unter deutscher Besatzung im Zweiten Weltkrieg," in: Docupedia-Zeitgeschichte, December 18, 2015. Accessed December 30, 2017 https://docupedia.de/zg/Besatzungsgesellschaften.

6 Manoela Patti, *La Sicilia e gli Alleati* (Roma: Donzelli, 2013); Isobel Williams, *Allies and Italians under Occupation. Sicily and Southern Italy 1943–1945* (London: Palgrave, 2013). Studies having more of a political history outlook: David W. Ellwood; *L'alleato nemico. La politica dell'occupazione anglo-americano in Italia 1943–1946* (Milan: Feltrinelli, 1977); Ennio di Nolfo and Maurizio Serra, *La gabbia infranta. Gli Alleati e l'Italia dal 1943 al 1945* (Bari: Laterza, 2010); see also some of the official histories of the occupation: Charles R.S. Harris, *Allied Military Administration of Italy 1943–5* (London: Her Majesty's Stationery Office, 1957); Harry L. Coles and Albert K. Weinberg, *Civil Affairs: Soldiers become Governors* (Washington DC: Office of the Chief of Military History, Department of the Army, 1964).

7 Nehal Bhuta, "The Antinomies of Transformative Occupation," *The European Journal of International Law* 16:4 (2005), 721-740; Susan L. Carruthers, *The Good Occupation* (Cumberland: Harvard University Press, 2016).

8 For instance Frank Trentmann and Flemming Just, eds. *Food and Conflict in Europe in the Age of Two World Wars* (Basingstoke: Palgrave Macmillan 2006); Lizzie Collingham, *The Taste of War: World War II and the Battle for Food* (New York: Penguin, 2012).

the touchstone of assessing the occupation. It helped transform perceptions and political structures as food was, instead of *too big to see* as recent governmental studies have highlighted, nowhere to be seen, which in turn made it a contentious issue and changed the perception of the Allies from liberators to *proper* occupiers.[9] This was particularly true for cities, and even more so for the city of Naples whose port became the "lifeline" for the Allies as far as reinforcements, both in logistical and manpower respects, were concerned.[10] At the same time, one is left to wonder if the evermore arriving Allied soldiers were embraced by the local Neapolitans as they rather hoped for ships bringing medical and food supplies. More Allied soldiers meant also more military mouths to feed which of course gained center stage. All in all, Naples therefore needs to be seen as a specific side and mode of occupation due to its pivotal character in the occupational regime and the vital role of the port.

While not necessarily embracing any ill-intended aspects of politics of food, I will point out the contingencies of the food security situation in Naples after 1943. This setting was as much a direct result of the supremacy of military necessity as it was a lack of priority and failure on behalf of the occupying Allies. In a lecture at the School of Military Government in Virginia, which prepared officers for the Civil Affairs tasks in occupied territories, it was openly stated that nothing could be more wrong than "the impression that the objective of promoting the welfare of the governed in occupied territory is almost as important as the objective of military necessity. In fact, you get the impression [...] that our principle objective in invading a foreign country is to bring light to the heathen. [...] There is only one legitimate objective of military government, and that is to win the war."[11] It therefore delineates a situation in which food may not have been used as a destructive weapon to weaken the enemy population, but which indeed comprised a system of privileges and in certain ways continuity with the fascist regime that was always cautious to provide food security for its own people but failed in its efforts to do so.[12] Any Allied

9 Carolyn Steel, *Hungry City: How Food Shapes Our Lives* (London: Chatto and Windus, 2008); Kevin Morgan, "Feeding the City: The Challenge of Urban Food Planning," *International Planning Studies* 14:4 (2009), 341-348.

10 Public Relations Branch of Allied Commission, Review of Allied Military Government and of The Allied Commission in Italy. July 10, 1943 D-Day Sicily to May 2, 1945 German Surrender in Italy (Rome: Public Relations Section, US Army, 1945), 30.

11 Quoted in Merle Fainsod, "The Development of American Military Government Policy during World War II," in *American Experiences in Military Government in World War II*, eds. Carl J. Friedrich and Associates (New York: Rinehart & Company, 1948), 27.

12 Charles Paul Vincent, *The Politics of Hunger: The Allied Blockade of Germany 1915–1919* (Athens, OH: Ohio University Press, 1985); for studies on German occupational policy: Christian Gerlach, *Kalkulierte Morde: Die deutsche Wirtschafts- und Vernichtungspolitik in Weißrußland 1941 bis 1944* (Hamburg: Hamburger Edition, 1999); Henri A. van der Zee, *The*

shortcoming to provide sufficient food thus always entailed a political dimension and carried the risk of legitimizing the toppled fascist regime, especially because the occupation in itself was as apparent as anywhere in Naples with the abundance of military personnel, headquarters and organizations in the city. Similarly, the ruins of bombed-out houses and places, dead bodies and the constant fear of mines left behind by the retreating German *Wehrmacht* served as a reminder that the war was ongoing too. The ability to have food available and allocate it to the local population can be regarded as a measuring stick for the success of any occupational activity, that is if occupation in itself conceives of a positive outlook and is not simply established to formalize and impose victory upon the defeated enemy nation. For Neapolitans, liberation – in a very crucial sense – meant to get fed and one of the most desirable purposes of living under Allied occupation was to make the acquaintance of an Allied soldier who seemingly disposed of unlimited access to food in the imagination of Italians.[13] If not having a direct contact to an Allied soldier, it was otherwise tough to figure out which of the administrative bodies one had to go to state their concerns or requests. Once having found the appropriate authority, it still meant waiting for hours or days before being received by the overstretched occupational apparatus. The political legacy of the liberation, with all its historiographical inscriptions, most famously expressed in the resistance myth, only compounded this situation and later blurred these experiences.

I will first outline the major events of the Italian Campaign and correlate them to domestic political Italian occurrences as well as embed them in Allied strategic contexts. To further this contribution's argumentation, the terms 'occupation' and 'military government' are then sketched out. The specific Italian case gains center stage next before narrowing it down to the occupational situation of Naples in World War II, with particular regard to the time span between late 1943 and the first half of 1944, that is the capture of Rome. The supply of food, which also serves to point out the shortcomings of the Allied occupation of Italy per se, shall be subsequently examined. Finally, concluding remarks on public memory and cultures of remembrance will be woven in as well.

Hunger Winter. Occupied Holland 1944–1945 (Lincoln, University of Nebraska Press, 1998); for Italian Fascism: Alexander Nützenadel, "Dictating Food: Autarchy, Food Provision, and Consumer Politics in Fascist Italy, 1922–1943," in *Food and Conflict in Europe in the Age of the Two World Wars*, eds. Frank Trentmann and Flemming Just (London: Palgrave Macmillan, 2006), 88-108.

13 Norman Lewis, *Naples '44. An intelligence officer in the Italian labyrinth* (London: Eland 1983), 166.

War in Italy: The Long Road to Rome

Nine months after Germany invaded Poland, Fascist Italy joined her Axis partner by declaring war on Britain and France in June 1940. This was chiefly a decision taken under the impression of the *Wehrmacht's* swift successes. The expected short and triumphant wars never materialized, however, and two years later – and after disastrous Italian military campaigns in Albania and Greece – Allied success came a lot nearer, with their armies both advancing politically as well as geographically throughout the Tunisian Campaign. The German-Italian armies finally surrendered in North Africa in May 1943. At the same time, Prime Minister Churchill and President Roosevelt agreed at the third Washington Conference (*Trident*) on the future Allied strategy.[14] Sicily was confirmed to be the target area for the Allied invasion of Europe. Recognizing Italy as the weak link of the Axis, Allied strategy intended to checkmate her as a political power. Besides the British geopolitical considerations to continue the war operations in the Mediterranean basin, with visions of resurfacing imperial ambitions in this area, it also needs to be seen in light of the employment of the Allied troops which now became available after the campaigns in North Africa had ended. Hence Italy was also a natural spot due to its geographical proximity and, as a consequence thereof, logistical reasons.

After some preliminary attacks, the Allied invasion of Sicily (*Operation Husky*) started on 9 July and lasted until 17 August 1943. From September onwards, the Italian Campaign crossed over to the mainland, most famously with the Allied landing in the Gulf of Salerno on 9 September 1943.[15] Naples was captured on 1 October and it was here that the Allied advance, which until then was gaining ground quickly, came to a halt. Between reaching Naples and liberating Rome, nine months passed before the Allies eventually got a hold of the Italian capital on 4 June 1944. It made Naples the political and military center of liberated Italy during this time. Political activity, albeit always banned by the AMG, played out on the streets and in the newspapers of Naples. By February 1944, this resonated even more as the Italian Government relocated its seat from Brindisi to Salerno, south of Naples. The agreement to postpone all Italian political matters, and most importantly the question of the form of

14 The minutes of the conference can be checked on the website of the Eisenhower Presidential Library, Museum and Boyhood Home's website. Accessed December 30, 2017. https://eisenhower.archives.gov/research/online_documents/d_day/Trident_Conference.pdf. It confirmed the decision taken at the Casablanca Conference in January 1943, a decision that amounted to a reversal of the strategic decision to fight Germany first.

15 The British reached the mainland on 3 September by entering Reggio di Calabria. They also landed in Taranto, Apulia on 9 September.

government and who should be a part thereof until Rome was reached now backfired; an agreement taken under the impression that the Italian Campaign would be an issue of mere months and not years. Also by early 1944, the Allied Force Headquarters (AFHQ) in the Mediterranean had established its base in the Royal Palace of Caserta, north of Naples and therefore much closer to the Gustav Line, the *Wehrmacht's* winter defense position.[16] In general, no less than eight headquarters concerned with military government were at one point in time in the city.[17]

Because of its exceptional value as the node for all military and occupational activity, the city of Naples itself would remain for the whole duration of the war under AMG. More and more reinforcements for the battle lines north of Naples arrived in the vital port and only the Allied landing at Anzio on 22 January 1944 relieved some pressure. It would take another half a year to get to Rome, however, as the Germans used the geographical conditions of Southern Italy to their advantage.[18] Further hampering progress was the withdrawal of many divisions in preparation for the Allied invasion of the Normandy (*Operation Overlord*) as the war in Italy was relegated to a sideshow. The Italian Campaign would end on 2 May 1945; Germans surrendered in Italy only a week before the war's official end.

Beyond the military actions, the campaign seemed to be paying off politically. After all, most severely affecting the conduct of war was that Italy itself underwent a profound change. In part because of the Allied invasion of Sicily, which further aggravated the existing discontent with the Fascist regime, Mussolini was overthrown on 25 July 1943.[19] Voted down by the Grand Council of Fascism, the King subsequently had him arrested. He then proceeded to instruct Field Marshall Pietro Badoglio to form a new government. Badoglio soon began armistice negotiations which brought about the odd status of Italian co-belligerency. While the King and Badoglio – whose government based in Brindisi came to be known as the Kingdom of the South (*Regno del Sud*) – were eager to earn Italy the status of an ally, Allied opinion differed on this matter. The US-Americans, who unlike the British did not fight Italy for the last three years in North Africa and also were carefully minding the Italian-American

16 The National Archives in the UK (TNA), WO 204-263, A.F.H.Q. move to Italy. Organisation of Allied forces.

17 Library of Congress (LoC), Manuscript Division, Maurice Neufeld Papers, Box 1. Diaries and Related Matter, 1931–1991, Feb. 1931–July 1957, 1931–1944, entry from January 18, 1944.

18 The best-known example for that might be the Battle(s) of Monte Cassino in the first half of 1944.

19 Philip Morgan, *The Fall of Mussolini: Italy, Italians and the Second World War* (Oxford, New York: Oxford University Press, 2010).

community, drew a more lenient line. But British tenacity insisted that the Italians were a former war enemy and could not be considered a proper ally. Taking this into account, yet likewise making the most of the Italian resources for the war effort, co-belligerency was to be found key to the solution, albeit no party involved seemed to know what this really meant or entailed. This would have far-reaching implications for the Allied occupational policy. The political events therefore outpaced the military successes, resulting in a severe test for Italian internal politics and for a concerted Allied strategy and effort.

Occupation and Military Government – Old Approaches to a New Phenomenon?

The awareness that occupation and military government would pose a major challenge, yet needed to be adjusted and redefined, rose only *after* the invasion of Sicily and mainland Italy. In large part because of this experience, the Allies soon realized that the old military textbooks and international treaties were outdated. Up until then, little regard was paid to the problem of occupation, if indeed realizing it as one after all. The US-Americans drew on their most recent experience with the Rhineland occupation in the aftermath of World War I and studying post-civil war occupations in the US south.[20]

The most serious attempt to elaborate on the issue came in the form of the Field Manual 27-5 which was published on 30 July 1940, roughly 18 months before the USA would eventually enter the war.[21] It marked a more pragmatic approach if juxtaposed to Field Manual 27-10, which was likewise published in 1940, laying out the legal leeway for enforcing occupations.[22] FM 27-5, on the contrary, tried to tackle the question of what was advisable to do while establishing military government. Its definition of military government was succinct: "Military government is that form of government which is established and maintained by a belligerent by force of arms over occupied territory of the enemy and over the inhabitants thereof." It was likewise the mechanism through which functions of civil government would be exercised to maintain

20 These two historical examples were part of teaching classes at Civil Affairs Schools in Charlottesville, Virginia for instance. U.S. Provost Marshal General's Bureau, box 1, Hoover Institution Archives.

21 FM 27-5 War Department, *Basic Field Manual Military Government 1940* (Washington DC: United States Government Printing Office, 1940). The following quotes can also be found there.

22 FM 27-10 War Department, *Field Manual. Rules of Land Warfare* (Washington DC: United States Government Printing Office, 1947).

public order. In addition, the principle of military necessity was laid down and reaffirmed once again. To underscore this point, it relegated military government to a second-tier task which could potentially harm the war effort because every man "engaged in military government is withdrawn either from the combatant forces or from productive labor at home." In a strange occurrence, the Army did not somehow consider military government to be part of the war effort – or at least not to be put on equal footing with pure fighting. With the theme of this chapter in mind, it is also important to note that there was no specific advisement regarding the occupation of different layers of government – apparently a city was to be administered the same way as villages. In any case, it was suggested to keep the existing political divisions in place and to station officers who would supervise civil affairs in bigger cities. That it specifically referred to "Kreise" as a governmental sub-division also underlined that already in 1940 occupation was conceived of rather with regard to Germany than to Italy for whose case any reference was missing.[23] Later on, Allied soldiers could consult a pocket guide for Italian cities where Naples was prominently mentioned as one of eleven Italian cities. It mostly served as a tourist guide though with a brief introduction to the city's history and geography, noting what sights were worth seeing and how to get there.[24]

How would the almost Weberian ideal type definitions of occupation and military government, which served as the guidelines for ACC and AMG and the idea that military government should always draw up on the existing personnel in the occupied territory, be applied to the Italian case in 1943? After all, if it was an enemy country, which by the time of the invasion of Sicily Italy certainly was, how could that then justify retaining its civilian personnel, usually of fascist background? And while for the invasion of Sicily, Italy was an Axis enemy nation, by the time of the arrival in Naples in October 1943, the armistice(s) had been agreed upon, and on 13 October 1943, Italy had declared war upon Germany which brought the co-belligerency about. So it was rather unclear whether it was indeed enemy territory that was to be occupied. Compounding the problem, most manuals at the time excluded liberation of Allied territory, an (oftentimes joint) international administration of territory or "the presence of armed forces in another state in accordance with some treaty or agreement."[25]

---

23 FM 27-5 War Department, *Basic Field Manual Military Government 1940*, 12.

24 United States War Department, *Pocket Guide to Italian Cities* (Washington: U.S. Government Printing Office, 1944).

25 Peter M.R. Stirk, *The Politics of Military Occupation* (Edinburgh: Edinburgh University Press, 2009), 33.

The Army also realized the problem of the sustainability for the Italian case. It is not for nothing that on 22 December 1943, a new Field Manual was published.[26] It now recognized that most of the 1940 provisions were rather academic because "[c]ivil administration may have broken down wholly or in part" in the occupied country. It also stated the need to remove public personnel from office which could be similarly read as a direct lesson learned from Italy. Remarkably, while the general definition remained by and large the same, military government was not "confined to belligerent occupation" anymore but could also be established pursuant to Allied or neutral territory dominated by the enemy and territory of which occupation was necessary for military operations. Both cases held true for the Italian example.

In some respects, and to borrow from the terminology of peace studies, the initial goal of any military government is to achieve a negative peace, defined by the absence of turmoil, tension, conflict and war. The long-term goal would consequentially be to reach a distinctly positive one.[27] Yet it always has to take careful consideration in achieving this as military government plays on the dialectic of subordination and legitimation. In order to enforce the occupation, it provokes a contradiction at the heart of the issue: "It has to subordinate before it can legitimate effectively, and the more it tries to subordinate, the harder becomes the legitimation."[28] In other words, we encounter an inherent contradiction of the institution of military government if we assume democratization as the utmost goal which should emanate from the occupation. The AMG in Italy after 1943 can basically be characterized as a temporary constitutional dictatorship which aimed to, if not bringing about democracy, at least prevent new forms of totalitarian dictatorship, meaning both new forms of Fascism and Communism.[29] The authority of the occupying power derives at any rate from its factual power and thereby from the potential to enforce its will upon the population. Owing to the factual power, as envisaged both theoretically by the Army Field Manuals but also by the actual situation in Italy after 1943, military government administrators had to a great extent *carte blanche*.

26 FM 27-5-War Department, *United States Army and Navy Manual of Military Government and Civil Affairs* (Washington DC: United States Government Printing Office, 1943). The FM 27-5 of 1940 was also heavily criticized in an US-American report on military government: TNA, WO 220-405, American report on A.M.G.

27 Resat Bayer, "Peaceful transitions and democracy", *Journal of Peace Research* 47:5 (2010), 535; Johan Galtung, *Peace by peaceful means. Peace and Conflict, Development and Civilization* (London et al: Sage, 1998).

28 Bhuta, "Antinomies", 724; the quote is on p. 739.

29 For a contemporary interpretation of this: Carl J. Friedrich, "Military Government and Dictatorship", *The Annals of the American Academy of Political and Social Science* 267 (1950), 1-7.

Matter-of-factly considered, the real test came anyway when Civil Affairs Officers who would administer, say a small village in Campania, had to put the theoretical guidelines and definitions to the practical test.

Allied Military Government in Italy

Allied Military Government for Occupied Territories (AMGOT) was activated on 1 May 1943 by General Eisenhower.[30] It was an army organization and chiefly served army needs, namely to ensure the security of the occupying forces and their lines of communication; it was only to further this end that law and order needed to be restored and food was to be provided as necessary among the civilian population. The Allied Control Commission was set up by virtue of Article 37 of the long armistice clauses as "*representative of the United Nations.*"[31] Then again, only British and US-Americans sat on the Commission with the Soviet Union being the most glaring omission. That this would set a bad precedent for future operations was already obvious to the Western Allies themselves.[32] AMG and ACC were the main institutional bodies for the implementation of military government and its execution.

In the first phase, military government was conducted directly by the advancing Army which put military needs first and subordinated all other tasks under this objective. In a second phase, the focus gradually shifted towards a more systematic approach and help to the civilian population. When an area was stabilized, it was turned into an AMG region which was then administered by a Regional Commissioner. It was also at that time that the ACC became the principal authority. The third phase, which coincided with the main goals of the second phase, comprised the preparation for the turnover of the respective territory to the Italian government and the actual turnover itself. This happened as early as February 1944 when most of the Italian South and Sicily got returned to the Italian Government and thereby greatly enlarged the *Regno del Sud.* ACC served a double purpose of being the headquarters for areas which were administered through military government and also being

30 Andrew Buchanan, *American Grand Strategy in the Mediterranean during World War II* (New York: Cambridge University Press, 2014). AMGOT would be later shortened to Allied Military Government to acknowledge Italy's new status.

31 Italian Armistice as quoted on http://avalon.law.yale.edu/wwii/italy03.asp, article 37). Accessed December 30, 2017. The commission's name would be shortened to Allied Commission (AC) in October 1944.

32 Bruno Arcidiacono, "*The dress rehearsal. The Foreign Office and the Control of Italy, 1943–1944,*" *The Historical Journal* 28: 2 (1985), 417-427.

the advisory body for those areas that were already restituted, thereby exercising its function to counsel the Italian government on all political matters and governmental appointments.[33] The consulting role, however, could also result in vetoing unpleasant political changes or appointments. At times, the overlap of military government, enacted and performed by different organizations, with rather similar administrative functions, also confused those who were a part of it. In that way, military government was much more complex than the rather straightforward US-American experiences after World War I.[34] For instance, as late as mid-1944, President Roosevelt confused Charles Poletti with being one of the heads of the ACC.[35]

Usually, the first act of Civil Affairs Officers upon arriving in the specific place they had to govern was to announce Proclamation No. 1, which served to establish the military government. The crucial aspect was its comprehensive authority: "All powers of government and jurisdiction in the occupied territory and over its inhabitants, and final administrative responsibility are vested in me [General Harold Alexander] as General Officer Commanding and Military Governor."[36] These Civil Affairs Officers who had eleven further proclamations and general orders with them and could usually consult a detailed handbook that precisely laid out what to do hour by hour in the first days of occupation, were the most visible representation of the military government. The invasion and occupation of Sicily therefore provided the first test. Charles Poletti, as Chief Civil Affairs Officer of the US 7th Army at the time, embarked with the first units in Sicily and was a natural fit for the position. He was of Italian descent, fluent in the language, and had studied in Italy for a while.[37] The best asset was perhaps his experience in local government, as Governor in New York in 1942 for example.[38] Yet people like Poletti remained the exception as

---

33 For the various sub-commissions of the ACC see National Archives and Record Administration, College Park (NARA), Record Group (RG) 331, 10000-105-50, Box 142_ Functions of the Sub-Commissions, Sept. 26-Oct. 22, 1943.

34 F.S.V. Donnison, *Civil Affairs and Military Government. Central Organization and Planning* (London: Her Majesty's Stationery Office, 1966), 86-87.

35 LoC, Manuscript Division, Maurice Neufeld Papers, Box 1, Diaries, entry from July 15, 1944.

36 Allied Military Government of Occupied Territory. Proclamation No. 1. Charles Poletti papers; Box 17; Rare Book and Manuscript Library, Columbia University Library. For a literary account, it is still enlightening to read John Hersey, *A Bell for Adano* (New York: Knopf, 1944).

37 Poletti studied Italian Civil Law and Roman Law while in Rome in 1924/1925 and even heard Mussolini speaking in public venues. See Charles Poletti papers, box 29; Rare Books and Manuscript Library, Columbia University Library. First draft of Poletti's article for the Italian magazine Epoca.

38 Poletti's former boss, Governor Herbert H. Lehman, was appointed by President Roosevelt with the task of creating an international relief organization. See Ben Shephard, *The Long Road Home: The Aftermath of the Second World War* (London: The Bodley Head, 2010), 36.

the Field Manual of 1940 even considered knowledge of the respective language as merely advisable but not indispensable.[39] Moreover, the Civil Affairs Officers were a tough act to follow in the Army of which they were part of as the traditional soldier lacked understanding for the work that went beyond the task of maintaining public order and safety.[40] On top of that, some felt envious as Poletti became almost a wartime celebrity for his work. This was not least owed to the military stalemate as the journalists, who waited in Naples for the advance to Rome, needed stories and Poletti proved both colorful and successful enough to warrant many of those.[41]

It might also be therefore that many soldierly accounts underlined that only AMG directly enforced by the Army would have worked and it was precisely when the ACC took on a more active role that it all broke down.[42] At any rate, the occupation of Sicily helped try to sort things out in many ways: as far as the main tasks of the occupation and its procedures were concerned, but also with regard to the relationship between different branches and the structural alignment of military government within the Italian Campaign. By the time the Allied armies crossed over to mainland Italy, however, the situation proved a far greater challenge than any Field Manual took into account. The overthrow of Mussolini meant that basically the hundreds of pages of civil affairs books devoted to the fascist organization of local government were now somehow redundant. What is more, it directly aggravated the implementation of military government as now the usual Civil Affairs Officer – or Regional Commissioner – could not simply enforce proclamations and rule the territory without any regard to politics. Italy was not an enemy in the strict sense any longer and by virtue of her co-belligerency, she assumed a status that was simply not foreseen in any handbook, Field Manual, let alone the Hague Convention of 1907. Co-belligerency fueled expectations that Italians would be liberated and treated on equal footing; certainly, it did not suggest further hardship after 1 October 1943 in Naples.

39 FM 27-5 War Department, *Basic Field Manual* 1940, 2.

40 There was also the contemporary joke that AMGOT was short for Ancient Military Gentlemen on Tour. See Hill, *In the Wake of War*, 17. *See* Also Robert Engler, "The Individual Soldier and the Occupation," *The Annals of the American Academy of Political and Social Science* 267 (1950), 77-86.

41 Charles Poletti papers; Box 12; Rare Book and Manuscript Library, Columbia University Library; the city of Rome also dedicated a bust to him: Archivio Centrale dello Stato (ACS), Presidenza del Consiglio dei Ministri, 1944-47, Fascicolo 14-5, Charles Poletti – Richiesta di Bronzo per fusione sul busto.

42 Paradigmatically for that: Thomas R. Fisher, "Allied Military Government in Italy," *The Annals of the American Academy of Political and Social Science* 267 (1950), 114-122.

The Real Test of Occupation: (the Lack of) Food in Naples

According to a publication by the ACC, Naples stood out for its organizational mess: "Naples, densely populated, badly shattered, and thronged with troops on leave and ready to spend freely on enjoyment presented, as might have been expected, every kind of problem: from the black market to venereal disease, from sanitation to threats of strikes, from lack of accommodations to inequities in the distribution of rations, from clandestine newspapers to political bickerings [sic!] by every shade of Italian opinion."[43] These were the problems that basically followed military government wherever it was established but nowhere was the problem as condensed and visible as in Naples. The damning assessment accurately pointed to the challenges posed to the AMG. As described, restoring public safety and order, and thereby protecting the communication lines of the army, were the primary duties of the initial phase of military government. After that, efforts towards a restoration of public life and reconstruction of the city began, under Allied and later Italian primary responsibility. Then again, because the Italian Campaign came to a halt, these phases of military government somehow overlapped and were not easy to distinguish. Various officers moved in these days from being directly employed by the Army to civilian agencies or to be seated at the ACC headquarters, often times without clearly recognizing if and how their tasks had shifted or to whom to report.[44]

As far as the AMG success rate is concerned, even Maurice Neufeld marked in his diary that he would give the AMG a mere "C Record and no more."[45] In his assessment, Neufeld particularly hinted at the issue of supply and the black market as being the most crushing factors undermining an effective government. This had to be particularly devastating in Naples where most personnel tasked with administering the occupation was stationed and which usually requisitioned lavish villas and hotels. All of that was naturally known and visible to the local population as was the black market where those locals had to buy their daily necessities at horrendous prices. That this all but put a strain on relations between occupiers and the occupied is easy to understand. Administrative policy did not help matters much either. Basically, four flaws impaired Allied food policy: the acquisition of food supplies, the distribution

43 Public Relations Branch of Allied Commission, Review, 30.

44 Robert M. Hill and Elizabeth Craig Hill, *In the Wake of War. Memoirs of an Alabama Military Government Officer in World War II Italy* (University, Alabama: The University of Alabama Press, 1982), 16-19.

45 LoC, Manuscript Division, Maurice Neufeld Papers, Box 1. Diaries, entry from January 6, 1944.

thereof, the pricing and the whole administrative chaos not least owed to the monstrous administrative machinery of the ACC which by its nature required many different sub-commissions and personnel to be involved with the nutritional situation. So people coming from different national, professional and generational backgrounds had to come to an understanding to get the food supply under control. By the time the Allies reached the Italian mainland, the food situation emerged clearly as the most central problem of AMG and it was hence particularly fatal that the respective sub-commission was understaffed and lacking experienced officers.[46] Moreover, it "confused administration with the issuance of rules, regulations, and restrictions which created even greater shortages."[47] The sub-commission, much as the ACC in general, filled its top administrative positions with inflexible, dogmatic office holders – oftentimes vocations based on reputation rather than merit – trying to run military government by the textbook.[48] Equally severe, the transportation sub-commission, also involved with ensuring the supply, suffered from the same shortcomings.

The main problem which affected the acquisition of supplies was tied to the expectations of the Italian Campaign. Each involved party anticipated a short war and thus took little measures to accumulate food stocks. The fascist regime, unable to create extra food stocks by any means, expected short triumphant wars.[49] The Allies, on the other hand, took the rather impromptu decision to invade mainland Italy and had high hopes of being in Rome by Christmas 1943. This, combined with the principle of military necessity and shortsighted militaries as principal actors formulating occupational policies, led to a situation in which no food stocks were prepared in the end. It was now especially valuable that the Italian Navy had made it intact to Malta after the announcement of the armistice as Italian ships and submarines were used to run food supplies.[50] In addition, by late 1943 the transportation sub-commission finally pushed through in its effort to declare food the number one priority for all civilian goods. The tonnage immediately rose from 3,000 in October 1943 to almost 300,000 a month later.[51] This was pivotal because of the initial naïve assumption that Italian cities could feed themselves. The

46 Maurice F. Neufeld, "The Failure of AMG in Italy," *Public Administration Review* 6:2 (1946), 142.

47 Ibid.

48 See the report in TNA, WO 220-404, Difficulties and defects in military government administration.

49 Nützenadel, "Dictating Food."

50 See NARA, RG 331, 1000-105-8, Box 140 for the meetings of the food committee of the ACC in late 1943; Public Relations Branch of Allied Commission, *Review*, 38.

51 Ibid, 58.

grandiloquent fascist propaganda was taken at face value and invading Allied troops were staggered to find that cities had only food for the first few days. For Catanzaro, it was reported that a mere ten percent of the necessary wheat to provide a ration of 150 grams of bread for the locals existed.[52]

Faced with the shortage of food, a debate emerged about whether to continue increasing food imports and setting up relief organizations or whether the objective of supporting local commercial agriculture would prove more beneficial in the end. Initially, the military government worked on the premise to be fed from local resources. The General Administrative Instruction No. 5 for "Civilian Supply and Resources" stated that it was the Civil Affairs Officer's duty "to assist in making the occupied area self-sufficient as far as minimum essential civilian requirements are concerned."[53] This dependence on local resources should have covered the first two months. The debate has to be seen against the backdrop of two larger contexts. First, there was an agricultural revolution in the United States which by 1946 produced a third more food than before the war with less labor.[54] This food surplus made any argument that the United States lacked food for relief implausible. What could be argued is that there were not enough ships to transport the food due to the principle of military necessity. This also puts the second context into perspective: it has been said that World War II and the immediate post-war years saw an increased US-American devotion to internationalism.[55] While this is true for the main part, it came with some caveats. The orientation towards internationalism led to the creation of the United Nations Relief and Rehabilitation Administration (UNRRA) for example, yet Congress made sure that the organization had to spend a substantial part of its budget on US-American agricultural products. Because these were much more expensive than products from other sources, it meant that less food could be bought. The idealistic internationalism of the United States therefore needs also to be seen in light of consumer politics that put US-American governmental interests first.[56] While the UNRRA was in operation in mid-1944, the occupiers decided to bolster local commercial

52 Report by Holmstrom for Catanzaro, 18 September 1943, 10214/115/37, box 4206, RG 331, National Archives Record Administration, College Park, Maryland. Holmstrom was the provincial Civil Affairs Officer; by mid-1944 the situation would improve: NARA, RG 331, 10220-115-26, box 4216.

53 Box 19, Daniel Lerner Collection, Hoover Institution Archives; Patti, "Il Pane Americano", 37-38. See also the Regional Administrative Instruction No. 3 that laid out this principle to agriculture officers in NARA, RG 331, 10210-101-7, box 4123.

54 Allen J. Matusow, *Farm Policies and Politics in the Truman Years* (Cambridge: Harvard University Press, 1967).

55 See for example the introduction by Trentmann and Just, eds. *Food and Conflict*, 1-10.

56 Shephard, *Long Road Home*, 252.

agriculture in Italy.[57] In March 1944, 32,000 tons of seed potatoes were distributed by the Agriculture sub-commission to Sicily, Campania and Puglia, of which Campania received the most. This would have theoretically been a much-needed remedy if not for the eruption of Mt. Vesuvius on 18 March 1944 which destroyed thousands of acres of the fertile Campanian land and the spring crops already in the ground, including some of the potato seeds.[58]

Once supplies arrived in Italy, there were four systems of distribution: legal shops, the black market, rationing schemes, and at a later time and closely connected to the rations, relief. Unsurprisingly, the usual market in terms of shops and stores was paralyzed by 1943. Most goods were not available, houses were either destroyed or requisitioned, and people simply could not afford to pay the prices. Furthermore, shopkeepers often suffered at the hand of Allies, who across all ranks, treated the shops as an entitlement. The attitude that now that the war was fought (and won), the country's goods and beauty could be enjoyed, pervades many sources and memoirs of the Allied occupation. Shopkeepers experienced that first hand when Allied soldiers bought, at a too low price, the supply they had available – usually wine.[59] This is partly why the large number of Allied soldiers in Naples was a burden. On top of those who were on regular duty in Naples, there were troops that arrived to reinforce the battle lines, worn out soldiers on convalescent leave, soldiers from all parts of Allied Italy visiting the city, and the future AMG staff for Rome which, among other things, trained some 3,000 Carabinieri waiting for their mission in Rome.[60]

So when the legitimate markets often broke down or became unaffordable, people desperately – and logically – turned to the emerging black market. This was the most visible and damning symbol of a misguided Allied food policy. It would be a mistake though to confuse the existence of the black market with the arrival of the Allied troops. Rather, a black market arose in Naples beyond any control in 1937, as many farmers hoarded their wheat and thereby undermined a compulsory legislation (*ammassi*) introduced by the fascist regime a

57 William I. Hitchcock, *Liberation. The Bitter Road to Freedom, Europe 1944–1945* (London: Faber and Faber, 2009), 215-248; Marvin Klemme, *The Inside Story of UNRRA. An Experience in Internationalism. A First Hand Report on the Displaced People of Europe* (New York: Lifetime Editions, 1949).

58 Public Relations Branch of Allied Commission, *Review*, 36ff.; Daniel Lerner Collection, Box 22, Hoover Institution Archives.

59 See for instance The Newberry Libary, Chicago, John Lardner Papers, Box 0, Chicago. Many Allied sources and accounts tell of Lucullan feasts in requisitioned villas. See also Lewis, *Naples '44*, 26.

60 Public Relations Branch of Allied Commission, *Review*, 30.

year earlier.[61] Even before the Allied invasion, families spent forty percent of their food budget on black market products.[62] The occupation all but aggravated this situation so that for those who could afford it, and who had no agricultural contacts, the black market was often the only viable option to get fed. In order to have the money to do so, Neapolitans sold their rare possessions just to be able to buy food. This, in turn, boosted the black market as more and more diverse items became available.[63] It invited speculation as it "could make a man rich overnight, while the bulk of the city population subsisted on a little black bread and dried pea soup."[64] Also, it led to a makeshift creativity: "Nothing, absolutely nothing that can be tackled by the human digestive system is wasted in Naples," wrote Norman Lewis in his famous account of his time as intelligence officer in Naples. He told stories of children prizing limpets off the rocks at the coast to sell them while also mentioning, only half-jokingly, that the cat population was considerably reduced.[65]

Most people engaged one way or another in the black market. Even those who qualified for rations usually had to buy supplementary food there as the rations were by no means enough. The rationing system carried the most obvious political implications since it enabled Neapolitans to directly compare living under Allied occupation with the experience under Fascism, even if only by means of their growling stomachs. Having a ration card meant being entitled to a diet provided by the Allies or authorities under Allied command. Because of the low rations, and exploiting the organizational mess during the occupation, most Neapolitans possessed many more ration cards than they could lay claim to. While within the rationing system there were many differences (dependent on whether somebody was a heavy worker, a mother, homeless etc.), more notably perceived were the varying rations from region to region. This made perfect sense considering that some of these regions were under different phases of military government and administered by different bodies. Yet it helped to spur envy and claims of discrimination. This was especially true for the South where the regional identity always triumphed over allegiance to the state and whose regional identity now considerably forged ahead. It did not

61 While the quota envisaged 95% of the harvest brought to public storages, it was estimated that for Campania less than 16% were actually delivered. See Nützenadel, "Dictating Food", 99-100.

62 Ibid.

63 Charles Poletti papers, Rare Book and Manuscript Library, Columbia University Library, Box 19, Report for February 1944

64 Quoted in David W. Ellwood, *Italy 1943–1945* (Leicester: Leicester University Press, 1985), 64.

65 Lewis, *Naples '44*, 15.

go unnoticed when Sicilians received 300 grams of bread early on (although it had to be reduced later) whereas Campanians got only 125 by December 1943.[66]

The argument worked the other way around too, however. Since the Italian South got a 300 gram ration by 1 July 1944, the Romans likewise demanded the same for them. Since they were not getting it, many Romans went out into the countryside to collect and buy whatever they could get their hold on – which in turn impeded the situation in Naples.[67] This group, checking the area around Naples for food, was only one of the new groups of people. Former Allied prisoners of war, of which only some of them reported to military units, while others decided to elude the war and remained with their newly made Italian friends, were present in the theater of war, as were Italian soldiers who were either able to make it back from the deployment in Greece or Albania for example or simply went home.[68] Similarly, Italian soldiers who could elude deportation to Germany as forced foreign workers were to be found in Campania.[69] The already mentioned arriving soldiers who would reinforce the battle lines were likewise an ever present occurrence in the winter of 1943/44. Because their arrival gained center stage with regard to supply for obvious military reasons, it further strained relations between locals and the Allies as the soldier's supply came at the expense of the locals. The number of war refugees rose as well; rumors spread about potential new beachheads established by the Allies and as a consequence surges of people moved to the alleged areas. Naples was full of refugees and during the month of November its number increased from 100 to 550 a day; until the end of 1943, some 30,000 new refugees would arrive in Naples.[70] Yet another group of people coming to the city were those living in villages nearby which found themselves now particularly cut off from any supply lines. Here it should suffice to draw attention to the transport means, or rather the lack thereof which basically prevented Allies

---

66 ACS, Ministero dell'Interno, Direzione Generale, Pubblica Sicurezza, Divisione Affari Generali e Riservati, Governo del Sud, Brindisi, 1943–1944, Busta 1. Report by Comando del Corpo d'Armata di Campania, December 21, 1943.

67 Public Relations Branch of Allied Commission, *Review*, 52.

68 See Roger Absalom, "Hiding History: The Allies, the Resistance and the Others in Occupied Italy 1943–1945," *The Historical Journal* 38:1 (1995), 111-131.

69 Overall, some 600,000 Italian soldiers were brought as forced laborers to Germany after the downfall of Mussolini and the armistice. See Ulrich Herbert, *Hitler's Foreign Workers: Enforced Foreign Labour in Germany under the Third Reich* (Cambridge: Cambridge University Press, 1997), 282-283.

70 Absalom, "Hiding History", 114-115.; Charles Poletti papers; Box 19; Rare Book and Manuscript Library, Columbia University Library. Report for February 1944, 10. Poletti remarked: *Refugees were handled under conditions little better than conditions under which cattle are handled at home.*

from getting food to these villages and left people with no other option than going to Naples, deprived of housing, clothes, and food.[71] This transformed the urban-rural relation: whereas rural Campania normally provided for its larger urban centers food-wise, this affiliation was turned upside down at that moment. It was now Naples that provided for the whole area, at least in theory, due to its pivotal port. Besides the supply organized by the army, cargoes from relief organizations such as American Relief for Italy or later UNRRA arrived there.[72] The port was notorious for its corruption where goods ended up on the black market almost the moment they arrived.[73] All of this led to a situation that was impossible to handle: While Naples was always a crowded place, the ongoing influx of people with their specific needs, at a time when the military campaign was not advancing, posed major obstacles.

While the problems with supply and the challenge of the crowds of people were to a great extent imponderable, other factors that contributed to the chaotic scenery were due to the military government's own actions. Initially, Proclamation No. 8 ensured that the present system of rationing and prices remained in force which soon tempered the rhapsodical atmosphere which the Allies encountered upon their entering the city.[74] Here again, it was fallacious to bank on Italian food stocks to regulate prices: the strategy envisaged to make food supplies available as necessary through local facilities under rigid controls to bring about a stabilization of prices.[75] The problem was that there was neither a sufficient food supply nor local facilities to distribute it. And even if stocks of food and transport had been available, the problem of electricity in the first days of occupying new cities loomed large, as it prevented flour mills from running for example.[76] In fact, when the mills started operating, it came at the expense of providing lighting and thereby literally creating dark zones that further enabled the black market exchanges, not to mention the way it facilitated crime and harbored a general feeling of unease. The original mistake of Allied food policy was then the issue of prices which did not

71 Lewis, *Naples '44*, 79.

72 By September 1944, UNRRA gave help to children and mothers while generally providing medical aid to the population. See UNRRA Program in Italy (October 9, 1945), in: Department of State Bulletin, Vol. 13, No. 329, October 14, 1945 Washington: US Government Printing Office, 1945). For American Relief for Italy see TNA, WO 204-9778, American Relief for Italy.

73 Public Relations Branch of Allied Commission, *Review*, 19-20.

74 Testimony by a British war correspondent's account upon entering Naples. Imperial War Museum London, Naples: Allied entry, October 1, 1943, Catalogue Number 1371.

75 TNA, WO 220-257, A.M.G. American and British division of responsibilities.

76 See TNA, WO 220-291, Preliminary survey of civilian position in occupied territory.

meet day-to-day realities at all.[77] For instance, the Allies would pay 500 Lire for grain per quintal until November 1943, when they lowered the payment.[78] Not surprisingly, most wheat found its way on the black market instead where prices of more than 2,000 Lire could be expected. So while the Allies constantly underpaid Italian farmers, prices on the black market were in turn incredibly high: 100 Lire had to be paid for fish or pasta and 2,000 Lire for shoes.[79] This amounted to the fivefold monthly pay of an average police man (*Carabinieri* earned 400 Lire in late 1943 a month) who, in a sort of irony, had to prevent crime and control the black market among his chief tasks. This encapsulated where Allied occupational policy went wrong.

All this must have deeply resonated with Italians who gradually experienced the Allied arrival not as the liberation it certainly was. Yet it was also an occupation, making clear that first of all this was necessary to set the reconstruction of law and order in motion again. While Allied and Italian relations under the occupational regime were always described as very good, the closer monitoring of the food situation casts doubt on these statements.[80] Rather they seemed to serve a mutual benefit. For the Americans, it assured them that they were *good* occupiers. It likewise enabled Italians to strike a good tone to prepare their re-entry on the world stage. Food politics all but put a strain on these relations. It might have carried additional weight as it came at a time when people were in disarray. After the short transitional period between 25 July 1943 (fall of Mussolini) and 9 September 1943 (announcing of short armistice), spirits changed.[81] When at first the armistice put the Badoglio government and the Allies into crosshairs and likewise caused a re-emergence of Fascists, both in reputation and in visibility (as movements like the *L'Uomo Qualunque* would lay credence too) the Allied food politics after October 1943 only seemed to reinforce these feelings.[82] Cynically put, it must have struck a chord with Southern Italians. After more than twenty years of Fascism, which

77 ACS, Ministero dell'Interno, Direzione Generale, Pubblica Sicurezza, Divisione Affari Generali e Riservati, Governo del Sud, Brindisi, 1943–1944, Busta 1. Report by Comando del Corpo d'Armata di Campania, December 21, 1943. See also NARA, RG 331, 10260-143-67, Box 4821; Paolo de Marco, *Polvere di Piselli. La vita quotidiana a Napoli durante l'occupazione alleata (1943–1944)* (Naples: Liguori Editore, 1996).

78 Later the price would rise again to combat inflation. See Ellery W. Stone Papers, Box 3, Hoover Institution Archives. Report by the Allied Anti-Inflation Committee, June 19, 1944.

79 LoC, Maurice Neufeld Papers, Box 1, Diary Entry from January 6, 1944.

80 See for instance the report mentioned in footnote 82.

81 Joshua Arthurs, "Settling Account: Retribution, Emotion and Memory during the Fall of Mussolini," *Journal of Modern Italian Studies* 20:5 (2015), 631.

82 ACS, Ministero dell'Interno, Gabinetto, Fase Permanenti, Relazioni dei Prefetti e dei Carabinieri 1944–1946, 1950-52, busta 198. Comando Generale dell'Arma dei Carabinieri Reali, monthly report for October 1945, November 6, 1945.

amongst other things promised a system of autarky when in fact people were starving well before 1943 and rations were consistently shortened, the Allied arrival offered the proverbial glimmer of hope.[83] Yet their inability to substantially change the food situation, indeed deteriorating it for the most part, also made people question the advantages of living under Allied occupation when living under the fascist regime was not so bad after all.[84] After all, fascism was mostly loathed for its system of privilege and patronage but rarely for its ideological impositions or the suppression of civil liberties.[85]

In this regard, the transference of authority over most of Southern Italy in February 1944 to the Badoglio Government passed the blame onto the Italians. Turning it over into Italian hands also meant considerably reducing the Allied organizations which were until then the biggest local employers. This led to a huge increase in unemployment which in turn exacerbated the inability to buy food on the black market. Then again the whole politics of food could also work the other way around. Maurice Neufeld reported that the Communist Party at least partly derived its huge surge in membership due to the allocation of food as relief (clothes and food) was distributed from the local party headquarters and people got more relief when they signed up in the Communist Party.[86] By May 1944, however, the food situation was improving and June 1944 saw the military breakthrough with the taking of Rome. Soon Italy was faced with another kind of problem: re-entry into the world of nations and infrastructural reconstruction while in the United States the debate over relief gained pace; these were however comfortable problems to have compared with the situation in Naples between October 1943 and the first half of 1944.[87]

Conclusion: The Legacy of Food and Occupation

The eventual success of the Italian Campaign should not obscure the fact that it was anything but a well-organized military venture. The rather impromptu decision to conduct the campaign thwarted any long-range, thorough planning.

---

83 Morgan, *Fall of Mussolini*, 60-71.

84 See for instance the nutrition report of school children in a school in Naples which according to Charles Poletti *exposed conditions that caused anxiety*. Charles Poletti papers; Box 19; Rare Book and Manuscript Library, Columbia University Library. Report for February 1944, 8.

85 Arthurs, "Settling Account," 629.

86 See LoC, Manuscript Division, Maurice Neufeld Papers, Box 1. Diaries entry from March 5, 1944.

87 Italy had "worked her passage" as Ellery Stone would argue. TNA, WO 204-420, H.Q. Allied Commission and United States Political Adviser, Stone to Supreme Allied Commander, June 23, 1945.

This was even exacerbated when Mussolini was pushed out and the Allies faltered in their quest to reach Rome. This had devastating effects on the occupational procedures in Naples too. Here, the campaign that arrived at a dead stop coincided with the logistical nightmare of having to feed overwhelming and diverse categories of populations while at the same time preventing unrest, fighting the black market and coping with all the soldiers, politicians, and war correspondents who would arrive with each day in bigger numbers in Naples.

With regard to a culture of remembrance, the chapter's topic did not find entry into the city's rich folklore and memory. The shortage of food and the catastrophic supply situation were remembered as part of a period of ongoing suffering; by virtue of this generalizing memory, the different developments from living under the fascist regime to the German occupation all the way to the Allied occupation – which only partly is remembered as such – became obscured. To celebrate the proud history of the city, the famous four days of Naples (*Quattro giornate di Napoli*) became a rallying point.[88] While they accurately refer to the popular uprising at the end of September 1943 that ousted the *Wehrmacht* from the city and thereby enabled the Allied armies to enter Naples without much fighting, it also served a higher political purpose to remember this event. It emphasized the fact that Southern Italy developed and experienced forms of resistance to the German invader as well.[89] This way the four days could register in the nation's celebration of the *Resistenza* and fuel the topos of the Italian liberation of mainland Italy, an identifying anchor which cannot be underestimated for its significance in building a post-war Italian identity. Moreover, highlighting the four days helped to thrust the memory of the Allied occupation aside. Because after all, it was precisely that: a liberation from Nazi dominion and occupation of Italian territory at the same time. Yet this memory got reduced to the Allied soldier who brought *cioccolata* and flowers upon entering liberated cities. While this was true for the first day or two, the subsequent situation, oftentimes worse than before, was forgotten and oppressed. It was particularly in cities where the initially good relations between occupiers and the occupied deteriorated. Soldiers soon vented their frustration over the stalemate in the campaign on the local population by committing crimes like sexual assault or stealing the little food the locals had available for themselves. Others seemed to enjoy the riches the city provided for its top military personnel as far as food, accommodation and general life-style was concerned. All that was plainly visible to the local population and this

88 See Luigi Longo, *Un popolo alla macchina* (Milan: Mondadori, 1947).

89 On that, see also the contributions in Enzo Fimiani, ed. *La partecipazione del Mezzogiorno alla Liberazione d'Italia (1943–1945)* (Florence: Le Monnier, 2016).

dynamic could only unfold in cities like Naples where enough soldiers were stationed and relations between locals and soldiers were somehow bureaucratized. While in little villages, many problems could usually be directly solved with the respective Civil Affairs Officer, oftentimes the only person on site, the situation in cities was different as evidenced by the seemingly endless breadlines outside of town halls. In the end, Naples might have presented the biggest challenge to military government throughout the Italian Campaign whereas Sicily was initially considered "*the golden age of AMG in this war*" and the occupation of Rome was termed "the smoothest in military government history."[90]

Strikingly enough, the Allied occupation of Italy inscribed itself also in some remarkable continuity to fascist policies: the promise of restoring law and order and food riots might have been all too reminiscent for the older generation that could remember the Fascist's battle cry in their quest for power in 1922. After all, Fascism too promised to reestablish law and order, albeit under different auspices, after the years before had seen food riots amongst other things (*biennio rosso*). More tangible, the adoption of the policy of collecting wheat and thereby upholding the despised *ammassi* system showed how little understanding the Allies had of the Italian situation.[91] Whenever it came to notable uprisings, which were usually grounded in the protest against Allied supply politics, they were usually understood by the Allies as militarily inspired.[92] The bigotry of the military policymakers and their myopia prevented the Allies from gaining more accurate insights into the nature of Italian society and life. Apparently, it never crossed their minds that their auspicious propaganda that promised increased food rations was taken at face value and raised expectations; the actual Allied policy must have therefore proved to be especially disappointing and provoking an angry reaction. Nothing gave more proof than the Italian dictum written on walls and shouted in the streets: "Dear Poletti: less talk, more Spaghetti!".[93]

---

90 See LoC, Manuscript Division, Maurice Neufeld Papers, Box 6. Correspondence, 1919–1990, Family, Neufeld, Hinda Cohen (wife), April-June 1944. Maurice Neufeld to Hinda Neufeld, June 18, 1944; Public Relations Branch of Allied Commission, *Review*, 41.

91 While changing the name to *Granai del Popolo* (grain of the people), the system remained in force until the Allies left Italy. See the Cereal Ammassing Report by the UNRRA's Italian Mission office from May 1947, Stanley Andrews Papers, box 1, Truman Library.

92 See Patti, "Il Pane Americano", 33-34.

93 Clare Boothe Luce, member of the House of Representatives and by 1953 ambassador to Italy, recited this wrongly upon the return from her visit to Italy in late 1944, when she said: "less Poletti, more Spaghetti." It might have also been an ill-concealed attack by the outspoken Republican representative on the equally outspoken liberal progressive Poletti. "Mrs. Luce says Administration lets Italy down," *New York Herald Tribune*, January 4, 1945.

While the article showed that this deteriorating situation was not the result of any ill-intended Allied policy, but rather found its origins in logistical and political shortcomings, concerns over Allied food policy were never really voiced in hindsight. After all it would have meant to inquire much more into the reasons for, and nature of, the Allied occupation in the first place and thereby run the risk of having to come to terms with a past that contained some uncomfortable truths supplanted by antifascism, *Resistenza* and the liberation of Italy. So without labeling the Allied occupation of Italy one way or another, it should be obvious that it is a particular case; ultimately choosing an appropriate description means more often than not reasoning from a political standpoint instead of a historical one.

Yet future research should not be discouraged by that. Dynamic definitions should consider that occupation is a phenomenon which is always negotiated and brokered *in situ*. An empirical study of the Allied occupation of Italy must hence take the supratemporal and ubiquitary definitions of the Army Field Manuals or other texts into account not so much as a fixed entity but as a starting point for investigating the curious case of occupations as a transitional phase between war and peace. It might be questionable to offer any remarks on how it should have been done with the benefit of hindsight. But one starting point might be to look closer at the occupational policies as they were formulated in Washington and London and subsequently enacted, modified or refused by local military government personnel. In the end, the success of military government might well come down to the question of how much power and independence these local officers were granted for making rapid decisions.[94] The top-down army structure as the central actor for not only making military but also political decision looms large here.

But then again we may also say that by the end of the war, the Allies had made an astounding contribution to Italian survival: By November 1945 they had brought foodstuff with an overall value of 340,901,318 million dollars to Italy since the onset of occupation.[95] Even more impressive, this happened while the war was going on. That "the soldiers brought inflation, starvation and prostitution to Italy" might be partly right too, but it does not say anything still about the reasons, backgrounds, or contingencies that provoked these issues.[96] For that, studying the occupation, taking both Italian and Anglo-American perspectives into consideration, with a particular regard to the local level, will be crucial.

---

94 See Neufeld, "Failure", 139.

95 See Ellery W. Stone Papers, Box 3, Hoover Institution.

96 Ben Shephard, *Long Road Home*, 43.

Works Cited

Archival Sources

Archivio Centrale dello Stato

Presidenza del Consiglio dei Ministri, 1944–47, Fascicolo 14-5

Ministero dell'Interno, Gabinetto, Fase Permanenti, Relazioni dei Prefetti e dei Carabinieri 1944–1946, 1950–52, busta 198

Ministero dell'Interno, Direzione Generale, Pubblica Sicurezza, Divisione Affari Generali e Riservati, Governo del Sud, Brindisi, 1943–1944, busta 1

Columbia University Library, Rare Book and Manuscript Library

Charles Poletti papers, Box 12, 17, 19, 29, 61

Hoover Institution Archives

Ellery W. Stone Papers, Box 1, 3

Daniel Lerner Collection, Box 19, 22

U.S. Provost Marshal General's Bureau, Box 1

Imperial War Museum London

Naples: Allied entry, 1 October 1943, Catalogue Number 1371

Library of Congress, Manuscript Division

Maurice Neufeld Papers, Box 1, 6

National Archives and Record Administration, College Park

Record Group 331, Box 140, 142, 4123, 4206, 4216, 4821

National Archives in the UK

WO 204-263 A.F.H.Q. move to Italy_organisation of Allied forces.

WO 204-9778, American Relief for Italy_distribution of supplies

WO 220-257, A.M.G. American and British division of responsibilities

WO 220-291, Preliminary survey of civilian position in occupied territory

WO 220-404, Difficulties and defects in military government administration

WO 220-405, American report on A.M.G.

WO 204-420, H.Q. Allied Commission and United States Political Adviser

Truman Library

Stanley Andrews Papers, Box 1

Published Sources

Coles, Harry L. and Albert K. Weinberg. *Civil affairs. Soldiers become Governors.* Washington DC: Office of the Chief of Military History, Department of the Army, 1964.

Department of State Bulletin, Vol. 13, No. 329, 14 October 1945. Washington: US Government Printing Office, 1945.

Engler, Robert. "The Individual Soldier and the Occupation." *The Annals of the American Academy of Political and Social Science* 267 (1950): 77-86.

Fisher, Thomas R. "Allied Military Government in Italy". *The Annals of the American of Political and Social Science* 267 (1950): 114-122.

FM 27-5 War Department. *Basic Field Manual Military Government.* Washington DC: United States Government Printing Office, 1940.

FM 27-10 War Department. *Field Manual. Rules of Land Warfare.* Washington DC: United States Government Printing Office, 1947.

FM 27-5-War Department. *United States Army and Navy Manual of Military Government and Civil Affairs.* Washington DC: United States Government Printing Office, 1943.

Fainsod, Merle. "The Development of American Military Government Policy during World War II", in *American Experiences in Military Government in World War II*, edited by Carl J. Friedrich and Associates, 23-51. New York: Rinehart & Company, 1948.

Friedrich, Carl J. "Military Government and Dictatorship". *The Annals of the American Academy of Political and Social Science* 267 (1950): 1-7.

Hersey, John, A Bell for Adano. New York: Knopf, 1944.

Hill, Robert M. and Elizabeth Craig Hill. *In the Wake of War. Memoirs of an Alabama Military Government Officer in World War II Italy.* University, Alabama: The University of Alabama Press, 1982.

Klemme, Marvin. *The Inside Story of UNRRA. An Experience in Internationalism. A First Hand Report on the Displaced People of Europe.* New York: Lifetime Editions, 1949.

Lewis, Norman. *Naples '44. An intelligence officer in the Italian labyrinth.* London: Eland 1983.

Longo, Luigi. *Un popolo alla macchina.* Milan: Mondadori, 1947.

Neufeld, Maurice F. "The Failure of AMG in Italy". *Public Administration Review* 6, No. 2 (1946): 137-148.

Public Relations Branch of Allied Commission. *Review of Allied Military Government and of The Allied Commission in Italy. July 10, 1943 D-Day Sicily to May 2, 1945 German Surrender in Italy.* Rome: Public Relations Section, US Army, 1945 War Department, *Pocket Guide to Italian Cities.* Washington: U.S. Government Printing Office, 1944.

"Mrs. Luce says Administration lets Italy down", New York Herald Tribune, January 4, 1945

Italian Armistice, 29 September 1943: http://avalon.law.yale.edu/wwii/italy03.asp, article 37

Minutes of Trident Conference: https://eisenhower.archives.gov/research/online_documents/d_day/Trident_Conference.pdf

Published Works

Absalom, Roger. "Hiding History. The Allies, the Resistance and the Others in Occupied Italy 1943–1945," *The Historical Journal* 38, no. 1 (1995): 111-131.

Arthurs, Joshua. "Settling Account: Retribution, Emotion and Memory during the Fall of Mussolini," *Journal of Modern Italian Studies* 20, no. 5 (2015): 617-639.

Atkinson, Rick, *The day of battle: The War in Sicily and Italy, 1943–1944*. New York, Holt: 2007.

Arcidiacono, Bruno. "The dress rehearsal. The Foreign Office and the Control of Italy, 1943–1944," *The Historical Journal* 28, no. 2 (1985): 417-427.

Bayer, Resat. "Peaceful transitions and democracy," *Journal of Peace Research* 47, no. 5 (2010): 535-546.

Bhuta, Nehal. "The Antinomies of Transformative Occupation," *The European Journal of International Law* 16(4) (2005): 721-740.

Buchanan, Andrew. *American Grand Strategy in the Mediterranean during World War II*. New York: Cambridge University Press, 2014.

Carruthers, Susan L. *The Good Occupation*. Cumberland: Harvard University Press, 2016.

Collingham, Lizzie. *The Taste of War: World War II and the Battle for Food*. New York: Penguin, 2012.

D Este, Carlo. *Lo sbarco in Sicilia*. Milan: Mondadori, 1988.

Donnison, F.S.V. *Civil Affairs and Military Government. Central Organization and Planning* London: Her Majesty's Stationery Office, 1966.

Ellwood; David W., *L'alleato nemico. La politica dell'occupazione anglo-americano in Italia 1943–1946*. Milan: Feltrinelli, 1977.

Ellwood, David W. *Italy 1943–1945*. Leicester: Leicester University Press, 1985.

Fimiani, Enzo (ed.), *La partecipazione del Mezzogiorno alla Liberazione d'Italia (1943–1945)*. Florence: Le Monnier, 2016.

Galtung, Johan. *Peace by peaceful means. Peace and Conflict, Development and Civilization*. London et al: Sage, 1998.

Gerlach, Christian. *Kalkulierte Morde: die deutsche Wirtschafts- und Vernichtungspolitik in Weißrußland 1941 bis 1944*. Hamburg: Hamburger Edition, 1999.

Harris, Charles R.S. *Allied Military Administration of Italy 1943–5*. London: Her Majesty's Stationery Office, 1957.

Herbert, Ulrich. *Hitler's Foreign Workers: Enforced Foreign Labour in Germany under the Third Reich*. Cambridge: Cambridge University Press, 1997.

Hitchcock, William I. *Liberation. The Bitter Road to Freedom, Europe 1944–1945*. London: Faber and Faber, 2009.

de Marco, Paolo. *Polvere di Piselli. La vita quotidiana a Napoli durante l'occupazione alleata (1943–1944)*. Naples: Liguori Editore, 1996.

Matusow, Allen J. *Farm Policies and Politics in the Truman Years*. Cambridge: Harvard University Press 1967.

Morgan, Kevin. "Feeding the City: The Challenge of Urban Food Planning," *International Planning Studies* 14, no.4 (2009): 341-348.

Morgan, Philip. *The Fall of Mussolini. Italy, Italians and the Second World War*. Oxford, New York: Oxford University Press, 2010.

Nolfo, Ennio di and Maurizio Serra. *La gabbia infranta. Gli Alleati e l'Italia dal 1943 al 1945*. Bari: Laterza, 2010.

Nützenadel, Alexander. "Dictating Food: Autarchy, Food Provision, and Consumer Politics in Fascist Italy, 1922–1943," in *Food and Conflict in Europe in the Age of the Two World Wars*, edited by Frank Trentmann and Flemming Just, 88-108. London: Palgrave Macmillan, 2006.

Patti, Manoela. "Il Pane Americano. La Politica Alleata degli Ammassi in Sicilia (1943–1945)," *Zapruder* 25 (2011): 26-42.

Patti, Manoela, *La Sicilia e gli Alleati*. Roma: Donzelli, 2013.

Shephard, Ben. *The Long Road Home. The Aftermath of the Second World War*. London: The Bodley Head, 2010.

Steel, Carolyn. *Hungry city: How food shapes our lives*. London: Chatto and Windus, 2008. Stirk, Peter M.R. *The Politics of Military Occupation*. Edinburgh: Edinburgh University Press, 2009.

Tönsmeier, Tatjana. "Besatzungsgesellschaften. Begriffliche und konzeptionelle Überlegungen zur Erfahrungsgeschichte des Alltags unter deutscher Besatzung im Zweiten Weltkrieg," *Docupedia-Zeitgeschichte*, 18 December 2015. https://docupedia.de/zg/Besatzungsgesellschaften.

Trentmann, Frank and Flemming Just (eds). *Food and Conflict in Europe in the Age of Two World Wars*. Basingstoke: Palgrave Macmillan 2006.

Vincent, Charles Paul. *The Politics of Hunger. The Allied Blockade of Germany 1915–1919*. Athens, OH: Ohio University Press, 1985.

van der Zee, Henri A. *The Hunger Winter. Occupied Holland 1944–1945*. Lincoln, University of Nebraska Press, 1998.

Williams, Isobel. *Allies and Italians under Occupation. Sicily and Southern Italy 1943–1945*. London: Palgrave, 2013.

CHAPTER 8

Rebuilding after the Reich: Sacred Sites in Frankfurt, Leipzig, and Wrocław, 1945–1949

Andrew Demshuk

The curse of Hitler ripped asunder the historic interconnectedness of urban spaces that had previously been part of Germany, and imbued their reconstruction with seemingly insurmountable ideological differences. Out of the ashes of the Third Reich, West German Frankfurt am Main was rebuilt as a showpiece of democratic transparency, capitalism, and humanism; East German Leipzig was refashioned along the ideals of socialist utopianism and anti-fascism; and, after the flight and expulsion of Breslau's over 600,000 German residents, Polish Wrocław was reinvented through a nationalist mythology that somehow the city had always been Polish despite a 700-year German "occupation." With such divergent destinies, it can be hard to believe that each of these historic trading cities had been part of the same country before 1945, much less that they could have had anything in common as they were rebuilt under rival regimes. Nonetheless, each city was reconstructed through local discourses that paralleled each other in their need to reinvent a usable past and forge a usable future out of the ruins of the Nazi German catastrophe. Regardless of which city is discussed, political and planning elites encouraged a selective and ideologically inflected memory of the unsavory past through architecture. Where once a Kaiser-era war monument may have stood before a grand historicist Wilhelmine edifice, a sleek modern façade could foretell a better tomorrow; or where bombs had wiped out a Renaissance gable that spoke to local civic pride, a replica might "come back" into being. Through investigating distinctive commonalities that stemmed from this shared quandary, the following analysis weaves all three cities back together into a common narrative across Cold War borders and highlights a corresponding pursuit by civic leaders who firmly believed that, with the right architectural language, they could redeem their society.

* Research for this essay was supported by a grant from the Alexander von Humboldt Foundation. I also wish to thank Rebecca Mitchell for her critical comments, as well as colleagues at talks I gave at CUNY, the Universities of Halle, Wrocław, Amsterdam, and Bremen, the GHI in Washington, and annual GSA and ASEEES conferences.

 | DOI:10.30965/9783657702787_009

After the traumatic ruptures and ignominies of Nazism, the immediate postwar era saw particular obsession with "sacred sites" that might rescue the city and nation.[1] As the first section shows, immediate postwar political and planning elites in all three successor regions expended considerable energy debating and executing the reconstruction of symbolic locations at a time when most residents lacked basic shelter and services, because they believed that the invention of a usable local contribution to a transfigured national story would inculcate a viable worldview for each traumatized populace. The second section furthers this contextualization by surveying how each region's planners and politicians exploited loosened property relations and embraced iconoclastic aesthetics to somehow "master" the moral and material ruins left by Nazism. The successive core sections then expound on how in each city a "sacred site" provoked passionate attention – Frankfurt's Goethehaus, Leipzig's resting place for Johann Sebastian Bach, and Wrocław's "medieval" cathedral island – as a means of fashioning a usable past that could redefine the city's local place in a crystalizing postwar national story. Regardless of how the monumental site was aesthetically realized, the ardent debates that arose around these architectural lynchpins for postwar identity evince three societies equally fixated on reimagining an historic architectural iconography to shape a usable narrative for the city's present and future.[2] As the essay's end gestures, early postwar sacred sites set the stage for each city's parallel urban planning experience through the coming decades.

Sacred Sites in Local and National Mythologies

The urgency with which leaders sought to enthrone their city in a transfigured national narrative was evinced by the considerable energy, resources,

1 For a broader canvas which juxtaposes urban planning quandaries, justifications, solutions, and reactions as they evolved in Frankfurt, Leipzig, and Wrocław throughout the latter half of the twentieth century, see Andrew Demshuk, *Three Cities after Hitler: Urban Reconstruction across Cold War Borders* (forthcoming).

2 My research represents a first major attempt to apply archival and other primary materials to compare urban reconstruction across the trifold division of post-1945 areas of former Weimar Germany. Building on earlier German-German comparisons, in 1987 Klaus von Beyme juxtaposed West and East German cities with some pages on urban spaces in the lost eastern territories. See his *Der Wiederaufbau. Architektur und Städtebaupolitik in beiden deutschen Staaten* (Munich: R. Piper, 1987). Michael Meng has since offered insightful analysis of how in West Germany, East Germany, and Poland synagogues emerged as an abject past few wanted in their new urban future. See his *Shattered Spaces: Encountering Jewish Ruins in Postwar Germany and Poland* (Cambridge, MA: Harvard University Press, 2011).

and "commemorative noise" they poured into choice showpieces at a time when bedraggled postwar survivors still huddled in the rubble.[3] To better understand how locals imagined their immediate past and future in this interim era before each state had crystalized in the late 1940s, Werner Durth and Niels Gutschow have coined the concept of "Träume in Trümmern": a double-sided phrase that implies both "ruined dreams" and "dreaming in ruins."[4] Ruined dreams were evident in the vast urban wreckage, unstable currency, and burden of occupying victorious Allied powers, who requisitioned scarce resources. Each of these harsh realities severely hampered progress toward reconstruction and so left city dwellers with reminders of broken dreams in their daily surroundings. Despite this everyday dreariness, politicians, planners, and the public were enraptured by dreamscapes of their imaginations, wherein gutted façades were perceived as a mutable heritage and singular opportunity to move forward and build a better city for the future – purged of past political and planning mistakes and embedded with uplifting, even utopian symbolic meanings. These dreamscapes centered especially upon what I call *sacred sites*: specific architectural landmarks whose reconstruction might fashion symbolic departure points that could overcome the Nazi catastrophe.[5] Here the application of *national* meanings was selective but essential in all three regions. In Poland's so-called "Recovered Territories," reconstruction took on a strongly triumphal-national flair: once-lauded German national landmarks fell into obscurity or disrepute, while long-neglected sites or fresh archeological digs were embedded with lofty national meanings; Stalinist rhetoric that "national" architecture bespoke proletarian interests (in contrast to historicist "bourgeois" styles under German rule) often gave way to dubious mythologies that certain sites embodied an ancient Polish nation that had never suffered Germanization throughout seven centuries of foreign rule.[6]

Whereas the emphasis on national redemption in Wrocław left little space for global meanings, stronger rhetoric in Frankfurt and Leipzig about a sacred site's global-historical importance was not a conscious attempt to "undo the

3 For early postwar "commemorative noise" about the past, see Rudy Koshar, *Germany's Transient Pasts: Preservation and National Memory in the Twentieth Century* (Chapel Hill: University of North Carolina Press, 1998), 199.

4 Werner Durth and Niels Gutschow, *Träume in Trümmern. Planungen zum Wiederaufbau zerstörter Städte im Westen Deutschlands 1940–1950* (Braunschweig and Wiesbaden: Vieweg, 1988).

5 Spiro Kostof surveys how sacred highlights like domes, towers, and other ritual centers have frequented Europe's cities over time. See *The City Shaped* (Boston et al: Little, Brown and Company, 1991).

6 For the Stalinist view, see Jan Minorski, "Die Baukunst im neuen Polen," *Blick nach Polen* 2:1 (1950), 33-37.

connection between the nation's historical memory and its architectural or urban forms."[7] Rather, an active campaign was waged to *redeem* the nation by infusing key architectural touchstones with usable historical memories. The idea of a German national architecture that dated back to Goethe, Herder, and nineteenth-century romantics had been deeply shaken by the catastrophe of Nazism, but it had not been destroyed. Postwar dreaming was thus dedicated to purging the urban environment of its Nazi past through clean modern forms punctuated by sacred sites that articulated the city's local part in a usable national story that had somehow made the world a better place. As Georg Wagner-Kyora observes in other immediate postwar cases, such projects "had less to do with the worth of the ruins as monuments than the political instrumentalization of history as a divergent chance for identification by German political elites in West and East Germany."[8]

In each city, the herculean cost and effort of fashioning sacred sites was justified by the perception that the very *worldview* of the public was at stake. As Jeffry Diefendorf observes, long before the Nazis took power "architects, planners, and politicians fundamentally agreed that the nature of the built environment largely shaped the behavior of the people living in that environment."[9] The East German Bauakademie gave typical expression to this idea with its motto: "first the person builds the city, then the city forms the people."[10] Formulating this outlook with democratic ideals, the West German Federal Planning Minister preached that "an inner reform of our society, which is one of the most important governmental tasks, is only thinkable through suitable measures in urban planning and its politics" that reflected the democratic will

7 For this view on national amnesia, see Paul Jaskot and Gavriel Rosenfeld, "Introduction: Urban Space and the Nazi Past in Postwar Germany," in *Beyond Berlin*, ed. idem. (Ann Arbor: University of Michigan Press, 2008), 3-4.

8 Georg Wagner-Kyora, ed., *Wiederaufbau europäischer Städte* (Stuttgart: Franz Steiner, 2013), 22, see also 108-109. Contributions in this volume catalogue symbolic energies that went into immediate postwar reconstructions and demolitions across East and West Germany, such as the remaking of the St. Marien church in West German Lübeck as an emblem of victims of aerial bombardments and expulsion from lost German eastern territories in Malte Thießen, "Wiederaufbau zum Sehnsuchtsort: Die Restaurierung der Lübecker Marienkirche als Symbolkirche des 'Deutschen Ostens'," (142-162) and the palace demolition in East German Schwedt in Philipp Springer, "'Machen sie das doch nicht so kompliziert ...'. Der Schlossabriss in Schwedt 1962 und die Zukunftseuphorie in der sozialistischen Industriestadt," (163-177).

9 Jeffry M. Diefendorf, *In the Wake of War. The Reconstruction of German Cities after World War II* (New York and Oxford: Oxford University Press, 1993), 43.

10 Deutsche Bauakademie Berlin, Institut für Städtebau und Architektur, Autorenkollektiv, ed., *Architektur und Städtebau in der DDR* (Leipzig: VEB E.A. Seemann, 1969), 13.

of the public.[11] Or to cast this in a more negative way, Alexander Mitscherlich contended in 1965 that preceding West German modernist planning had *damaged* minds and made society *unhealthy*, concluding: "a literally fatal cycle is shaping our destiny: people fashion their living space in the cities – a field of expression with thousands of facets – but this shape of the city also steadily fashions the social character of the residents."[12] Finally, in western Poland reconstruction had to convince settlers that they were actually living in ancient Polish "Recovered Territories." As party secretary and Minister of the Recovered Territories Władysław Gomułka professed during a visit to Wrocław in 1946, "you return as the lawful possessors of your land, taking it in possession as your ancestral native soil. The Germans could Germanize this land through force and pressure, through centuries of de-nationalization and colonization, but there are no means to Germanize history."[13] Given this profound belief in the urban environment's ability to imprint minds, it is small wonder that early postwar politicians and planners threw such passion into debates about sacred sites and dreamt at length about how to reconfigure the city overall – a process with serious implications in much that was executed after 1949.

Regional-Level Mechanisms for Immediate Postwar Reconstruction

In each coalescing country of the formerly unified state, various degrees of destruction and population upheaval upended preceding property relations and placed redistribution in the hands of the authorities, ensuring top-down control and the promise of "rationalization" on a level previously unimaginable. Considerable top-down direction did not imply Allied intervention, however; although the occupiers monitored what was printed and proclaimed, they seldom intervened in urban planning. Greater constraint on local decision-making came from national leaders, especially in Leipzig and Wrocław, and special priority was given to the historic capital, as for instance West Berlin

11 Bundesminister für Städtebau und Wohnungswesen, *Unsere Städte. Probleme von heute, Lösungen für morgen* (Bad Godesberg: Presse- und Informationsamt der Bundesregierung, Städtebaubericht 1970), 1.

12 Alexander Mitscherlich, *Die Unwirtlichkeit unserer Städte: Anstiftung zum Unfrieden* (Frankfurt/Main: Suhrkamp, 1965), 9.

13 Quoted in Marek Zybura, *Der Umgang mit dem deutschen Kulturerbe in Schlesien nach 1945* (Görlitz: Senfkorn Verlag Alfred Theisen, 2005), 12. See also Władysław Gomułka, "Musimy odnowić kulturę polską," *Głos Ludu* 158 (May 20, 1946), 3.

received one-third of American reconstruction assistance by 1958.[14] Finally, despite differing interpretations on what "reconstruction" was to imply, each region witnessed considerable diversity in stylistic approaches to reconstruction from city-to-city. But ever the need to exhibit a usable past for the present and future compelled considerable investment in planning debates and even funds for the construction of singular sacred sites as post-Nazi urban highlights.

In the Western occupation zones, wealth and property redistribution only differed in extent from that in the Communist regions. From the late 1940s through the early 1950s, money for rebuilding efforts tended to come from an equalization of burdens that included taxes on undamaged property. An August 1947 reconstruction law (Aufbaugesetz) in Lemgo was soon adopted with variations across much of western Germany to allow local authorities to impose five-year bans on building in designated areas (such as old towns) and expropriate private property in the name of the common good – with compensation usually in the form of resettlement. Only by 1955 did the Federal Constitutional Court rule that expropriation which failed to allow for "sufficient" compensation was unconstitutional, undercutting future expropriations (but not undoing those which had already reshaped so many cityscapes).[15] Despite such incursions into private property relations, however, the lack of unified urban planning laws even after the formation of West Germany in 1949 resulted in wide divergences in planning outcomes based upon local choices. While cities like Münster and Nuremberg ultimately adopted more restorative approaches, however, even the most modern cities retained a so-called "reservation for historical monuments" [Denkmalinsel], usually a collection of restored or reconstructed highlights such as the old town hall with a few adjoining buildings – a retreat from the modern city strongly invested with usable symbolic meanings.

In the Soviet Zone, a March 1947 property law paralleled that in the West, allowing for the confiscation and combination of properties to ensure that private interests gave way to the perceived greater good. Under Communism, however, this usually meant that property reverted to the State. Also mirroring the West was the inconsistency in aesthetic and approach in cities across the zone, exacerbated by rival visions about how each new cityscape might embody a usable past. Whereas Weimar's reconstruction fostered a humanist image as

---

14 Jeffry Diefendorf, "America and the Rebuilding of Urban Germany," in *American Policy and the Reconstruction of Germany, 1945–1955*, ed. idem., Axel Frohn, and Herman-Josef Rupieper (Washington D.C.: German Historical Institute and Cambridge University Press, 1993), 334.

15 Diefendorf, *In the Wake of War*, 230-231, 240.

the city of Goethe and Schiller (rather than Nietzsche) and Dresden restored choice monuments and retained symbolic ruins that made it an emblem of German victimhood after Anglo-American "terror" bombing, Chemnitz was ultimately wiped clean of all but a few historic highlights as it was remade into the utopian-socialist metropolis Karl-Marx-Stadt.

Finally, whereas the Nazi catastrophe compelled both German regions of the former *Reich* to select reconstruction narratives that might salvage something from German history, it understandably prompted hatred for German history in Poland, where the Polish nation was elevated as an eternalized victim whose heroic struggle must now be realized through the creation of a homogenous nation-state. The architectural accompaniment for this national motif was problematic, not just because Poland had historically been one of the most heterogeneous states in Europe, but also because the restoration of Polish statehood was accompanied in 1945 by the cession of one-third of Polish territory to the Soviet Union and acquisition of about one-quarter of prewar German territory. While Polish inhabitants were expelled from the East, Poland's Recovered Territories were ethnically cleansed of most German inhabitants and redefined as an eternally national space. Although the Soviets tried to make discussion of Poland's lost eastern territories a taboo, here too the Allied occupiers showed little interest in urban planning, and iconography related to the lost Polish city of Lwów was soon inscribed into Wrocław's postwar urban topography. As Polish authorities dreamt of how to weave an anti-German narrative whilst taking possession of landmarks across formerly German territories, the Polish School of Conservation was founded under General Conservator Jan Zachwatowicz,[16] who argued that willful German eradication of Polish landmarks compelled preservationists to "reconstruct them, rebuild them right from their foundations, to show future generations, at least, exactly what they looked like – the form still alive in our memories and accessible in our records – even if it is not authentic."[17] Warsaw's old town formed the prototype for what Zachwatowicz and his colleagues intended for all of Poland: façades interpreted as nationally Polish were tacked onto fully

16 Zachwatowicz always rejected the idea of a Polish "school," insisting that historical reproductions were simply "good work done by Poles." Tadeusz Polak, "In Memoriam," in *In Memorial Professor Jan Zachwatowicz, 1900–1983*, ed. Jolanta Fajkowska, trans. Charles Vincent (Warsaw: Wydawnictwo Geologiczne, 1983), 25.

17 Jan Zachwatowicz, "The Program and Principles for the Conservation of our Cultural Heritage" (Warsaw, 1946), in *In Memorial Professor Jan Zachwatowicz, 1900–1983*, 5. The longevity of this 1946 tract is proven by its endless citation. See for instance Olgierd Czerner, "The Conservation of Lower Silesian Historic Monuments," *Annales Silesiae* 3 (1966/7), 53.

modern interiors.[18] Indeed, the search for a unified "national" style resulted in just as much stylistic disunity as in each of the German zones of the former Reich. Whereas the creation of a nationally "Polish" style mandated preference for Neoclassical pillars in Warsaw or Renaissance gables in Gdańsk, the Gothic and Romanesque styles won preferential treatment in Wrocław, whose Polish history was said to be "older" than the rest of the country. Such reasoning gave further ideological justification for tearing down Kaiser-era buildings as "foreign" impositions. Polish hatred for Kaiser-era construction was hardly singular, however: planners in both German states spared no aspersions against historicist façade encrustations as unhealthy impediments to the renewing qualities of modern construction.

The Frankfurt Goethehaus

As in Leipzig and Wrocław, Frankfurt's early postwar politicians and planners exchanged monumental dreams in the ruins left from Nazism. Yet while Leipzig was imagined as a cultural mecca and Wrocław as a reborn center of ancient Polish civilization, dreams of future grandeur in Frankfurt were nourished by profound political and economic success, as functions once centered in Leipzig, Breslau, or Berlin moved to the Main metropolis. At the same time that Frankfurt seized much of Leipzig's prewar tradition as a trade-fair city and publishing center, it was rebuilt in no small part by expellees, among them architects informed by cutting-edge modernism pioneered in interwar Breslau. By May 1947, Frankfurt had become the seat of the bizonal administrative offices of the American and British Zones; already the center for bizonal postal services, finance, and military coordination, it became a hub for economic, transit, and agricultural administration. In accelerating discussions about statehood, Frankfurt arose at the top of the list as a suitable, even preferable replacement for Berlin itself. The city's first popularly elected mayor, Walter Kolb (SPD) explained Frankfurt's good fortune, not just due to its central geographical location, but also its international economic reputation and democratic tradition.[19] As Dieter Bartetzko observes, Frankfurt's good fortune

18 For a survey, see Grażyna Ewa Herber, *Wiederaufbau der Warschauer Altstadt nach dem zweiten Weltkrieg: Im Spannungsfeld zwischen denkmalpflegerischen Prinzipien, politischer Indienstnahme und gesellschaftlichen Erwartungen* (Bamberg: Universitätsverlag, 2014), 332.

19 Walter Kolb, "Frankfurts neue Aufgaben," May 19, 1947, Frankfurt Institut für Stadtgeschichte (ISG-Ffm): S6a/577.

destined it to be "the stage for the struggle over the past and the future," not least in debates about reconstructing the Paulskirche and Goethehaus.[20]

By 1948, the city was poised as favorite to become provisional capital of West Germany – and in this context it was essential to demonstrate the city's worthiness as a center of humanism embodied in Goethe and as an emblem of democracy enshrined in the Paulskirche, which had been home to the first liberal German parliament in 1848. In tandem with debates about the Goethehaus, the gutted shell of the Paulskirche was envisioned as the centerpiece in Frankfurt's future as capital of a redeemed German democracy. That the aesthetic language of German salvation was to be modernist was all but assured when Kolb appointed Eugen Blanck as minister for architecture and planning; at once, Blanck staffed city planning offices with fellow colleagues who had been active under the interwar Breslau and Frankfurt modernist Ernst May. Brushing off stiff resistance from local activists, architects favored by this clique stripped away what remained of the structure's neoclassical religious interiors, recrafting it into an austere oval that some critics claimed was reminiscent of Nazi aesthetics. Thus "cleansed" of its historicist décor and divorced from its Protestant community, the Paulskirche was all but complete for the centenary in 1948 to serve as a hallowed commemorative hall for the 1848 parliament. Big dreams that the remade Paulskirche might become a parliament building for a transfigured German state first faltered as it became clear that the structure was simply too small for so grand a purpose, prompting wild construction efforts on a massive rotunda just north of town. Although Bonn's victory as capital foreclosed on that construction site's political destiny (it was later sold to Hessian radio), the sparse Paulskirche lived on as a museum to Frankfurt's inherently democratic identity, underpinned by occasional festivities such as the annual conferral of the Goethe prize.

Modernist success in reconfiguring the Paulskirche exacerbated debates about how to aesthetically pay tribute to the city's worthiness as a center of humanism at the site of Goethe's childhood. As in Wrocław and Leipzig, in Frankfurt it was never debated *whether* something should be done to honor its usable icon, but rather *how*. Should the Goethehaus be rebuilt as it had formerly appeared, should it take new form as a modern museum, or should the site of Goethe's birth be left as a ruin to prove that the loss was irrevocable?

20 Dieter Bartetzko, *Denkmal für den Aufbau Deutschlands: Die Paulskirche in Frankfurt am Main* (Königstein: Langewiesche-Köster, 1998), 41. For comparison of the Goethehaus with post-1989 debates about Dresden's Frauenkirche, see Susanne Vees-Gulani, "From Frankfurt's Goethehaus to Dresden's Frauenkirche: Architecture, German Identity, and Historical Memory after 1945," *Germanic Review* 80:2 (2005), 143-163.

A host of politicians, architects, preservationists, and public figures insisted that any reproduction would be a gross falsification, a pretense that what was gone could ever return. Erasure was a fact of life, and only a monument amid the ruins or a sleek modern museum offered a way forward without grievous moral and aesthetic consequences. On the other side of the debate, vocal local activists, another host of national figures, and above all the Freie Deutsche Hochstift (Independent German Foundation), which owned the site, wanted an historic replica to house the many relics from Goethe's house that Hochstift members had saved from bombardment. After Nazism had sullied so many markers of German identity, was it not healthier to allow this sacred site to return as a sign of what Germans aspired to become?

As with most sacred sites, everyone agreed that Frankfurt's Goethe shrine (whatever its form) had to be completed in time for an anniversary, in this instance the 200th anniversary of the poet's birth. Already upon his tour of the rubble that remained of the Goethehaus in August 1946, Ernst Beutler (head of the Hochstift since 1925) insisted that Goethe's spirit would return within the walls of a copied house.[21] As it became clear in March 1947 that the contemporaneous reconstruction of the Paulskirche was taking place in a largely modern style, Beutler became anxious that Frankfurt's planning offices might use some legal trick to seize the property (as they were seizing the Paulskirche from its community), and he demanded confirmation from the mayor and city building authorities that the Goethehaus would indeed be reconstructed with its former appearance.[22] Disturbed by the city's coyness, he formally presented all of his demands before the city council (Magistrat) when it made its decision on April 19, 1947.[23] And his fears were not entirely misplaced, since none other than Eugen Blanck tried to force an architectural competition; when Beutler ultimately prevailed on grounds that the Hochstift had owned and preserved the house since 1865, Blanck voted against reconstruction with the argument that the city should not approve a project it could not oversee.[24] For all the fervent argumentation on both sides in letters, speeches, and articles, it was ultimately Beutler's ability to retain possession of the Goethehaus as property

21 Kulturamt, "Besichtigung des Goethe-Hauses zusammen mit Herrn Prof. Dr. Beutler," August 16, 1946, ISG-Ffm: Kulturamt 78.

22 Kulturamt an Kolb, "Wiederaufbau des Goethe-Hauses," February 25, 1947, ISG-Ffm: Kulturamt 78; Kulturamt, Vermerk an Herrn Stadtrat Seliger, March 24, 1947, ISG-Ffm: Kulturamt 78.

23 Hans-Reiner Müller-Rämisch, *Frankfurt am Main. Stadtentwicklung und Planungsgeschichte seit 1945* (Frankfurt/Main: Campus-Verlag, 1996), 43-45.

24 Andreas Hansert, *Bürgerkultur und Kulturpolitik in Frankfurt am Main: eine historisch-soziologische Rekonstruktion* (Frankfurt/Main: Kramer, 1992), 217.

Figure 8.1 Max Göllner, Goethehaus, 1945, ISG-Ffm BA S7B 1998/936

of the Hochstift that prevented the city's modernist hegemons from intervening with their plans. As was ultimately the case with the Paulskirche as well as sacred sites in both Leipzig and Wrocław, determination of ownership and thus jurisdiction played a crucial role in the physical outcome, in this case a replica of the original edifice.

Regardless of the aesthetic result, however, impassioned debate had turned the pulverized foundations of Goethe's house into a testing ground for discussing how to confront (or escape) quandaries left by the previous regime and its misdeeds. Arguments that Germany must *redeem* or *salvage* something from the ruins were paralleled by urging that Germany must not *forget* or *falsify* the recent past, and these positions took on aesthetic expression through calls for a modernist museum, an historic reproduction, or a memorial in the ruins.[25] As in Leipzig and Wrocław, debate about this symbolically loaded site awoke passions and forged alliances that cut across political lines and personal pasts.

Responding in part to an appeal from Beutler's Hochstift, waves of letters swamped the mayor's office over the ten days before the city's April 19 decision. Poets, professors, philosophers, and even the university presidents in Frankfurt, Munich, Marburg, and Tübingen urged for restoration of Goethe's house to prove that the best of German culture lived on for future generations. As one writer asserted, a replica would "establish the connection between yesterday and tomorrow" for future generations – skipping over the unspoken Nazi interim.[26] This would serve, a Göttingen editor argued, as "a sign that we have not lost our belief in the German spirit and courage to live on."[27] A letter from Upper Bavaria imbued the discussion with philosophical idealism: "we experience through what we see, through imagination. And certainly here we want to help ourselves to imagine the right thing." Positive memories had to be made visible so that people could embody them. Leaving the site in ruins would be Nazi-style "heroism," he concluded, but a Goethe cult (succeeding the Hitler cult) could enrich the nation: "Goethe lives. He must become more alive in us with each year. To make this easier for ourselves, we have to continue to

---

25 For summary of how "engaged democrats" like Dirks debated the Goethehaus, see Sean Forner, *German Intellectuals and the Challenge of Democratic Renewal: Culture and Politics after 1945* (Cambridge and New York: Cambridge University Press, 2014), 138-145

26 A.P., Frankfurt/Main, April 11, 1947, "Wiederaufbau des Goethehauses – pro und contra," 1954, ISG-Ffm: S1/172, 2112.

27 N., *Die Sammlung*, Göttingen, March 20, 1947, "Wiederaufbau des Goethehauses – pro und contra," 1954, ISG-Ffm: S1/172, 2112.

experience in spirit the atmosphere of Goethe's youth and the consciousness of Goethe's being."[28]

Most letters calling for a replica were careful to add that this exceptional case in no way threatened modernist plans elsewhere. Although he was "no friend of historicist architecture," the director of the Karlsruhe state art museum insisted that "the exception proves the rule, and the exception is the Frankfurt Goethehaus."[29] A Frankfurt writer put it in poignant local terms, insisting: "one naturally thinks about what should happen with the old town, which is dear to us all. It is both materially and ethically impossible to reconstruct it. But the Goethehaus should be an exception, a sample of what once was, of something out of the ordinary, even if it can only have the form of a museum."[30]

Meanwhile, some of Germany's most famous architects, artists, poets, and art historians rejected the very idea of reconstruction. Whereas a replica was somehow "anti-Goethe," one commentator noted, a clean and simple but "monumental" modern structure would be "humble in its exterior scale, just like Goethe himself."[31] A Cologne journalist likewise granted modernism an "ethical" standing opposed to the "petit-bourgeois" desire for imitation, self-deception, and illusion. The sad fate of the Goethehaus was a chance to teach the people, even educated people, "that death is reality. A destroyed Goethehaus is and remains destroyed."[32] Soviet Zone architect Karl Wilhelm Ochs, upheld by his West German colleagues at a Zürich meeting, went so far as to argue that, after decades of "cultural decline" and "lying to ourselves and being lied to," a replica would "lie to us again." The only answer was to "carry through nonetheless to reflectiveness and truth, however painful and full of resignation such a step may be," and construct a modern museum.[33] The most influential letter against a replica came on 18 April 1947 – the afternoon before

---

28 W.M., Murnau/Oberbayern, March 28, 1947, "Wiederaufbau des Goethehauses – pro und contra," 1954, ISG-Ffm: S1/172, 2112.

29 M., Karlsruhe, April 12, 1947, "Wiederaufbau des Goethehauses – pro und contra," 1954, ISG-Ffm: S1/172, 2112. A replicated site, he argued, would give him "courage and hope again for my own work."

30 W.S., Frankfurt/Main, circa April 2, 1947, "Wiederaufbau des Goethehauses – pro und contra," 1954, ISG-Ffm: S1/172, 2112.

31 O.V., Munich, March 26, 1947, "Wiederaufbau des Goethehauses – pro und contra," 1954, ISG-Ffm: S1/172, 2112.

32 H.S., Cologne, March 27, 1947, "Wiederaufbau des Goethehauses – pro und contra," 1954, ISG-Ffm: S1/172, 2112.

33 Karl Wilhelm Ochs, "Goethehaus," in *Der Architekt im Zerreiß-Punkt. Vorträge, Berichte und Diskussionsbeiträge der Sektion Architektur auf dem Internationalen Kongreß für Ingenieurausbildung (IKIA) in Darmstadt 1947*, ed. Ernst Neufert (Darmstadt: Roether, 1948), 171.

the city was to reach its decision – from noted Frankfurt political commentator Walter Dirks, who argued in a published statement *Mut zum Abschied* [Courage to say Goodbye] that the destruction of the hallowed structure had not been some random act of nature, but a direct result of the fascist turn away from Goethe; the only solution, he argued, was to accept the loss as a reality of history.[34] Echoing Dirks, modernist architect Otto Bartning asserted that one had to accept the "truth" of destruction and reject the "lie" of reconstruction: the "spirit" of the house had been forever lost.[35]

The city council's April 1947 resolution in favor of a replica only passed by one vote against speeches citing Dirks and Bartning.[36] Henceforth the storm of discussion actually intensified, so that by November Beutler was citing support from the Goethe Society in Weimar and a host of architects to warn Blanck and city planning office chief Werner Hebebrand away from contravening the council's decision.[37] To explain himself at the consecration of the ruined site three months after the city council decision, mayor Kolb asserted: "we undertook this project as an *allegory* to the original house, as a memorial to the poet and his youth, as a symbol of our faithfulness and devotion to the spirit of Goethe." Germany had "too many graves" already, and thus need not leave Goethe's house "a romantic grave, an unfortunate monument to this unfortunate war." The old town would arise in a "new form," but the sacred site of Goethe's youth was to return as a "call for resurrection and new life."[38] By the formal inauguration of this "national monument to German culture" and "symbol of peace and understanding among the nations" on 10 May 1951 Goethe prize winners such as Fritz von Unruh and Thomas Mann expressed their satisfaction with the structure's restoration, and no less than President Theodor Heuss defended it as far more suitable than the "feeling of frost" that surrounded Goethe's Weimar house under Communist administration.[39]

In fact, the Communist authorities were just as interested in using Goethe as a usable legacy for Weimar as they were in upholding Bach in Leipzig. By 1952,

34 Walter Dirks, "Mut zum Abschied," *Baukunst und Werkform* 2 (1948), 27-28.

35 Otto Bartning, "Entscheidung zwischen Wahrheit und Lüge," *Baukunst und Werkform* 2 (1948), 28-29.

36 Magistrats-Beschluß 60, April 19, 1947, ISG-Ffm: Kulturamt 78.

37 Ernst Beutler an Stadtrat Eugen Blanck, Frankfurt/Main, November 7, 1947, ISG-Ffm: Kulturamt 78.

38 My italics, Walter Kolb, "Weiheakt vor dem Goethehaus in Frankfurt am Main zu Beginn des Wiederaufbaues," July 5, 1947, ISG-Ffm: S6a/577, 3, 1.

39 Walter Kolb, Invitation to the Consecration of the Goethehaus, April 1951, ISG-Ffm: Kulturamt 1.004, 123; Walter Kolb, "Rede zur Weihe des wiederaufgebauten Goethe-Hauses," May 10, 1951, ISG-Ffm: S6a/577; "Goethehaus eingeweiht. In Anwesenheit des Bundespräsidenten," *Frankfurter Neue Presse* (May 11, 1951), 1.

Figure 8.2 Frankfurt Goethehaus, July 2013, Author's Photograph

the communist authorities had seized the ducal mausoleum of Säxe-Weimar for a Goethe and Schiller mausoleum, redesigned with stark, almost fascist aesthetics. The problem with Bach, however, was that history had scattered sites of veneration across Leipzig: which would best embody a symbolic center as Leipzig's most important sacred site?

A Bach Mausoleum for Leipzig[40]

Newly appointed by the Soviets, Leipzig mayor Erich Zeigner and his chief architect Walter Beyer (SPD) at first pursued a reconstruction plan based on historic precedents, in which sweeping new development would be reserved for areas either totally destroyed or previously slated for new construction.[41] As with the sacred sites in Frankfurt and Wrocław, however, political and planning elites were soon at odds in their fantastic dreams about how to architecturally honor Johann Sebastian Bach as Leipzig's symbolic centerpiece. Should

40 For a more extended discussion of Leipzig's Bach Mausoleum affair, see Andrew Demshuk, "A Mausoleum for Bach? Holy Relics and Urban Planning in Early Communist Leipzig, 1945–1950," *History & Memory* 28, no. 2 (Fall/Winter 2016): 47-89.

41 Walter Beyer, "Messestadt Leipzig im Jahre 1948." *Bauhelfer* (Heft 5, 1948): 121.

a grand mausoleum appear in place of a ruined church over Bach's grave on Johannis Square (proposed by Beyer and supported by leading State representatives and preservationists, as well as the Johanniskirche community), or should his body be moved to the Thomaskirche, where the great composer had first performed many of his most famous works and directed the Thomas Boys' Choir (proposed by leading Thomaskirche musicians like Thomaskantor Günther Ramin and Barnet Licht and supported by Mayor Zeigner, as well as the Saxon church). So protracted and bitter did this dispute become that it began to look like nothing would get done for Bach before the 200th anniversary of his death in 1950.

Discussions about moving Bach to the Thomaskirche had already begun under Nazism. Before he was tortured in the Theresienstadt concentration camp, Jewish choir director and Bach admirer Barnet Licht had sent a letter in 1936 to Mayor Carl Goerdeler (before he became an anti-Nazi resistance leader), but Licht and his supporters were denied: Goerdeler declared that Bach would remain in the Johanniskirche "for all time."[42] Then the bombing campaign of 4 December 1943 decimated Johannis Square, so that amid the church's scorched outer walls only the Baroque tower (which dated from the time of Bach) and the crypt containing Bach and Christian Fürchtegott Gellert (a famed Enlightenment poet and teacher of Goethe) remained intact. In August 1945, Beyer protected the crypt from weathering with a cement cover. By the end of the first postwar Bachfest weeks in April 1946, leading citizens of all stripes had offered orations as to why "no German city has such a right to celebrate Bach as Leipzig," and how Leipzig was thus specially positioned to "give expression to its cultural will in the person of Bach in the new Germany."[43]

Fully aware that he could never convince Ramin or Licht, Beyer produced a richly illustrated book filled with models and sketches of his Mausoleum on a reconstructed city plan to potential supporters including the Saxon church, Mayor Zeigner, and the International Bach Society (unaware that Ramin himself had just taken a central position on the Society's executive board).[44] Beyer argued his case to Zeigner in March 1947 with "conviction that it is precisely Leipzig, favored by the Bach question, that should take leadership in establishing a humanitarian course that shows the world that it no longer has to

---

42 Italics added, Kirchenvorstand zu St. Johannis an Goerdeler, October 15, 1936, in Walter Beyer, "Zur Frage eines Bach-Mausoleums in Leipzig," 1947, Stadtarchiv Leipzig (StadtAL) Bibliothek XVIII/131 2410, 12-13.

43 Franz Jost, "Leipziger Bach-Festwochen 1946," StadtAL StVuR 4291, 119.

44 Walter Beyer, "Zur Frage eines Bach-Mausoleums in Leipzig," 1947, StadtAL Bibliothek XVIII/131 2410. Of the twelve copies of Beyer's book, at least those in the Leipzig city archive and German National Library survive.

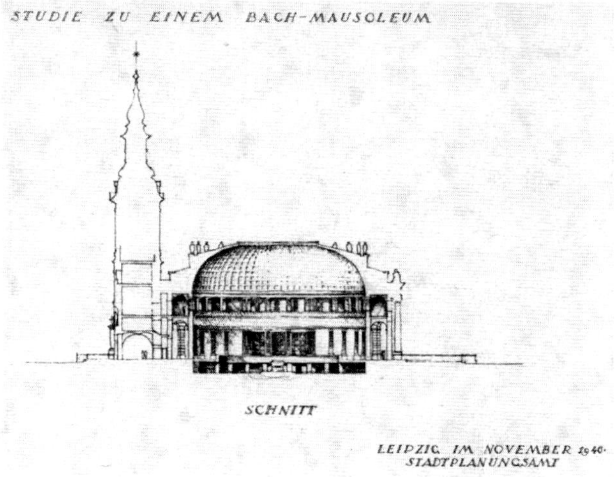

Figure 8.3 Walter Beyer's 1948 plan for a Bach Mausoleum, StadtAL Bibl.2410 Anlage 20

Figure 8.4 Walter Beyer's Plan for a Bach Mausoleum at Johannis Square (center top). A largely intact and restored Karl Marx Square can be seen at the lower center. StadtAL Bibl.2410 Anlage 21b

fear our Volk, because it has learned to respect living harmoniously in the family of nations."[45] Zeigner rejected the Mausoleum plan and campaigned for moving Bach to the Thomaskirche, a position soon supported by the Saxon church. Beyer reacted in an August 1948 internal report to the city council, observing that, for instance, no less than Frankfurt "rebuilt the totally destroyed Goethehaus for the 200th anniversary of J.W. Goethe's birth. Here one sees far-reaching and decisive ways by which a city can take hold of opportunities, not least to raise its reputation, despite all the surrounding deprivations of this difficult time. This would hardly be possible if the remains of J.S. Bach were merely transferred to the Thomaskirche."[46]

Indeed, by retaining Johannis Square as a symbolic highlight in his transfigured cityscape, Leipzig's urban planning head was striving against what he saw as an unnecessary "concentration of all Bach veneration" as proposed by Thomaskantor Ramin in 1946.[47] Leipzig should in fact be sculpted with "two imposing Bach sites," he asserted, which could be further enhanced by renaming Johannis Square the "Bachplatz" and the street by the Thomaskirche as the "Bach Ring."[48] Although the crippling dispute stretched on for another year until the mayor's death in office and Beyer's subsequent replacement with the new chief architect Kurt Brendel in 1949, the decisive moment had already come with the city assembly's vote on 13 October 1948 to move Bach to the Thomaskirche, along with the city's compromise to retain the Johannis tower as "one of the few architectural monuments from the time of Bach … which has indisputably high architectural value for the cityscape."[49] Unfortunately, Bach's departure on 28 July 1949 permanently damaged Johannis Square's legitimacy, and the Johannis tower was torn down despite protest in 1963.[50]

Bach himself, however, prevailed as an emblem of usable identity throughout East Germany. The program for the 250th anniversary of Bach's call to

---

45 Italics in original. Dezernent Bau- und Verkehrswesen Walter Beyer an Herrn Oberbürgermeister Dr. Zeigner, April 9, 1947, StadtAL StVuR 4292, 44.

46 "Bericht an den Rat und die Stadtverordneten zu Leipzig über die vom Dezernat Bau- und Verkehrswesen bisher unternommenen Schritte zur Klärung der Frage über J.S. Bachs endgültige Ruhestätte," August 1, 1948, in "Bachs Grab," StadtAL Bibliothek 2405, 5-6.

47 "Wo soll Johann Sebastian Bach ruhen? Konzentration der Bach-Pflege," *Leipziger Zeitung* (October 10, 1946), in Walter Beyer, "Zur Frage eines Bach-Mausoleums in Leipzig," 1947, StadtAL Bibliothek XVIII/131 2410, 20.

48 Stadtbaurat Walter Beyer, "Wo soll Johann Sebastian Bach Ruhen? Zwei große Bach-Stätten für Leipzig," *Leipziger Zeitung* (October 30, 1946), StadtAL StVuR 4768, 12.

49 Der Rektor der Universität Leipzig an den Oberbürgermeister der Stadt Leipzig Herrn Professor Dr. Zeigner, October 19, 1948, StadtAL StVuR 4292, 152.

50 For a report on the transfer, see Oberbaumeister, "Bericht über die Überführung von Bach und Gellert in die Thomas- bzw. Universitätskirche," August 1, 1949, StadtAL StVuR 4292, 190.

Leipzig in 1973 praised socialist Leipzig's exemplary honoring of the greatest German composer, not least through his already eternalized resting place in the Thomaskirche.[51] By 1977, the Honecker regime praised Bach as "a core piece in the heritage of our Volk's musical culture" to be defended from misreading by Western imperialists.[52] At first honored under a stark cement block designed by former Nazi architect Kunz Nierade, Bach's surroundings in the Thomaskirche evolved into their present, eternalized state in a "cleansing" spree from 1962–1964. Rather than reconstruct Baroque interiors to make the church emulate its condition at the time of Bach, preservationists and architects stripped virtually all intact historicist decorations from the walls to expose barren interiors said to evoke the church's medieval appearance – a fit of iconoclastic streamlining fully in keeping with how all surviving décor was eliminated for the purified "democratic" hall of Frankfurt's Paulskirche and how destruction of post-medieval artifacts "Polonized" brick Romanesque and Gothic churches in Wrocław.

Wrocław as City of the Piasts

Fully intact until the final year of the war, the Silesian capital was all but dead when it finally capitulated – of all the cities inside of Poland's postwar borders, only Warsaw suffered greater destruction. Even after hostilities had ended, a wave of looting and vandalism wrecked much of what remained; many who first came to the new Wrocław only sought loot or temporary shelter before escaping to less damaged hamlets in Poland's new "Wild West" or back "to Poland" across the prewar borders. By 1948, city planner Józef Rybicki complained that, in a city once populated by over 600,000 (nationally unnamed) people, 300,000 now resided in the relative squalor of divided apartments, often without kitchens, making ends meet by bartering plunder (the so-called "*szaber*" economy).[53] In no small part because the city's diverse, mostly Polish inhabitants did not feel at home, politicians and planners worked hard to build modern facilities

51 "Textprogramm für 11. März sowie 4./5. Mai," 1973, StadtAL StVuR 22145, 84-85.

52 Gehrke, Rat der Stadt Leipzig, Abteilung Kultur, "Konzeption zur Schaffung der Nationalen Forschung- und Gedenkstätten Johann Sebastian Bach Leipzig," August 15, 1977, StadtAL StVuR 986, 60-65.

53 Dyrektor Inz. J. Rybicki, "Sprawozdanie z wyniku działalności Wrocławskiej Dyrekcji Odbudowy w czasie od 1945 r. do 1948 włącznie," (Archiwum Państwowe we Wrocławiu (APWr) WDO 239, 45-46. Gregor Thum also discusses the szaber economy in *Uprooted: How Breslau Became Wrocław during the Century of Expulsions* (Princeton, NJ: Princeton University Press, 2011), 129-135.

and invent sacred sites that inspired the people to dream with them in the ruins about a hopeful future and proud past. Otherwise, the people would vote with their feet and leave, and Poland might lose its claim to the once-German metropolis – an added pressure absent in Frankfurt and Leipzig.

In keeping with official perspectives that invention of an eternally Polish Wrocław would facilitate appropriation, leading planner Emil Kaliski declared in 1946 that architects and planners had to reconstruct a city more Polish than Cracow by restoring medieval monuments that embodied "the city's Polish birth certificate."[54] In his influential monograph on Breslau's postwar transformation into Wrocław, Gregor Thum goes so far as to identify a "sacralization of Gothic," which architects and planners embraced at the expense of other styles, because it would harken to the Piast dynasty that had once ruled the city.[55] Nonetheless, the national use of style was too malleable to be circumscribed to Gothic alone: this was a sacralization of anything that could be salvaged for the nation. Restoration highlights ultimately included the Romanesque St. Martin chapel, Renaissance gables on the market, the Baroque University, and the Neoclassical Opera. Hardly a brick Gothic Disneyland, reconstruction of the particularly symbolic "Piast" Cathedral Island included allocation of 708,464 zloty to renovate the bishop's palace in 1946, even though it was a "neoclassical building from 1794." Due to its "character as an historic monument," this landmark was given a faithful restoration.[56] The fad of stripping away ornamentation to expose bare brick was also fundamentally modern and in keeping with trends in each German state. Responsible for the Polonization of numerous inner-city landmarks, Marcin Bukowski chose to strip interwar stucco from the Wrocław town hall façade to expose "medieval" brick that often included modern bricks harvested from other ruins.[57]

Perhaps the most profound sacred site for the newly Polish city was its war-ravaged cathedral, whose 1946–1952 restoration Bukowski felt had offered "a testing ground, in which the Wrocław chapter of the Polish school of conservation formed, and the first group of young architects and conservators took shape" to build an edifice so Polish that it "inherently reminds one of the Wawel cathedral" in his native Cracow.[58] Indeed it was fortunate, Bukowski observed in 1948, that "by a happy chance the bare walls and the towers with their spires

54 Quoted in Thum, *Uprooted*, 327.

55 Thum, *Uprooted*, 363, 331-333.

56 Inż.Arch. Marcin Bukowski, "Kosztorys," October 7, 1946 APWr WDO 126, 38.

57 A full description of the renovation is offered in Marcin Bukowski and Mieczysław Zlat, *Ratusz Wrocławski* (Wrocław: Zakład Narodowy Ossolińskich, 1958).

58 Marcin Bukowski, *Katedra Wrocławska* (Wrocław: Ossolineum, 1974), cover. Bukowski insisted that his Wrocław restorations were reminiscent of Cracow throughout his career.

blown away have revealed the Gothic construction of the church, which shows its light, though monumental and even severe outline."[59] As in Leipzig and Frankfurt, contestation about *how* to restore this sacred site emerged when provincial conservator Jerzy Güttler assailed Bukowski on archeological excavations he felt failed to meet conservation standards. Having "learned in secret from bystanders" that Bukowski had ordered a dig to expose the cathedral's Romanesque foundations, Güttler asserted that, although national "research of this sort is essentially valid," it was "being technically undertaken in a half-dilettantish manner, without proper scientific controls, just to get a quick result."[60] To Güttler's concerns, Bukowski protested that he was merely checking on the state of the cathedral foundations.[61]

Figure 8.5 Wrocław Cathedral, 1955, Sammlung Stefan Arczyński, Herder Institut Bildarchiv (HI-BA) 148712

See for instance his *Wrocław z lat 1945–1952: zniszczenia i dzieło odbudowy* (Warsaw: Państwowe Wydawnictwo Naukowe, 1985), 44.

59 Marcin Bukowski, "The Restoration of the Architectural and historical monuments of Wrocław," in *Lower Silesia and the City of Wrocław*, ed. Silesian Institute Branch in Wrocław (Wrocław: Drukarnia Uniwersytetu i Politechniki we Wrocławiu, 1948), 51.

60 Urząd Wojewódzki Wrocławski Wydział Kultury i Stuki do Naczelnej Dyrekcji Muzeów i Ochrony Zabytków w Warszawie, "Dotyczy sprawy badania stanu fundamentów w katedrze we Wrocławiu," November 19, 1947, APWr UWW XVII/101, 189.

61 Urząd Wojewódzki Wrocławski Wydział Kultury i Stuki do Naczelnej Dyrekcji Muzeów i Ochrony Zabytków w Warszawie, November 21, 1947, APWr UWW XVII/101, 190.

However, no one disputed that the cathedral imbued Wrocław with deep national significance. Years later, Bukowski decreed that, by restoring the cathedral of the Piasts, they had "demonstrated our vitality and our commitment to be the capital of Lower Silesia and the Western Territories."[62] As a local pastor declared in 1955, the people of Wrocław not only struggled to save their churches after the war for religious services, but also because they were "documents of the Piast past." Thanks to state investment, the restored cathedral was said to "exude reverence for Wrocław's historical past and convey an impression of the strength and moral resolve of our nation, which in its common efforts is able to reawaken old forms in order to fill them with new meaning."[63] No less than Cardinal Stefan Wyszyński, a leading regime opponent and figure behind the letters of reconciliation between German and Polish bishops at the Second Vatican Council, gave a fiery nationalist sermon at Wrocław cathedral in 1965 celebrating that the building's "stone relics, marvelous signs of the past, tell us: we were here, and we are here again. We have returned to our ancestral house." Calling from the walls, from the bones in the crypt, these stones spoke to them "in our mother tongue," entreating everyone that, "when we see this Piast house of God, when we listen attentively to its language, we know for sure that this is no German inheritance. It is the Polish soul."[64] In particular for his commentary that Poland had at long last returned to its lost territories, Pope John XXIII was honored with a monument on the island in 1968. Symbolic appropriation of the Odra islands continued even after major landmarks had been reconstructed by the early 1950s, such as when the medieval foundations of the Piast fortress were rebuilt knee-high and the shattered Romanesque church of St. Martin was bricked back together as though it had always been the vanished fortress chapel. Meanwhile, the cathedral's Piast makeover continued through the 1960s, ultimately with the addition of Gothic spires in 1991, which conservator Edmund Małachowicz admitted were based upon his own fantasies.[65]

Finally, as with Goethe and Bach, dead personages of the Piast era also had to be architecturally repositioned to serve postwar narratives. By 1968–1970, Małachowicz pieced together a brick Gothic/poured cement Piast Mausoleum in the basement of the St. Clara and Hedwig cloister out of fragments from Piast gravestones that included the sarcophagus of Wrocław's last Piast duke.[66]

62 Marcin Bukowski, *Katedra Wrocławska* (Wrocław: Ossolineum, 1974), 73.

63 Jan Puzio, "Wir bauen die Kathedrale auf," *Union Pressedienst* (November 11, 1955), 23.

64 Quoted in Zybura, *Der Umgang mit dem deutschen Kulturerbe in Schlesien nach 1945*, 15.

65 Piotr Kuroczyński, *Die Medialisierung der Stadt. Analoge und digitale Stadtführer zur Stadt Breslau nach 1945* (Bielefeld: Transcript, 2011), 93.

66 Edmund Małachowicz, *Stare Miasto we Wrocławiu: Rozwój urbanistyczno-architektoniczny zniszczenia wojenne i odbudowa*, 2nd ed. (Warsaw and Wrocław: Państwowe Wydawnictwo Naukowe, 1985), 171.

Asserting that Germans had deliberately destroyed the ashes of the Piast family in the preceding Baroque mausoleum, a 1970 description praised Małachowicz for putting back "the lost tombs of the Piast princes," as this offered "valuable material for studying the history of this land."[67] As former preservationist Janusz Przyłęcki recalled in 2012, the mausoleum was Małachowicz's "personal work" and, in service of official propaganda, one of the greatest Piast "mementoes."[68] It was a place where generations of local schoolchildren came to venerate the empty graves of their imagined national ancestors, in much the same way that they paid their respects at Goethe's reconstructed birthplace or set flowers before Bach's new final resting place. Pilgrimages to each sacred site imbued them with an air of unchanging eternity, authenticity, and sanctity: assets all in short supply for cities and nations whose topography had been cursed by the Nazi catastrophe.

Figure 8.6 Wrocław Piast Mausoleum, October 2011, Author's Photograph

67 Lesław Kaliński, "Cenne odkrycie we Wrocławiu. Mauzoleum Piastów w średniowiecznej kaplicy," *Express Wieczorny* (March 14, 1971), HI-PAS P0385.

68 Elżbieta Grodzka, interview with Janusz Przyłęcki, September 28, 2012, Archiwum Ośrodka Pamięć i Przyszłość (AOPP) AHM 350.

Conclusion

Looking back in 1975, Wrocław preservationist Waldemar Łysiak rhetorically asked why Polish settlers had devoted such attention to restoring monuments in a formerly German city. His answer – to show that Hitler's barbarism against centuries of European culture would not triumph – could just as easily have come from a figure in Leipzig or Frankfurt.[69] Through their parallel obsession with identity and memory, immediate postwar debates about sacred sites reveal a common post-Nazi story under three divergent states and societies. In each immediate postwar city, lofty dreams arose in answer to the comparable dilemma of how to rebuild from the same ruins. Sacred sites offered a means for political and planning elites to forge a new and usable local identity for a revised national narrative after Hitler's barbarism. Very often the site was related to venerating a dead body (Leipzig's Bach Mausoleum or Wrocław's Piast crypt) or perhaps its spirit (Frankfurt's Goethehaus).[70] On time for a key anniversary, the sacred site was to be upheld as an ideal representation of the transfigured urban self-image.[71] In many respects, this era of greatest disorientation was also that of greatest public optimism and good-will, when residents in each city worked with authorities to grasp for a usable past as they gazed firmly forward toward building what they envisioned as a better future.

After 1949, each city's architectural dreams moved beyond isolated sacred sites to find realization in 1950s showpiece ensembles which portrayed that a better future had arrived. In a relatively conservative, still decorative variant of modern designs, Frankfurt's Römer ensemble resurrected with sleek gables that featured the tile mosaic of a phoenix rising from wartime ashes; Leipzig witnessed the creation of a triumphal Stalinist trade fair hall and monumental Opera; and in addition to crafting a gabled old town over new poured-cement structures, Wrocław fused Stalinism with surviving Kaiser-era structures on a grand city block at Kościuszko Square. By the 1960s, this urge for utopia spread across each cityscape in futuristic high-modern towers and blocks. Whereas the resulting meld of history and modernism generally satisfied uprooted

69 Michaela Marek, "Können alte Mauern 'deutsch' sein?" in *Deutsche Geschichte und Kultur im heutigen Polen*, ed. Hans-Jürgen Karp, 103-117 (Marburg: Herder Institut, 1997), 108.

70 The immediate postwar years saw many bodies so revered. See for instance Anna von der Goltz's analysis of Hindenburg's grave in Marburg in *Hindenburg: Power, Myth, and the Rise of the Nazis* (Oxford: Oxford University Press, 2009), 202-204.

71 For a collection of article-length treatments of anniversaries as formative moments for the self-identity of specific twentieth-century German urban examples, see Adelheid von Saldern, ed., *Inszenierter Stolz. Stadtrepräsentationen in drei deutschen Gesellschaften, 1935–1975* (Stuttgart: Franz Steiner, 2005).

Wrocławians who lacked prewar memories, however, strident and tyrannical high-modernist devastation prompted public outrage in each German city, before by the late 1970s and especially 1980s new efforts at stylistic synthesis arose in the hope of somehow restoring a sense of historical appropriation after the traumatic ruptures, not just of the Third Reich and wartime devastation, but also the "second destruction" of German cities that had followed.

Indeed, from the vantage point of the 1980s, symbolic projects such as the Goethehaus in Frankfurt or a Bach commemorative site in Leipzig were isolated but laudable exceptions that might have been extended more fully throughout the city. Finding themselves once more confronted by "dreams in ruins" – this time due to modernism's explosion of history and humane proportions – German political and planning elites yearned to recover the promise which the previous generation appeared to have offered through early postwar sacred sites: an ideal apparently attained through Polish reconstructions in a formerly German city like Wrocław. Given the current fad of demolishing high-modern ensembles such as Frankfurt's Technisches Rathaus, where a small-scale, partially replicated old town has appeared in its stead, the imagined potential of early postwar dreamscapes appears to carry considerable capital for contemporary urban planning and marketing. It is hoped that this trend will include informed circumspection, just as early postwar critics on at least some occasions voiced compunction against selectively remembering or even whitewashing the traumatic past.

Works Cited

Bartetzko, Dieter. *Denkmal für den Aufbau Deutschlands: Die Paulskirche in Frankfurt am Main*. Königstein, Langewiesche-Köster, 1998.

von Beyme, Klaus. *Der Wiederaufbau: Architektur und Städtebaupolitik in beiden deutschen Staaten*. Munich: R. Piper, 1987.

Bukowski, Marcin and Mieczysław Zlat. *Ratusz Wrocławski*. Wrocław: Zakład Narodowy Ossolińskich, 1958.

Bukowski, Marcin. *Katedra Wrocławska*. Wrocław: Ossolineum, 1974

Bukowski, Marcin. *Wrocław z lat 1945–1952: zniszczenia i dzieło odbudowy*. Warsaw: Państwowe Wydawnictwo Naukowe, 1985.

Bundesminister für Städtebau und Wohnungswesen. *Unsere Städte. Probleme von heute, Lösungen für morgen*. Bad Godesberg: Presse- und Informationsamt der Bundesregierung, Städtebaubericht 1970.

Czerner, Olgierd. "The Conservation of Lower Silesian Historic Monuments." *Annales Silesiae* 3 (1966/7): 5-54.

Czerner, Olgierd. *Wrocław: Landscape and Architecture*. Warsaw: Arkady, 1976.

Demshuk, Andrew. "A Mausoleum for Bach? Holy Relics and Urban Planning in Early Communist Leipzig, 1945–1950." *History & Memory* 28, no. 2 (Fall/Winter 2016): 47-89.

Demshuk, Andrew. "Preservationism, Postmodernism, and the Public across the Iron Curtain in Leipzig and Frankfurt/Main, 1968–1988." In *Re-framing Identities: Architecture's Turn to History*, ed. Ákos Moravánszky and Torsten Lange, 245-260. Basel and Berlin: Birkhäuser/De Gruyter, 2017.

Demshuk, Andrew. *Demolition on Karl Marx Square: Cultural Barbarism and the People's State in 1968*. Oxford and New York: Oxford University Press, 2017.

Deutsche Bauakademie Berlin, Institut für Städtebau und Architektur, Autorenkollektiv, ed. *Architektur und Städtebau in der DDR*. Leipzig: Seemann, 1969.

Diefendorf, Jeffry. *In the Wake of War: Reconstruction of German Cities after World War II*. Oxford: Oxford University Press, 1993.

Diefendorf, Jeffry. "America and the Rebuilding of Urban Germany." In *American Policy and the Reconstruction of Germany, 1945–1955*. Edited by idem., Axel Frohn, and Herman-Josef Rupieper. Washington D.C.: German Historical Institute and Cambridge University Press, 1993, 331-351.

Durth, Werner and Niels Gutschow. *Träume in Trümmern. Planungen zum Wiederaufbau zerstörter Städte im Westen Deutschlands 1940–1950*. Braunschweig und Wiesbaden: Vieweg, 1988.

Durth, Werner, Niels Gutschow, Winfried Nerdinger, and Thomas Topfstedt, eds. *Neue Städte aus Ruinen. Deutscher Städtebau der Nachkriegszeit*. Munich: Prestel, 1992.

Forner, Sean. *German Intellectuals and the Challenge of Democratic Renewal: Culture and Politics after 1945*. Cambridge and New York: Cambridge University Press, 2014.

von der Goltz, Anna. *Hindenburg: Power, Myth, and the Rise of the Nazis*. Oxford: Oxford University Press, 2009.

Hansert, Andreas. *Bürgerkultur und Kulturpolitik in Frankfurt am Main: eine historisch-soziologische Rekonstruktion*. Frankfurt/Main: Kramer, 1992.

Herber, Grażyna Ewa. *Wiederaufbau der Warschauer Altstadt nach dem zweiten Weltkrieg. Im Spannungsfeld zwischen denkmalpflegerischen Prinzipien, politischer Indienstnahme und gesellschaftlichen Erwartungen*. Bamberg: University of Bamberg Press, 2014.

Koshar, Rudy, *Germany's Transient Pasts: Preservation and National Memory in the Twentieth Century*. Chapel Hill: University of North Carolina Press, 1998.

Kostof, Spiro. *The City Shaped: Urban Patterns and Meanings through History*. Boston, Toronto, London: Little, Brown and Company, 1991.

Kuroczyński, Piotr. *Die Medialisierung der Stadt. Analoge und digitale Stadtführer zur Stadt Breslau nach 1945*. Bielefeld: Transcript Verlag, 2011.

Małachowicz, Edmund. *Stare Miasto we Wrocławiu: Rozwój urbanistyczno-architektoniczny zniszczenia wojenne i odbudowa.* Second Edition. Warsaw and Wrocław: Państwowe Wydawnictwo Naukowe, 1985.

Marek, Michaela. "Können alte Mauern 'deutsch' sein? Zum Problem 'deutscher' Baudenkmäler in Polen zwischen Nostalgie, Politik, Wissenschaft und Denkmalpflege." In *Deutsche Geschichte und Kultur im heutigen Polen: Fragen der Gegenstandsbestimmung und Methodologie.* Edited by Hans-Jürgen Karp, 103-117. Marburg: Herder Institut, 1997.

Meng, Michael. *Shattered Spaces: Encountering Jewish Ruins in Postwar Germany and Poland.* Cambridge, MA: Harvard University Press, 2011.

Mitscherlich, Alexander. *Die Unwirtlichkeit unserer Städte. Anstiftung zum Unfrieden* Frankfurt/Main: Suhrkamp, 1965.

Müller-Rämisch, Hans-Reiner. *Frankfurt am Main. Stadtentwicklung und Planungsgeschichte seit 1945.* Frankfurt/Main: Campus-Verlag, 1996.

Rosenfeld, Gavriel and Paul Jaskot, eds. *Beyond Berlin: Twelve German Cities Confront the Nazi Past.* Ann Arbor: University of Michigan Press, 2008.

von Saldern, Adelheid, ed. *Inszenierter Stolz. Stadtrepräsentationen in drei deutschen Gesellschaften, 1935–1975.* Stuttgart: Franz Steiner, 2005.

Thum, Gregor. *Uprooted: How Breslau became Wroclaw during the Century of Expulsions.* Translated by Tom Lampert and Allison Brown. Princeton: Princeton University Press, 2011.

Wagner-Kyora, Georg, ed. *Wiederaufbau europäischer Städte. Rekonstruktionen, die Moderne und die lokale Identitätspolitik seit 1945.* Stuttgart: Franz Steiner, 2013.

Zachwatowicz, Jan. "The Program and Principles for the Conservation of our Cultural Heritage" (Warsaw, 1946). In *In Memorial Professor Jan Zachwatowicz, 1900–1983.* Edited by Jolanta Fajkowska. Translated by Charles Vincent, 5-16. Warsaw: Wydawnictwo Geologiczne, 1983.

Zybura, Marek. *Der Umgang mit dem deutschen Kulturerbe in Schlesien nach 1945.* Görlitz: Senfkorn Verlag Alfred Theisen, 2005.

Contributors

Jonathan A. Beall
earned his master's and doctorate degrees at Texas A&M in 2004 and 2014, respectively. He has taught history at Norwich University in Northfield, Vermont and is now assistant professor at the University of North Georgia in Dahlonega, Georgia. At North Georgia, he teaches history courses in the History, Anthropology, and Philosophy Departments as well as for the University's Strategic and Security Studies Program.

Simon Davis
is professor of history at Bronx Community College and Graduate Center of the City University of New York. He specializes in imperial and colonial history, has written previously on the Cold War, Anglo-American relations in the Persian Gulf, and on the Middle East during the Second World War. He is presently working on British Mandate policy towards Arab Palestine in the 1920s and 1930s. Professor Davis is Director of the CUNY Graduate Center's Masters' Program in Middle Eastern Studies.

Andrew Demshuk
(American University) researches post-1945 Central European history. Fellowships including DAAD and Humboldt have supported his publications on Cold War-era nostalgia, territorial revisionism, and processes of reconciliation among Germans expelled from areas annexed to Poland, as well as the politics of urban planning and demolitions in East Germany. His forthcoming book *Bowling for Communism* investigates how local officials and residents sought to combat urban decay and fashion a livable city before Leipzig's Peaceful Revolution in 1989. His pending monograph *Three Cities after Hitler* measures the politics of memory in urban reconstruction across prewar German cities divided by Cold War borders.

James Horncastle
is an assistant professor and holder of the Edward and Emily McWhinney Professorship in International Relations at Simon Fraser University. His recent manuscript, *The Macedonian Slavs in the Greek Civil War, 1944–1949*, examines how the Macedonian Slavs participation in the conflict, and the attempts by other groups to manipulate them, gave rise to modern issues that continue to affect politics in the region today. His research interests include: Refugee and Migration studies; International Relations; History of Modern Greece; and Yugoslav Studies.

Tim Keogh
is an assistant professor at Queensborough Community College of the City University of New York. His pending monograph, *Suburbs in Black and White: Struggling to Live and Work in Postwar Long Island*, investigates the role of military defense spending in suburbanization and urban inequality from World War II through the end of the Cold War. His research interests include the history of poverty, the intersection of military spending and urban development, and social policy history.

Stefan Laffin
is a research associate of History of Modern Societies at the Department of History and member of the Bielefeld Graduate School in History and Sociology at Bielefeld University in Germany. He has studied History and British and American Studies there while also taking classes in history at the University of Bologna. His PhD project engages with the Allied occupation of Sicily, Calabria and Campania in the context of World War II. He has been awarded grants from the German Historical Institutes in Rome and Washington, D.C. as well as the Harry S. Truman Presidential Library & Museum among others. In his research, he deals with Italian history of the 20th century, especially Fascism, and US-American history in its international dimension.

Dr. Linda Parker
is an independent scholar and author. She has published five books on the British Army chaplaincy in both World Wars for Helion and Co, the most recent a biography of Geoffrey Studdert Kennedy, A *Seeker After Truths* (Helion: 2018). She had contributed essays to edited volumes on twentieth century military and religious history in the UK and the USA and travels widely for international conferences. She is a member of the Royal Historical Society and the Western Front Association, the American Commission for Military History and an active member of the Toc H Movement.

Alexander Querengässer
studied Medieval and Modern History at the University of Leipzig and earned his PhD at Potsdam University in 2016 researching the Saxon Military in the Great Northern War. He is the editor of the Series "Beiträge zur Geschichte des Militärs in Sachsen" (Contributions on the History of the Military in Saxony), as well as the author of fifteen books and various articles and essays about Military History ranging from the Late Middle Ages to the twentieth century, the history of State Building and Saxon History.

Index

1st Infantry Division 10, 19-21, 24-27, 31, 35-36, 39-43
16th U.S. Infantry Regiment 20, 35-36
18th U.S. Infantry Regiment 20, 22, 35
26th U.S. Infantry Regiment 20, 27, 39

Aachen 20, 27-32, 35-43
Acre 2, 118, 129, 134-135
Air Raid Precaution Act, 1938 73
Air raid warning 69-70
Allied Control Commission (ACC) 139, 146, 148-152
Allied Military Government for Occupied Territories (AMG) 11, 139, 143-144, 146-154, 161, 164
American Relief for Italy 157, 163
Ammassi 139, 154, 161
Andrews, British District Commissioner Lewis 123
Anne I of England 63
Arab Higher Committee 105, 112
Augustus II of Poland (See Frederick August I of Saxony)
Augustus the Strong (See Frederick August I of Saxony)
Autarky 159

Bach Mausoleum, Leipzig 181-184, 190, 192
Badoglio, Pietro 144, 158-159
Baldwin, Stanley 72
Barracks War 92
Bartning, Otto 180
Beersheba 107, 125, 127, 129
Ben Gurion, David 116
Berthold, Johann Gerhard 56
Beutler, Ernst 176, 180
Beyer, Walter 181-184
'Big Red One' (See 1st Infantry Division)
Black market 11-12, 151, 154-160
Blanck, Eugen 175-176, 180
Blitz Spirit 72-73
Bombardment, aerial 5, 8-9, 23, 67-75, 82, 91, 176
Bonn 11, 35-37, 40
Bosnia 88-89, 95, 101, 103-104
Brendel, Kurt 184
Bukowski, Marcin 186-188, 191

Carabinieri 154, 158, 163
Cathedral Island, Wrocław 168, 186-188
Caumont 25
Charles XII of Sweden 45, 49-51
Chemnitz 47-48, 54, 58, 173
Churchill, Winston 73-74, 77, 81, 143
Clausewitz, Carl von 3, 18, 41
Co-belligerency 144-146, 150
Cold War 12, 86-87, 93, 98, 167
Colonial Office, British 106-109, 113, 119-121, 132, 134
Communist Party of Yugoslavia (KPJ) 86
Cracow 186
Croatia 85-104
  Independence of 89, 93-97, 102
Croatian Democratic Union 94
Culture of remembrance 142, 160

Daniel, Lieutenant Colonel Derrill 28, 34, 39
Deep shelters 81
Democratization 147
Deptford 77-82
Dill, British Lieutenant General John 120-124, 135
Dippoldiswalde 59
Dirks, Walter 180
Döbeln 54
Dresden 47-51, 55-61, 65, 100, 173
Dubrovnik 85-86, 100

Eisenhower, Dwight D. 148

Field Manuals 147, 162
  Field Manual (FM) 27-5 145, 164
  Field Manual (FM) 27-10 145, 164
  Field Manual (FM) 31-50 24-26, 37, 43
Flemming, Jacob Heinrich von 59
Fog of war 3
Frankfurt am Main 167, 191-193
Fraustadt 49, 62
Freiberg 47, 50, 55-57, 65
Freie Deutsche Hochstift, Frankfurt 176
Fürstenberg, Anton Egon von 51-52

Gaza 38, 41, 107, 115-116, 127, 129-131, 136
Gellert, Christian Fürchtegott 182

Goerdeler, Carl 182
Goethehaus, Frankfurt 168, 174-181, 184, 190-191
Goethehaus, Weimar 180-181
Gomułka, Władysław 171
Görlitz 47-48, 62, 193
Gotha Bombers 67-68, 82
Great Northern War 11, 45-48, 61-63, 65
Great Rebellion 11, 105-109, 132
Gustav Line 144
Güttler, Jerzy 187

Hague Convention of 1907 150
Haifa 109-110, 112, 115-116, 119-128, 133-134, 138
Haining, Sir Robert 126-133, 135
Hamoukar 1, 14
Harris, British Air Commodore Arthur 107, 128-129, 133
Harvest Moon raids 70-71
HDZ (See Croatian Democratic Union)
Hebebrand, Werner 180
Hebron 107, 125-131
Heuss, Theodor 180
Hicks, William Joynson 69
Humanitarian crisis 98
Hume, Edgar E. 139
Hürtgen Forest 32-35, 39-42
Husseini, Haj Amin, al- 113, 123, 131, 137

Ingram, Bishop Arthur Foley Winnington 69
International Bach Society 182
Invasion of Normandy (See *Operation Overlord*)
Invasion of Sicily (See *Operation Husky*)
Italian armistice 144, 146, 148, 152, 158, 164
Italian Campaign 139-140, 142-144, 150-152, 159-161

Jaffa 11, 105, 110-122, 125-127, 130-131, 134, 136-138
Jenin 112, 115, 118, 131
Jericho 8, 14, 107, 129
Jerusalem 105-119, 122-130, 134, 136-137
JNA (See Yugoslav People's Army)
Johannis Square, Leipzig 182-184
Johanniskirche, Leipzig 182
Jović, Borisav 89-91, 102
Jüterbog 52

Kaliski, Emil 186
Karl Marx Square, Leipzig 173, 183, 192
Keith-Roach, British District Commissioner Edward 128-129, 136
Kolb, Walter 174-175, 180
Kościuszko Square, Wrocław 190
KPJ (See Communist Party of Yugoslavia)
Kučan, Milan 89

Lauban 53
Leipzig 12, 47-51, 54-63, 65-66, 167-171, 174-175, 178-187, 190-192
Lesson learning 25, 31, 37
Levy, Bert 21, 26
Lewis, Norman 155
Licht, Barnet 182
Lydda 124, 134
Łysiak, Waldemar 190

MacDonald, British Colonial Secretary Malcolm 130
MacMichael, Palestine High Commissioner Sir Harold 126, 129
Małachowicz, Edmund 188, 189, 193
Manshiyeh 105, 112, 119, 126
Mass observation 80
May, Ernst 175
McDonnell, Chief Justice of Palestine Sir Michael 117
Medicines sans Frontieres 92
Merode 32-37
Military history 4-7, 12
Military training 10, 18-24, 30-32, 36-38, 90-92
Milosević, Slobodan 85-91, 95-99
Minckwitz, Hans Rudolf von 49
Montgomery, British Major General Bernard L. 107, 128-129, 133
Morrison, Hubert 74-75
MSF (See *Medicines sans Frontieres*)
Mussolini, Benito 144, 150, 158-160, 165, 172

Nablus 112, 115, 118, 127, 130-131
Naples 11-12, 139-146, 150-151, 154-157, 159-161, 163-166
Nashashibi family 123-124, 127, 130-131
Nazareth 115, 123, 129
Neufeld, Maurice F. 139, 151, 159, 163-164
Nierade, Kurt 185

North Africa 10, 19, 21, 32, 41, 143-144
'Notes on Imperial Policing' 113, 119

O'Connor, British Major General Richard 107, 128-130, 133, 135
Occupation 10-12, 73, 116, 118, 124, 126, 140-142, 145-151, 154-155, 158-162, 164-166, 167, 172
Ochs, Karl Wilhelm 179
Operation Anchor 117
Operation Husky 143
Operation Overlord 144
Ormsby-Gore, British Colonial Secretary William 113, 117, 123, 126

Palestine 11, 106-138
Palestine Police 106, 136
Paramilitaries 92
Paulskirche, Frankfurt 175-178, 185, 191
Peace studies 147
Peel Commission (see Royal Commission on Palestine)
Peenemunde 74
Peirse, Richard, British Air Commodore 115-120
Peter I of Russia 45, 51
Piast Dynasty 186, 188-189
Piast Mausoleum, Wrocław 188-190
Poletti, Charles 139, 149-150, 161, 163
Polish School of Conservation 173, 186
Przyłęcki, Janusz 189
Public memory 12, 139, 142

Qassam, 'Izz al-Din, al- 112, 137-138
Followers 112, 120, 123

Ramin, Günther 182, 184
Rationing 154-157
Ration cards 155
Reconstruction 9-10, 12-15, 151, 167-173, 176, 179-181, 186, 192
"Recovered Territories" 169, 171, 173
Regno del Sud 144, 148
Reisenflugzeugen 71
Reprisal raids 69
Resistenza 160-162
Restitution of occupied territory 149
Rhineland occupation 145

Römer Ensemble, Frankfurt 190
Roosevelt, Franklin D. 143, 149
Royal Air Force, British 112
Royal Commission on Palestine 121
Report 122-123, 130
Royal Navy, British 115
Rybicki, Józef 185

Sacred Sites 12, 168-172, 176-181, 186-191
Safad 122, 126
Sandys, Duncan 74-75
Saunders, Palestine Police Inspector-General Alan 125-128
School of Military Government, Charlottesville 141
Schulenburg, Johann Matthias von der 49, 62
Second Vatican Council 188
Serbia 88-91, 96-97, 101
Šešelj, Vojislav 91-92
Siege 11, 50-53, 85-100, 132-133
Slovenia 87, 89-91, 104
Independence of 89
St. Cloud 22, 27, 36
Stalinist architecture 169, 190
Stolberg 26-27, 30, 36-38
Stone, Ellery W. 139, 163
Sun Tzu 3
Šušak, Gojko 88, 94
szaber economy 185

Technisches Rathaus, Frankfurt 191
Tegart, Sir Charles 125-130, 135, 137
Tel Aviv 105, 108, 112-114, 119-122, 130, 133, 136-138
Thomaskirche, Leipzig 182-185
Tiberias 122, 127
Torgau 50, 53-54
Total National Defence (TND) 87-90, 102
Trident Conference 143, 165
Troina 23
Tudjman, Franjo 88-89, 92-97, 101, 104
Tulkarm 116, 118, 125

United Nations Relief and Rehabilitation Administration (UNRRA) 153, 157, 164
Upper North Street school 68-69, 82
urban combat 17-27, 37

urban history 3-7, 12, 14-15
urban operations 8, 10, 12, 18-21, 25, 28, 31, 35-39, 42
urbicide 8-9, 11-12, 13-14, 85-87, 98-100
Ustaša 94, 97, 99

Vergeltungswaffen
V1 67, 73-75, 78, 80-81
V2 67, 75-82
Vesuvius eruption 154
Vukovar 86
Siege of 11, 85-104

Warsaw Old Town 173
Wauchope, Palestine High Commissioner Sir Arthur 105-126, 131
Wavell, Lieutenant General Sir Archibald 124, 126
Wehrmacht 23-25, 139, 142-144, 160
Weymouth 23-25, 36
White Paper on Palestine 130-132
Wilhelmine Construction 167
Wittenberg 49-53, 60-62, 65
Woodhead Commission 130
World War I 37, 43, 68-73, 145, 149
World War II 12, 14, 17-43, 73-82, 140-165, 192
Wrocław 12, 167, 169, 171, 174-175, 178, 181, 185-191, 192-193
Wyszyński, Stefan Cardinal 188

Yugoslav People's Army 85-101
Yugoslav Wars 85-86, 92, 96

Zachwatowicz, Jan 173, 193
Zeigner, Erich 181-184
Zeppelin 67-68
Zionism 105-116, 122
Zwickau 58-59